HOW TO BE A GARDENER

Alan Titchmarsh

HOW TO BE A GARDENER
BOOK TWO

secrets of success

Photographs by Jonathan Buckley

ACKNOWLEDGEMENTS

How to be a Gardener has been one of the most rewarding projects I've ever undertaken, but then when something starts as a vague idea over lunch, and develops over a period of five years into two television series and two books, there is always a degree of wonder and, with any luck, a sense of fulfilment if things turn out well. If the reception granted to the television series and the book are anything to go by, that is certainly the case.

Much of that combined success is due to two talented and forbearing sets of people whose hard graft and endless good humour made things happen. In the production of the television series I have been helped tremendously by Dick Coulthurst, Helga Berry, Cassie Walkling and Rachel Malin, while Russell Jordan, Neil Woodger and Ross McInnes constructed the gardens on time and with great care.

The ever affable Jo Swift was generous with design help, and my regular cameraman Paul Hutchings and sound engineer Gordon Nightingale turned even the wettest days into something worth turning out for. Tim Shepherd again stunned us with his wonderful slow-motion footage, achieved thanks to months of patience in his studio. To the editors I owe especial thanks, for turning my disparate pieces to camera into a cohesive and inspiring whole.

Sue Thompson and the staff at the Royal Horticultural Society's gardens at Wisley were always tremendously helpful when we filmed there, and made sure we never went short of refreshments.

The National Trust staff at Hinton Ampner in Hampshire were equally welcoming.

The patient garden owners have, I hope, ended up with something better than anticipated. I most certainly have, thanks in the main to my producer Kath Moore. I am at a loss to find words that say a big enough thank you to her. Like Sam Goldwyn, she has managed to make something bigger than both of us, as well as making the journey stimulating, rewarding and a bit of a laugh.

The book has been a mammoth undertaking and could not have been accomplished without the encouragement of Nicky Copeland, the considerable editorial skills of Helena Caldon, and the design flair (and baking skills) of Isobel Gillan, who kept the patient photographer Jonathan Buckley and myself well supplied with cake and buns while trying to work out what shape each picture had to be. Jonathan deserves plaudits for making me and my gardens look so good, and for keeping his figure.

To Sue Phillips I am indebted for her unparalleled research skills, and to Lin Hawthorne for her patient checking of details. Amanda Patton has produced the clearest of artwork from my vague sketches with endless patience.

And finally I must admit that without Sue Richards and Bill Budd my garden would not be half so beautiful as it is. I owe them more than I can say.

How to be a Gardener has been a team effort, and team efforts are usually not without their trials. I can honestly say that this one was.

The photographer would like to thank the following owners and designers for kindly allowing their gardens to be photographed:

BBC Gardens: Cottage Garden designed by Joe Swift & Sam Joyce for The Plant Room 2, 14, 38, 84, 123; No Space Garden designed by Joe Swift & Sam Joyce for The Plant Room 15, 50, 51, 74, 203b; No Time Garden designed by Russell Jordan 16, 120; Hot Garden designed by Joe Swift & Sam Joyce for The Plant Room 20, 34, 169, 303; Natural Garden designed by Joe Swift 7 Sam Joyce for The Plant Room 21, 28; Blank Canvas designed by Joe Swift & Sam Joyce for The Plant Room 30, 31, 43t, 53, 243; Water Garden designed by Sandy Worth 202.

Other Gardens: Barleywood, Hampshire (Alan Titchmarsh) 122, 136t, 160, 223, 244, 282; Barry Road, London (Jonathan Buckley) 137; Beth Chatto Gardens, Essex (Beth Chatto) 150, 176; Canning Road, London (Erica Hunningher) 110t; Chelsea Physic Garden, London 10; Chelsea Flower Show 2001, A Real Japanese Garden designed for the *Daily Telegraph* by Professor Masao Fukuhara 12; Chelsea Flower Show 2002 Visual Retreat designed by Wynniatt-Husey Clarke 13; Chelsea Flower Show 2002, High Fliers Haven designed by Chloe Wood & Tamsin Woodhouse 22; Chelsea Flower Show 2002, The Accenture Garden designed byMiriam Book 23l; Chelsea Flower Show 2002, Kelly's Creek designed by Alison Wear & Miranda Melville 23r; Chelsea Flower Show 2002, Sanctuary designed by Steve Woodhams 24; Chelsea Flower Show 2000, Zen Inspired designed by spidergarden.com 110; Chelsea Flower Show 1999, A Chef's Garden designed by Sir Terence Conran 238; Chiltern Road, Buckinghamshire (Jo Chatterton) 76r; Church Lane, London (Paul Kelly) 70, 109; Coton Manor, Northamptonshire (Ian & Sue Pasley-Tyler) 250; Crystal Palace Road, London (Sue Hillwood Harris) 98; Culverden Road, London (Nick Ryan) 36; Grafton Park Road, London (Robin Green & Ralph Cade) 35, 37t, 125, 129t, 227, 251, 280; Great Dixter, East Sussex (Christopher Lloyd) 80t, 83, 170c, 189t, 192, 216l, 266; Glen Chantry, Essex (Sue & Wol Staines) 170r, 198t, 210, 218, 226; Eastgrove Cottage, Worcestershire (Malcolm & Carol Skinner) 178; East Ruston Old Vicarage, Norfolk (Alan Gray & Graham Robeson) 270t; Hinton Ampner House, Hampshire (The National Trust) 42, 44, 144; Hollington Herbs, Berkshire (Judith & Simon Hopkinson)252; Ketley's, East Sussex (Helen Yemm) 26, 85, 228, 254; Ladywood, Hampshire (Sue Ward) 54, 58, 86l, 87, 145; Longstock Water Gardens, Hampshire (John Lewis Partnership) 204; Meynell Crescent, London (designed by Steve Woodhams) 127; Peachings, Hampshire (Gill Sidell) 283; Pentridge House, Dorset (Mr & Mrs King) 264r; Perch Hill, East Sussex (Sarah Raven) 194; RHS Garden Wisley, Surrey 170l; Rofford Manor, Oxfordshire (Mr & Mrs J. Mogford) 248; Sheffield Park, Sussex (The National Trust) 11; Shepherd's Bush (Deidre Spencer) 108; Spencer Road, London (Anthony Goff) 132; Sticky Wicket, Dorset (Pam Lewis) 273; Stoneacre, Kent (The National Trust) 79; Sycamore Mews, London (designed byPenny Smith) 114; Upper Mill Cottage, Kent (David & Mavis Seeney) 119, 182; Valentine Cottage, Hampshire (Mr & Mrs Brown) 41, 59, 86r, 90, 104r, 126, 173, 264t, 278; Welcome Thatch, Dorset (Diana Guy) 27, 40t, 146, 298; West Dean Gardens, Sussex (Edward James Foundation) 240; West Green House, Hampshire (Marylyn Abbott) 60; West Green House Cottage (David Chase) 18, 33, 62t, 115.

This book is published to accompany the television series entitled *How to be a Gardener*, the second series of which was first broadcast in 2003.
The series was produced by BBC Bristol.
Executive producer: Dick Colthurst
Producer: Kath Moore

Published by BBC Worldwide Ltd,
Woodlands, 80 Wood Lane, London W12 0TT

First published in 2003
Text copyright © Alan Titchmarsh 2003
The moral right of the author has been asserted.

Photographs copyright © Jonathan Buckley 2003

Except the following photographs from: A–Z Botanical p 65 (5), p103 (2) photographer Anthony Seinet, 103 (3) Ian Gowland, 172 (1) BON, 172 (6) Adrian Thomas, 198 (3) J Malcolm Smith, 217 (3) Yves Tzaud, 268 (1) F Merlet, 269 (3) Chris Martin Bahr; Arcaid/MHK 291 Martine Hamilton Knight; Ardea 260T and 263 John Daniels; David Austin Roses 175(i) BBC Worldwide 62B, 129B, 168, 203 and 296 Tim Shepherd; Garden Picture Library 91 (1) Neil Homes, 94 (1) Janet Sorrell, 133 (5) Howard Rice, 183 (3) David Cavagnaro, 213 (4) and 214 (1) Howard Rice, 217 (5) Sunniva Harte, 220 (1) J S Sira, 265TR Sunniva Harte, 288 (7) John Glover; Harpur Garden Library 99 (5), 157 (6), 221 (5), 287 (2 and 4); Andrew Lawson Photography 288 (10), 290, 293 (5 and 6); Marianne Majerus Photography 66 (4), 78 (6), 118 (3), 152 (3), 249 (2), 294 (10), 294 (11); Clive Nichols Garden Pictures 80 (2), 92 (1), 156 (3), 165 (3), 172 (2); Oxford Scientific Films 216 (1) Gordon Maclean, 217 (4); Photos Horticultural 95, 103 (5), 105 (3), 154 (3), 175 (6 and 7), 197 (5), 216 (2) 287 (5).

BBC Worldwide would like to thank the above for providing photographs and for permission to reproduce copyright material. While every effort has been made to trace and acknowledge all copyright holders, we would like to apologize should there be any errors or omissions.

ISBN 0 563 53405 2

Commissioning editor: Nicky Copeland
Project editor: Helena Caldon
Copy editor: Lin Hawthorne
Art director and designer: Isobel Gillan
Picture researcher: Susannah Parker
Artist: Amanda Patton
Production Manager: John Martin

Set in Sabon and Akzidenz
Printed and bound in Great Britain by Butler & Tanner Ltd, Frome
Colour separations by Kestrel Digital Colour, Witham

CONTENTS

Introduction

It has always struck me that gardening is a basic skill that is not so much learned as uncovered. Why else would academics and intellectuals suddenly go off into raptures about the simple task of growing their own courgettes, or raising busy lizzies from seed? It is, purely and simply, because gardening is deeply instinctive. It satisfies our basic urges in a way that few other pursuits can.

It seems to me perfectly obvious that we were always meant to grow things. Other people are convinced that we are meant to understand how a mobile phone works. I am happy not to be of their number; new mobile phones appear that are ever more complex and that offer facilities I am never likely to demand. Nature, bless her, has no need for such frequent 'improvements'.

In *How to Be a Gardener Book One* I explained simple growing techniques and showed how plants work. If you understand how something works, you can better equip yourself to deal with it – which is probably the root of my mobile phone problem. Once you know how plants grow, and how to make them grow, you have become a gardener. But that does not mean that you will have a beautiful garden. To do that, you need to know how to put different plants together: you need to know which plants will grow best in which situation, and then how to group them with other plants of a similar disposition that will make them look even better.

The architect Sir Frederick Gibberd said that gardening was the most complicated of all art forms because as well as using shape, form, colour and texture, it also used time. Time changes the picture – over the seasons and over the years. What was once a perfectly formed planting scheme can become overblown and over the hill.

By now you have probably convinced yourself that you will never become a proper gardener. But take heart – none of us has ever cracked it completely. Provided you know the pitfalls, you can anticipate them. You won't always avoid them, but you might learn to enjoy the challenge.

How to Be a Gardener Book Two lets you in on the ways to make your garden look good and feel right. There is no accounting for taste, or for fashion, but even allowing for these influences, there are still ways of having a garden that reflects your own personality. And that is the key – your garden is for you – not for the neighbours, who will have their own likes and dislikes, or who may be slaves to fashion.

Oh, you will be influenced by current trends – if you are a receptive sort, you will have no option. But basic rules of thumb are as valid in the garden as they are on the catwalk, and you can get to grips with them more easily than you would think. A bit of planning, and a few basic design guidelines will avoid most pitfalls, and you will have great fun trying different designs and different planting schemes over the years.

It is a mistake to think that a garden is ever finished. It is not a room filled with inanimate objects. It is a living, breathing, passionate, fiery creation. Or it should be. Anyway, you'll see what I mean – I hope. And you will get more out of your garden as a result.

1 YOUR DESIGN

Garden design in history

In the beginning, nobody set out to design gardens at all. They just happened. But then, in the beginning, the garden as we know it today did not exist. Early gardens were either strictly practical or for limited recreational use. Gardeners simply endeavoured to make the best use of the space and the small range of plants and materials available. Down-to-earth common sense was there in spades, but for anything fancier, you'd have to wait several centuries.

Medieval practicality

For medieval peasants, the space around the family hovel was little more than a farmyard and, if they wanted a few herbs for the pot within easy walking distance of the back door, they had to fence them off to stop livestock eating the lot. People didn't much go in for vegetables at that time; meat, bread or a 'potage' made from dried peas, beans or cereals made most meals, and the staple ingredients came from a personal strip in a communal field. Flowers didn't get a look in because hard-working folk didn't waste their time on anything they couldn't eat.

At grand establishments like castles, gardens were enclosed within fortifications where the ladies could walk safely and sit and talk, but there wasn't much to grow except wild flowers that came up naturally, so you had flowery meads and turf seats to take away the smell of dawning civilization. The serious horticulturists were in monasteries. Monks – the doctors of the day – grew medicinal herbs in well-ordered beds with paths in between, so they knew where everything was. Later, the same layout of beds and paths was used in apothecaries' or 'physic' gardens, placed close to 'hospitals', since plants were still used for medicines. There's still a good example in London, at the Chelsea Physic Garden, and a smaller one at Petersfield, not far from Barleywood.

Better times

As living standards improved, Elizabethan English peasants evolved into self-sufficient cottagers. At the back of the dwelling, they'd have a well-stocked vegetable garden and a pig in the sty, and out front would be a cottage garden where they kept bees, a jumble of wild flowers and a few cultivated plants grown from bits passed on between neighbours. These treasures were shoved in anywhere there was room. Smallholders became yeomen farmers, with bigger houses, more livestock and several employees.

In the apothecary's garden, plants were cultivated for their medicinal properties rather than their beauty.

As the big landowners grew richer, their houses were enlarged, and their gardens became places to show off. They would surround themselves with formal grounds, creating wonderful views of fountains, parterres and clipped hedges from the terraces. Rare flowers, such as tulips, would be displayed in flower beds that were like a stage set, with bare earth and contrived backgrounds that were intended to drive visiting toffs wild with envy.

But it was no good showing off if you couldn't keep one jump ahead of the Joneses, so just as everyone who was anybody had finished creating their formal gardens, fashions changed. In the early 18th century, the craze for Arcadian landscapes came in. William Kent, Lancelot 'Capability' Brown, Humphry Repton and co. were brought in to turn upper-crust grounds into vistas of trees and lakes decorated with grottoes, follies and ruined temples. The idea was to improve on nature. One wag remarked that he hoped he died before Capability Brown did so that he could see heaven before Brown had 'improved' it. The parkland beyond the house would be full of deer and prize herds of cattle, which were kept at a suitable distance by a ha-ha – a steep-sided ditch that didn't obstruct your view. It gave the distinct impression that you owned everything as far as the eye could see – an early example of what garden designers today call 'borrowed landscape'.

Ostentation was the name of the game in the 18th century when the 'Arcadian' landscape was all the rage.

Victorian and Edwardian gardens

By Victorian times, for anyone concerned with keeping their place in society, a conservatory and walled kitchen garden – complete with a range of greenhouses – were essential for entertaining guests at country-house parties. Elaborate, formal carpet-bedding schemes came into fashion, showing the world that you could afford both the tender plants and the greenhouse to produce them, and that you had a properly trained staff capable of tackling the latest fashions, however outlandish. Mathematical geometry was a vital part of a gardener's training in those days.

As the 19th century progressed, the style became more romantic, so at country houses you'd see formal lily ponds, pergolas and rose gardens for a quiet tryst. William Robinson published his *English Flower Garden* in 1883 in which he made a plea for naturalness and lack of formality in gardening. By Edwardian times, Gertrude Jekyll, often designing in collaboration with the architect, Sir Edwin Lutyens, was being creative with her book *Colour Schemes for the Flower Garden* (1908), and the sort of themed 'garden rooms' you see at Sissinghurst and Hidcote Manor were beginning to evolve. It was to be a century of gardening contradictions and extreme variety.

Modern times

Since the early part of the 20th century, gardens have gone through several short, sharp phases. During the Second World War, gardening was all about Digging for Victory, so you dug up your back lawn to grow vegetables and planted marrows on top of your Anderson shelter.

Then came 'fifties formal', when you'd have cut a geometrically shaped flower bed out of the middle of your front lawn and filled it with straight rows of salvias. During the 'low-maintenance' sixties, you crammed the garden with shrubs and ground cover, or heathers and conifers, to save work.

In the 'sun-loving seventies', you pulled it all out again to make a patio, which gradually grew until the garden became, for a lot of people, a complete outdoor living room. Organic gardening took off in the 'earthy eighties' and it's been growing ever since.

Instead of just being a genteel hobby for the retired generation who'd become real enthusiasts, by the nineties, gardening had become the height of fashion for younger people and families with children, who would make the type of gardens they'd all enjoy. Everybody was at it, and the thing you needed was style. Wild gardens, Mediterranean gardens, water gardens – you name it, you could have it. If you had a big enough space, you could enjoy the lot all at once by dividing your space up into separate 'rooms' and 'decorating' each one differently. Oh, yes. And decking arrived. It had been popular in the States for decades, and took off here on account of its relative cheapness and all-weather attributes. Suddenly, you could go out into the garden and come back indoors without being muddy – even in winter. Gardens became fun instead of hard work, and hard-bitten traditionalists sniffed in despair.

The future

We've been pinching design tips from gardens of the past ever since I can remember, but with the dawn of a new millennium, we have – at last – started to look ahead and develop totally new ways of thinking about what goes into a garden. That's why you see so many contemporary gardens in magazines, at shows and on the TV these days. Yes, I know some of them are experimental and not necessarily the sort of thing you'd want to live with every day, but there are lots of bright ideas you can adapt to suit yourself. And what today seems difficult to live with may well be commonplace tomorrow.

Now that we tend to stay put instead of moving house every few years as we once did, we are more inclined to make changes to our present plot instead of just trading it in for a new model somewhere else – so the trend is to make the most of the space and really develop it to the full. There's never been more scope.

Today, gardens are individually created to suit the needs and artistic preferences of their owners, but they are still influenced by changing fads and fashions.

What's right for you?

The way most people make a garden is very hit-and-miss. You know the sort of thing – first-time buyers move into a starter home, put up a whirligig washing line and park dustbins where they won't be bumped into, plonk some paving down outside the patio doors, put in a patch of grass for the kids to play on, and a path down to the shed. The rest slowly fills up with whatever takes their fancy at the garden centre. They'll probably move on before the lot gets overgrown, leaving the result for somebody else to sort out. Well, it doesn't have to be like that.

Evolution versus revolution

A garden should suit both house and owners. This dull patch (*below*) has been transformed into a cottage garden (*above*) that complements both dwelling and family.

In my experience, people are either evolutionists or revolutionists when it comes to making a garden.

Evolutionists like to start with something that's already there and alter it gradually. There's a lot to be said for this method. You never have to put up with a plot that looks like a building site, you complete one project at a time, and you can stagger the work – and the cost. When the children grow older, you can turn their play patch into something more adult and, if you spot something on the telly that takes your fancy, you can replace an old feature with something new. If you take over a big garden, as I did at Barleywood, you don't have to try and finish it all at once. You can tackle a different bit every year or so, as I did, then start redeveloping the original bits when you think up better ideas.

An evolutionist's garden is never finished, but then, no garden ever is. The big problem with this type of development is that it's very easy to wander off track and end up with a mess, so you do need to make long-term as well as short-term plans.

Revolutionists are the exact opposite. They prefer to scrap everything, start with a completely clean slate, and get the whole job over with at once so they can spend the next few years just enjoying it. They are the type of people who are most likely to sit down and plan the garden fastidiously, or call in a designer and a team of landscapers to do everything. This is very much the way we work on *Ground Force* – we have to, if we are to get the job done in the time – and, at home, it suits a lot of people with small gardens who want to see the full effect straight away. But you can take things too far and end up with plans so detailed that you hardly dare impulse-buy so much as a single flower in case it throws your whole scheme out of synch. Don't get me wrong, having a plan is a good idea. Just don't get bogged down in the fine details at the start, and be flexible.

You don't have to be a professional designer to transform a tiny rectangular patch of ground (*above*) into a well-crafted garden (*below*). Once you know a few secrets, you can achieve wonders by doodling and playing around with lines on a sheet of paper...

Thinking it through

Whichever approach best suits your natural instincts, begin by asking what you are trying to achieve. Otherwise you can spend a lot of time and money, but just end up with a collection of ingredients that don't make a garden. It's like trying to pick two socks that match without turning on the light; you stand no chance. Look at your lifestyle and what you want from your garden.

Do you want a stylish space for outdoor entertaining in summer? In which case a courtyard garden in a Mediterranean-style or contemporary look is worth considering. Or, if you lead a busy life with no time for chores, then a low-maintenance garden that looks good all year round might be the best choice. Think about gravel and paving instead of grass, a fountain or pebble pool instead of a pond, and a few outstanding, all-year-round specimen plants instead of lots of time-consuming flowers and containers. Maybe you want to grow your own produce, encourage wildlife, or cultivate special plants you've enjoyed collecting at garden shows or propagated yourself? These gardens need more time, but you'll spend it doing those things you enjoy, so it won't feel like a chore.

If your home has period character, with masses of architectural detail, then a garden with lots of curving beds, winding paths and small features will look very much at home, but, if you have a very

This garden has been designed to suit a family with little time to spare. The plants are easy to maintain, there is little lawn to mow and somewhere to sit in the sun during precious leisure time. Perhaps an hour or two's work a week is needed, that's all.

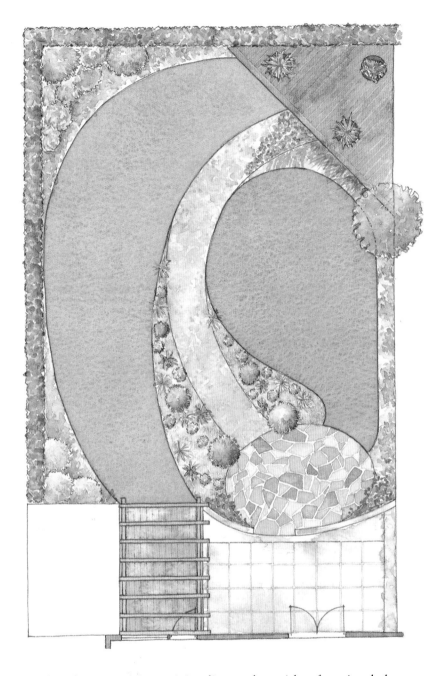

This plan of the low-maintenance garden opposite shows the following time-saving features:

1 Low-maintenance planting scheme of shrubs and grasses.
2 Small lawn area, which is quick to mow.
2 Decking made of railway sleepers, positioned to catch the evening sun.
4 Slate mulch in planting beds to minimize watering and weeding.
5 Pergola to provide shady and scented seating area.

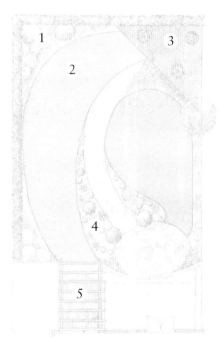

modern house, a more minimalist garden with a few simple but stylish shapes will be the best match. The style that suits you will be different in each case. It sounds obvious, I know, but if you don't ask yourself the right questions, you'll be amazed at how easy it is to end up with the 'wrong kind of garden'.

So the first rule of garden designing is: always start with the big picture and leave the details till last. From pages 22–44 there are some of the possible garden 'looks' that are available to you, but, before you go straight to choosing a style, there is another important factor you should consider that might influence your decision.

Working with nature

Some gardens start out with natural characteristics that are very difficult and expensive to alter, so if you have seriously boggy ground, a patch of shady woodland, or a steep rocky site, my advice is: don't fight it. Instead, see the 'problem' as nature's way of telling you that this is the perfect place to develop a particular style of garden. That will be a heck of a lot cheaper than trying to change the soil type, clear trees, or level rock, and because you've built on the garden's natural characteristics you'll end up with a garden that's the envy of your friends and that people with 'normal' sites would have spent a fortune to achieve.

Which brings me to rule number two of garden design: the easy way is often the best.

This seaside garden makes good use of plants that can endure a maritime location. The nautical atmosphere continues with a shingle path, a painted shed and a stripy deck chair.

Problem solving with style

Even in places where you might think a 'proper' garden is out of the question, there's a lot you can do just by following the lead that the landscape gives you. The result is a garden that looks totally at home in its surroundings, and which is very easy to look after because you are only doing what comes naturally.

Gardens near the sea

Strong winds, often laden with sand or salt, are a feature of coastal gardens. The soil is usually pretty grim – all pebbles and sand and with hardly any fertility to speak of. In these conditions normal garden plants don't stand a chance of flourishing.

Design solution There are two real choices; a normal-ish garden or a seaside-style one. The late Derek Jarman's garden at Dungeness is a great inspiration. Team plants with beach paraphernalia, such as a bit of breakwater, driftwood, chunks of chain or hemp hawser, a mulch of cockle shells – which you can now buy in bags for the purpose – and lots of pebbles.

Suitable plants If you want a normal-ish garden, then plant a defensive barrier of tough plants round the edge for some protection. Inside your shelter belt of plants, such as Corsican pine, (*Pinus nigra* subsp. *laricio*), maritime pine, (*P. pinaster*), Monterey cypress (*Cupressus macrocarpa*), or *Euonymus japonicus*, you could go for a summer garden of hardy fuchsias, escallonias and annuals. If you want to leave your sea views open, stick to really tough seaside plants that'll stand the conditions, such as sea holly, (*Eryngium*), thrift (*Armeria*), and pinks (*Dianthus*). If, however, you want to make a seaside-style garden inland, you can use plants that look nautical, but don't actually enjoy coastal conditions, such as euphorbias and ornamental grasses.

Wet ground that never dries out, even in summer

Most normal garden plants need reasonably good drainage because their roots rot if they are left standing in 'soil soup', particularly in winter.

Design solution Make a bog garden, adapting features found in real swampy places, such as knotty branches and chunks of tree trunk, willow panels, a rustic gazebo on stilts, banks and ditches.

Suitable plants Stick to plants that are naturally adapted to living with their feet in water. Most marginal plants will grow in anything from very wet ground to a couple of inches of water. Use this type of plant in the lowest lying places, where puddles collect in winter. For the not-quite-so-soggy bits round the edges, choose moisture-loving perennials, such as hosta and candelabra primulas, and plants like *Darmera peltata*, which is found on the banks of streams in the wild. Where you have a large space and you need what designers call 'a bold statement', then the giant prickly rhubarb *Gunnera manicata* is perfect. But in a small garden it will eat you out of house and home.

Hunt for inspiration

It takes imagination to find a stylish solution for seemingly impossible spots, so don't be afraid to borrow ideas from people who have already done it. Visit other gardens in your locality and take a camera and notebook and pencil with you. You'll discover a lot of good private gardens on your doorstep by visiting those that open in aid of good causes for a few days each year under the National Gardens Scheme. Their famous 'Yellow Book' – Gardens of England and Wales Open for Charity *– comes out each spring, and is on sale in bookshops and garden centres.*

On boggy land, use plants whose roots are naturally adapted to growing in soggy earth – they'll happily thrive.

Sunny, sloping sites

The ground dries out quickly, plants suffer from drought and, in heavy rain, the soil is washed down the slope.

A bare, sun-baked terrace (*above*) can be turned into a flower-filled garden (*below*) using plants that are naturally equipped to cope with hot, dry situations.

Design solution Unless you fancy a vineyard – and this is a good spot for one – then the best plan might be to turn the steepest part of the slope into a series of shallow terraces. Create winding paths between the stone retaining walls of the terraces and make beds on the terraces for naturally drought-tolerant plants. If there's good rock just under the surface, expose it and make the most of it.

Suitable plants Go for sun-loving shrubs, perennials and rock plants that don't mind drying out a bit in summer. Use plenty of evergreens so the view doesn't just evaporate in winter; if the ground is well covered there's less risk of soil erosion. Don't worry about using lots of small plants, because on a sloping garden they are brought closer to eye level.

Shady gardens under woodland trees

Summer shade makes it difficult to create a colourful garden using normal border plants.

Design solution Make a woodland garden. Big trees would be a problem if the soil is dry underneath, but proper woodland is different. It has a light canopy of branches overhead with deep, rich leaf-mould or a thick layer of organic matter on the ground, making perfect growing conditions for all sorts of choice shade lovers and woodland treasures. If you need to let more light in, call a tree surgeon in to thin out or lift the crowns of big trees.

Suitable plants Choose spring bulbs, which complete their growing cycle before the tree leaves emerge, as well as perennials, such as hellebores and violets, that love damp shade. Where shade is light, grow Japanese maples (*Acer palmatum* cultivars), shade-tolerant grasses and woodland wild flowers, such as bugle (*Ajuga reptans*) and primroses (*Primula vulgaris*) and cut 'rides' through for access. If the soil is acid, which it often is in this situation, then lime-hating woodland plants, such as rhododendrons and camellias, will thrive.

There are plants to suit every situation, however difficult, so the third rule of garden design is: if you don't have a problem, then don't look for one. Think about the style of garden you'd like and don't feel pressurized by current trends – remember that the garden is there to please you and yours. Do show off a bit, but not at the expense of the garden's original purpose – to provide pleasure and relaxation.

There is a world of difference between a patch of dreary and unkempt wilderness (*below*) and a wild garden (*above*), but with a little crafty planning and planting the one can be transformed into the other.

Contemporary gardens

Contemporary gardens are all about breaking away from tradition. They are not plant-lovers' gardens; they generally appeal to younger, or more design-conscious people, who may or may not know much about gardening – but they know what they like. This sort of garden looks quite out of place around a traditional house, but if you have an unusual space to fill, such as a roof-top terrace, or modern-style home or office surroundings to landscape, then a contemporary exterior is often a very good choice.

By using a small selection of hard landscaping materials and utilizing bold and dramatic curves, a garden instantly takes on a contemporary look.

What's it all about?

Contemporary style is all about shapes, textures and patterns. Plants are only part of the picture. If you go contemporary, you'll use fewer plants than in a more conventional garden, but they will need to be the architectural kinds that look almost like living sculpture. Alternatively, you could go for carpets of plants contrasted with blocky shapes of clipped hedging to create a more formal contemporary style. Colour is often provided by the walls, furniture or floor, with the plants providing the plain green. The secret of this rather abstract look is that the empty spaces become as much a part of the design as the plants.

Hard surfaces, containers and abstract artefacts are major ingredients, and the more way out they are, the better. Glass nuggets, stainless steel catering vats, and lengths of copper water pipe are *de rigueur* in contemporary gardens, but what you are really trying to do is to use materials in unexpected ways. You can dream up all sorts of creative uses for things most people would never think of putting in a garden. Don't bother trying to achieve a natural look; that's not what this style of gardening is all about, and that really gets up the nose of some traditionalists. If you like it, don't worry about them!

Contemporary gardens aren't easy to make unless you have a naturally artistic eye or some design training, but a good one is certainly eye-catching. If you feel like dabbling with this style, I'd strongly suggest taking a look at some examples that really work and using one of these for inspiration. Adapt it to suit your own taste, of course, but don't be frightened of using it as a starting point. You'll see superb examples in the display gardens at the Chelsea and Hampton Court Flower Shows, and they sometimes turn up on television in more off-the-wall make-over programmes and in the trendier type of home and gardening magazines.

There's one thing you can say about a contemporary garden, and that is: because there are very few plants and probably no lawn, it will be a lot less work to look after than a more traditional garden. Routine chores? It's more like housework. Which may be a good or a bad thing, depending on how you look at it.

A restrained use of colour creates a clean, cool and highly sophisticated atmosphere in this modern water garden (*below left*). Take care not to create a multicoloured nightmare when using coloured gravels. This garden (*below right*) just about gets away with it.

Choosing paintwork to complement the shades of the planting scheme has a unifying effect.

Good contemporary plants

The way many designers go about choosing plants for contemporary gardens is to think first of the shape they want, and then put a plant name to it. For spiky shapes, go for plants like the New Zealand flax, (*Phormium tenax)* and hardy yuccas, if you have to leave them outside all winter. If you have a sunroom to overwinter containers, you can use less hardy plants, like *Agave americana* and Chusan palm (*Trachycarpus fortunei*). If you want to make a carpet of identical plants, then low ornamental grasses are good – and, no, you don't have to mow them – but don't forget that if you choose a species that dies down in winter, you will lose the effect. Evergreen grasses, such as blue fescue (*Festuca glauca*), or the red sedge (*Uncinia rubra*), are a better bet for year-round looks, and the leaves make a repetitive pattern that reeks of the trendy. Block-shaped, evergreen knee-high hedges, low pillars or other architectural shapes can be clipped in box (*Buxus sempervirens*), thuja, or plain evergreen euonymus – choose a cultivar with small leaves, as large leaves, which you can't help cutting in half when you use shears or hedge-trimmers, end up looking tatty.

Hard surfaces

Contemporary gardens at shows contain lots of novel combinations of paving and other hardware, including some outlandish materials. I've even seen paths made from rusty washers and broken windscreen glass. This strikes me as a touch uncomfortable, but there's big business in recycling glass from bottle banks as coloured nuggets about the size of cough lozenges to use in the garden, and they also make glass gravel. The edges are supposed to have been rounded for safety, but I'd still wear gloves for handling them, just to be firmly on the safe side. These sorts of materials are too expensive to use for paths, but you can use them for top dressing containers, for mulching or for making imitation pools.

Garden artefacts

Don't think you can't have water features just because you've gone contemporary. You can, but a traditional lily pond won't look good in an ultra-modern setting. This is the place to take off on a flight of fancy with a floodlit fountain, or go the other way entirely with something very stark like a plain, shiny bowl of water.

Reflective surfaces are very fashionable, so besides stainless steel for covering vertical surfaces, look at mirror acrylics from DIY stores, which are a lot cheaper. You don't have to spend a fortune to be stylish; some of the trendiest containers are just large tin cans that have been washed out and stood in a row with plants in them.

Which brings me to rule number four of garden design: it's not how much you spend, it's the forethought that counts.

Five ways to make your garden contemporary

Materials	Colour	Lighting	Plants	Keep it simple
Be adventurous – think manufactured materials rather than traditional ones, such as glass, stainless steel, copper piping or rendered concrete.	Look beyond planting to introduce colour. Paint walls, fences, floors and outbuildings in bright colours as an effect in their own right, or as a background to dramatic planting.	Whether for practical or fun use, lighting can create instant contemporary impact. Use lights to highlight dramatic plants, focal points, water features or reflective surfaces, or simply to illuminate paths or dining areas.	Choose dramatic, architectural plants with well-defined shapes, such as phormiums, tree ferns, Chusan palms, agaves, ornamental grasses or clipped evergreen plants such as box or euonymus.	Contemporary gardens are about order, incorporating strong shapes, clean lines, a few simple textures and bold, minimalist planting schemes – this is not the place for packed, busy borders and the natural look!

Natural gardens

Conventional gardening involves rearranging the landscape and planting non-native species and plants that have been mucked about by plant breeders, but these days a lot of us are feeling the call of the wild. Natural gardens are firmly back in fashion. They'll suit anyone who likes the idea of a slice of countryside on the doorstep, even if they live in the town. It doesn't matter if your garden is measured in square feet instead of acres; a corner at the bottom of a normal garden is enough. It helps if you have the leave-it-alone philosophy, because this isn't the type of garden for a control freak or a serial tidy-upper.

What's it all about?

Natural-style gardens use flowers, trees and shrubs that grow wild in this country, planted very informally to mimic the way they grow in nature. They aren't evenly spaced out in the way you find plants in a 'proper' border, and you won't find the tallest at the back and the shortest at the front. You might not find any borders at all; wild flowers are often just grown in grass, and paths may only be roughly marked out with fallen logs and surfaced with bark chippings.

It takes a degree of planning and careful planting to create an apparently artless wild flower bank.

Natural-style gardens are quite cheap to create, since wild flowers are easily raised from seed and, once your favourite kinds are growing, they'll usually spread by self-seeding. Bulbs like daffs and bluebells only need to be planted once and then left to spread naturally, and native species of trees and shrubs are usually the cheapest kinds to buy from nurseries and garden centres. You don't always have to *buy* wild flowers and native trees and shrubs – very often if you give up conventional gardening, they'll find you.

There's no reason why you shouldn't stop using weedkiller on your lawn if you are happy to call it a wild flower meadow!

Good plants

It is plants that give a natural, wild-looking garden its character. Go for native trees like rowan (*Sorbus aucuparia*), birch (*Betula pendula*), or bird cherry (*Prunus padus*), but plant them in close groups of three if there's room. That's the way they often grow out in the countryside.

If you want a hedge, forget about cultivated conifers and go for the sort of mixed hedge you see out on a country walk, made from a mixture of hazel, hawthorn, elder, dog rose and blackthorn – the prickly tree with the white spring blossom followed by a crop of sloes. You don't have to clip a mixed hedge tightly – a relaxed row of plants allowed to grow into small trees makes a good, bird-friendly windbreak – but if you do clip it more tidily, let the occasional hawthorn or elder, or maybe a holly seedling, grow up through the hedge and turn into a small standard tree.

Wildflowers like primroses and cowslips are good for growing in short grass, while corncockle and annual poppies give long grass more character. Choose woodlanders, such as foxgloves and bluebells, for shady areas under trees.

Inspiration taken from the wild can be used to give any garden a more natural feel, even where quite hard curves and lines are employed.

Try to include as many different habitats as you can. A patch of flowering hay meadow looks truly rural and only needs cutting in spring and autumn. Otherwise, encourage a grassy lawn to grow short wildflowers, such as dog violets (*Viola riviniana*) and heartsease (*Viola tricolor*), by not using fertilizers and weedkillers, and topping it at about 8–10cm (3–4in) instead of cutting it short.

If there's room, have a small wooded area – birches are good here as they don't cast too much shade, so woodland plants and bulbs will thrive underneath. If your site is suitable, have a shallow pond or a patch of boggy ground, as they both lend opportunities for increasing the range of wild plants and flowers you can grow. They're also great for encouraging birds and amphibians, such as frogs, toads and newts, into the wild garden.

Don't feel you have to stick only to genuine wild plants; if you want to add 'tame' ones feel free, but plant them in random drifts, so they look as if they grew wild, and go for those that look the part so they don't stick out like sore thumbs. You'll find that anything too big, blowsy and brilliantly coloured will look really out of place.

Five ways to make a natural garden

Plants	Water	Materials	Wildlife	Natural boundaries
Use native plants – flowers, trees and shrubs that grow wild in this country rather than cultivated species. Don't plant them up as you would for a conventional border: go for a more informal feel, as they would grow in nature.	Dig a shallow pond or set aside a patch of boggy ground to encourage wildlife to visit and set up home. Damp areas also increase the range of wild flowers and plants you can grow.	Go back to nature – incorporate logs, hazel hurdles, timber, willow and stones in your design. Reclaiming natural materials can be environmentally friendly – as long as you are getting them from reputable sources!	Attract wildlife into your garden by planting trees and hedges with berries, wild flowers and grasses to supply food and hiding places for small animals and birds. Leave the garden undisturbed and they will seek you out.	Natural gardens look best with boundaries made of natural materials. Willow and hazel hurdles blend into the planting, as do wild hedges. Other fences can be smothered with climbers to give a more natural effect.

Other ingredients

The simpler and more back-to-nature your scheme is, the better it will look. Tree stumps and old logs are vital – rotting wood supports 40 per cent of forest life, so don't be too tidy. You don't have to leave them littered about, if you can't bear it; they will be just as attractive to wildlife in a stack.

Even a wild garden deserves a few decorative touches. Natural dips and hollows in the ground can be enlarged or emphasized. Woven hazel hurdles or heather panels make good natural arbours, route markers and dividers. Or you can even add 'wild' ornaments, like wooden mushrooms, a willow sculpture or a tree house. But don't try to be too clever – let the plants have the limelight.

Wildlife accommodation is very in-theme. You can make or buy hedgehog hibernating boxes, woven coir roosting pockets to wedge in hedges for birds, and insect 'hotels' made of hollow canes or dried grass stems crammed into wooden frames to hang in trees. One thing I wouldn't be without is a seat. A fat fallen log is all you need for a quiet afternoon's nature study.

Family gardens

This is a good example of what I said earlier about choosing the type of garden that will suit everyone who uses it. Most people need a garden like this at some stage in their lives. If you have a huge place in the country, it's not hard to have a great family garden, but it's not so easy to create something attractive behind a suburban semi with a typical pocket-hanky-sized patch.

You can have lots of different gardens in one, so that every member of the family has a spot they feel happy in. At this end of the garden the patio provides a place to sit and soak up the sun...

What's it all about?

A growing family needs room to run around, so it's no good planning a garden full of fragile flowers and breakable features. But it still needs to look attractive. After all, you'll be looking at it for several years. Play safe with a garden filled with child-friendly features, but don't forget to include things the whole family can enjoy: a sunny patio, a barbecue for Dad to play with (yes, I know there are only three days a year when he can fiddle with it, but it's the thought that counts), and some flowers, herbs and a salad bed somewhere out of harm's way. You can easily alter the playground feeling to something more sophisticated later.

Family-friendly plants

The perfect plant for a family garden is one that you can fall into, but which bounces back without either of you coming to any harm. Into that category I'd put most of the reliable old favourites – dogwood, forsythia, flowering currant, mock orange and winter jasmine. An ancient apple tree is good for a natural climbing-frame-cum-summer-sunshade; two are even better for hanging a hammock, and it's not a bad idea to have some tough ground cover, such as *Cotoneaster horizontalis*, that withstands most things.

Whatever else you grow, a patch of lawn is essential for running around, but I wouldn't worry about laying a top-quality lawn: something rough and ready is the answer. As long as it's well fed and not cut too closely, it'll stand up to a heck of a lot of hard wear.

It's worth thinking about what to leave out of a family garden if there are small children around. Steer clear of poisonous plants – laburnum and aconitum are among the worst offenders. Even so, it's best to teach small kids not to put anything they find in the garden into their mouths, unless it is presented to them on a plate.

…and at the far end of the garden a curved path surrounds a lawn where toddlers can have a rough and tumble.

Avoid prickly plants, such as berberis, roses and pyracantha, and anything sharp, which includes many ornamental grasses and bamboos. Irritants, such as euphorbias, which have very unpleasant sap, and fremontodendrons, whose leaves are covered in tiny hairs, can both cause severe skin reactions.

While children are small, I'd give ponds a miss, even if they are only shallow, or you'll always worry. Water features are something to save until they are a bit older and wiser. If you want one while they're small, I'd stick to a fountain or pebble pool in which most of the water is kept safely in a reservoir underground.

Other ingredients

It's worth putting things into a family garden that children will enjoy – a wildlife corner, or a place to keep pets such as guinea pigs, safely fenced from foxes. Start them on the right tracks by showing them how to grow their own sunflower seeds to feed the

Five ways to make a family garden

Plants	Water	Play area	Grow your own	Lawns
Think robust – the plants might be victim to a stray football and trees might become climbing frames for children. Also know your poisonous plants and try to remove them from the garden, or at least out of reach of small, tempted hands.	If you have children, avoid open water features, such as ponds, and choose water features that keep water in secure, underground reservoirs, where it doesn't present a danger.	Devote a section of the garden to the children for swings, slides, sandpits and climbing frames. Cover the floor area with bark chippings – they are a good, soft alternative to lawn.	Encourage children to take an interest in plants while indulging an adult passion for growing your own fruit and veg. Even a few pots of tomatoes on the patio can be very satisfying on a summer's day.	If your family garden is not complete without a lawn, make sure the grass you choose is a hard-wearing variety. A more expensive, delicate variety won't stay immaculate for long when your lawn becomes a football ground.

birds, or salad leaves for the rabbit. Specialize in things that grow quickly, such as lettuce and nasturtiums. Children can be impatient but fast-growing plants will harness and retain their interest.

If the garden is big enough, you can create a special play area covered with bark chippings – they are a lot kinder to tiny knees than gravel, and won't go muddy in wet weather as grass does. Use it to park a Wendy house, swing and slide. If you are talked into building a sandpit, make a cover for it – trellis will do – to stop cats using it for their personal convenience.

Fruit, vegetables and herbs have a great place in family gardens and kids usually enjoy helping to grow things they can eat or cook on the barbecue. But because time is bound to be short, think about growing just a few things that everyone likes, say cherry tomatoes in tubs on the patio. If you are serious about growing edibles, then make a couple of deep beds where you can grow a lot in a small space without too much work. Family gardens, in particular, are the kind it does pay to cultivate organically; there's no risk of kids coming in contact with pesticides or weedkillers. If you really must use garden chemicals, lock them safely away when they aren't in use, and keep kids and pets off treated areas until the stuff has dried, even when it's been diluted and properly applied.

You don't need vast amounts of space to create a family garden – it can be achieved almost artlessly in the tiniest of spaces.

Paved gardens

A paved garden is probably one of the easiest kinds for a novice garden planner to make a big hit with, because half your plants are in containers so the 'garden' is portable. This makes it easy to shift things round every time you come up with a better design idea, and you can also update the area each season just by buying a few new plants or containers. A paved garden is ideal for first-time gardeners, small gardens and for fashion victims who like to update their 'look' regularly. For anyone, in fact, who appreciates stylish outdoor living without making a lot of work for themselves.

What's it all about?

Families with small children need a decent-sized patio to double as a play area, especially when the lawn is soggy. But if the surrounding planting is used to soften the effect, it need not look like an airport runway.

The hot, sleepy siesta style goes down well in sunny patio and courtyard gardens, where there's no grass to cut, just gravel and paving with terracotta pots and a few sun-loving plants. It's a garden with a natural holiday feeling that you can build on by adding a state of the art barbecue, sophisticated outdoor furniture, an awning or parasols, outdoor lighting and all the trimmings. Go as high-tech as you like.

In summer, sheltered corners of a patio make a good home for house plants and potted tender perennials.

Typical paved garden plants

Plants in pots are essential in a paved garden. Annual bedding plants are the traditional choice, but don't feel tied to them – use something that will create the particular effect you have in mind.

On very hot, sunny paving you can create a Mediterranean look by using terracotta pots planted with pelargoniums and aromatic, evergreen herbs. A lean-to pergola can support a grape vine. In summer, you can stand tubs of bougainvillea up against trellis on a sunny wall, or dot potted lemon trees and tubs of oleander all around the place.

Without changing the structure of the patio, you can give it the tropical treatment by using containers of canna, pittosporum and gazanias, with *Trachelospermum asiaticum* growing up the wall – that's the evergreen climber with white jasmine-scented flowers all summer long. You could almost think you are in Hawaii.

Alternatively, you can create a desert-island paradise decorated with palm trees – the tougher ones anyway, such as cabbage palm, (*Cordyline australis*), and the dwarf fan palm (*Chamaerops humilis*), with some potted bamboos and banana plants (*Musa basjoo*). All it takes is a little imagination and somewhere warm to keep tender plants in winter, as they won't stand frost.

Other ingredients

Don't over-decorate a paved garden, or it'll end up looking like an architectural salvage yard, but there's no doubt that pots are very good scene setters. Don't just settle for cheap plastic kinds. Terracotta is a classic material for pots, but bright-coloured ceramic looks more tropical, and the understated earth shades with brush-stroke markings are inscrutably oriental. A lot of people pick the pots first and then find plants that go with them; it doesn't matter which way round you do it, just so long as you know what you are aiming at. Unity of theme is important whatever your garden style.

A variety of textures underfoot add enormously to the interest in a paved garden, especially in winter when you only have your evergreens for company. Don't design your paving so it's dead square, and do leave out the odd slab, either for planting, or to allow you to vary the texture by covering the soil with gravel, or with cobblestones set into a bed of cement. You don't want to become bored with your flooring, because it's the one thing that's difficult to change once it's down.

A variety of textures and colours work well in a garden space and add interest to your scheme, but keep them to a minimum for maximum effect.

Furniture is likely to be your biggest item of outlay, so pick something you'll be happy to live with for a few years. It needs to be comfortable and suit your chosen style. Unless you have lots of room in your garage, go for hardwood (taking care to look for the tag that shows it is from sustainable forests), or cast aluminium because it looks classy, and most important, you can leave it outside all year round. Just be sure to bring the cushions in when you aren't using them to keep them dry.

The smallest sitting area can be made spectacular with the bold use of paving, containers and plants. This one isn't subtle, but it's individual and exhilarating.

Five ways to make a paved garden

Flooring

Paving slabs are the most conventional material, but add a bit of interest to it by removing (or leaving out) some slabs and replacing them with gravel, cobbles, lawn or ground-cover planting.

Pots

There is a wide range of containers available from terracotta to glazed pots and more contemporary steel ones, which come in all different shapes and sizes to suit any style of garden.

Plants

There are many plants that will happily grow in pots – from summer bedding plants, to herbs and even palms or small trees. Your only restrictions are the size and aspect of your plot.

Hi-tech

A paved garden is perfect for technology extras such as lighting, outdoor heaters and barbecues – and anything else to lure you outdoors on a sunny day!

Furniture

This might be the most visible part of your garden, and will probably be the highest outlay, so choose carefully to make sure you select the most comfortable and the most aesthetically pleasing pieces for your plot.

Cottage gardens

Here the box balls provide a touch of formality alongside the paved and gravel path, and are a nod to the old cottagers' love of topiary. Horizontal lines – the path and the pergola – are perforated by verticals – the pots and the verbascums and delphiniums.

The romantically cluttered look of a cottage garden makes it an ideal style for plant lovers. You can cram a lot of different plants into a small space, without losing the overall character. A quaint country cottage isn't essential. There are people who make cottage gardens on modern housing estates or in towns. If you can't stop buying plants, or if you are a compulsive plant propagator, this could be just the kind of garden for you – a patchwork quilt of your own particular floral pleasures.

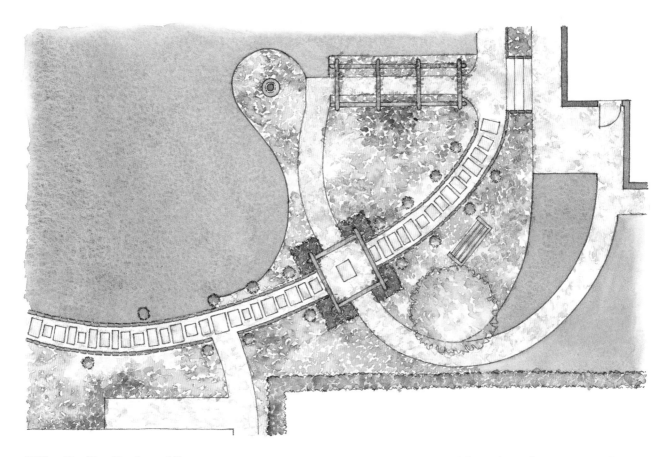

What's it all about?

Cottage gardens are all about plants and very little else. The original cottage gardeners didn't bother with grass because it took up valuable growing space. Clinker paths, which nowadays have been replaced by gravel, did for getting round, and everything else was wall-to-wall plants, all jumbled together with recycled bric-a-brac. Cottage gardeners simply stuck things in wherever there was room. Design didn't come into it – the garden just 'happened'.

Even today, cottage gardeners are the sort who'll keep nipping a bit out of the lawn to enlarge the flower beds any time they need more room. RHS guidelines? Forget 'em. This type of garden breaks all the rules. If there's a tree, it will have a couple of climbers growing up it and a shrub underneath. Every shrub will be underplanted with perennials *and* bulbs. The porch will be weighted down with climbers and the steps congested with plants in geriatric clay pots.

Although it goes against the grain for anyone with an instinct for cottage gardening to do any garden planning, it's still well worthwhile. It's the only way you'll see all the various plant characters properly and to make sure that they don't end up swamping each other. You also need a little bit of architecture or hard landscaping to set them off, or you end up not seeing the garden for the flowers.

The paths in this cottage garden are supremely practical in that they lead from the door of the house to the garage and garden gate, but the planting and design softens the hardness of the practicality, and the chosen plants give a truly cottagey feel.

Cottage garden plants

Old cottage gardens were stuffed solid with easy-going plants like hardy annuals and the sort of spreading perennials that would probably be called 'thugs' in most modern gardens. They'd also have old roses, useful plants like herbs and vegetables, and wild flowers and plants providing nectar for bees because every garden had a couple of hives.

The only trees and shrubs would have been the sort that provided fruit for the house. Flowers like gladioli, sweet peas and dahlias were often grown in rows to sell as cut flowers at the garden gate – few evergreens would have found a place at all. The emphasis was on self-sufficiency, with the chance to earn a little pocket-money on the side.

Nowadays, you can make a low-maintenance cottage garden border by teaming self-seeding hardy annuals with rampant, spreading perennials, or you can make a nostalgic border by mixing together flowers for cutting and the prettier vegetables and herbs.

Five ways to make a cottage garden

Plants	Hard landscape	Climbers	Recycling materials	Containers
In a cottage garden, the more plants, the merrier. Plant whatever you fancy – from flowers to trees, shrubs, bulbs.	Most cottage gardens avoid this except for the occasional small path to allow access to the garden or beds – plants are the key ingredient.	If you don't happen to have a porch, try and introduce some verticals in the garden over which climbers can grow. Pergolas, gazebos, trellis or trees can provide good support.	Old sinks, chimney pots and other antique or second-hand paraphernalia add a cosy, relaxed feel to a cottage garden.	Cottage gardeners soon run out of space in their beds and borders, but containers provide room for yet more plants and can be snuck on paths and patios and into gaps throughout the garden.

But your average cottage garden houses a huge mixture of choicer plants too. It might contain flowering shrubs, a clematis collection, a formal herb garden, unusual perennials, topiary, natural-looking ponds and streams, or containers of alpines shoehorned into every inch of available space. The 21st-century cottage garden is definitely an enthusiast's garden.

Restraint is not a familiar word in the cottage gardener's vocabulary. The planting wraps right around the house (*opposite*) and billows out over snaking paths (*above*) as you amble down the garden.

Other ingredients

Cottage gardeners are born recyclers; the Victorians did so out of genuine poverty, but today it's usually because they would rather spend their money on more plants. If a wall came down, if the kitchen sink was replaced, or a bucket sprang a leak, or a tile floor was re-laid, the plunder would be re-used somewhere in the garden.

Nowadays, to achieve the look, people will buy (or better still, acquire) second-hand items, such as old chimney pots or stone butler's sinks from salvage yards. Twist-topped tiles are good for edging paths, and old bricks make good raised beds for special treasures. Rickety rustic structures made from pruned tree branches, and plant supports made out of rural materials, such as hazel and willow wands, look very much at home in this sort of garden. And so do distressed, reproduction antique garden knick-knacks. But go easy on the paraphernalia – the final effect should give more of a nod towards Sissinghurst than the junk yard of Steptoe and Son.

Formal gardens

Formal gardens are a carry-over from the grand gardens of the past, and what makes them stand out is their geometry. They don't even try to look natural. Lines are straight, angles are right, and corners are squared. You might think you need a junior stately home to carry it off, but not so. A lot of tiny town gardens look good with a formal layout, but if you have a big enough space to divide into several 'rooms', there's something peculiarly refreshing about wandering straight from a wildly casual patch into an area with a strong sense of order and calm.

What's it all about?

The character of a traditional formal garden is created by rectangular blocks of grass, clipped evergreen hedges and elaborate topiary with bags of architecture, whether it's walls and paving,

Squares and circles, rectangles and avenues are the backbone of the formal garden (*below*). You don't need acres of space to create a similar feel: this style can work well even in the smallest area and with a limited range of plants (*opposite*).

or classical sculptures – there is none of your abstract stuff here. Only Corinthian columns, stone cherubs and Grecian urns need apply. Water features might be the square, lily pond variety, or the circular sort complete with a skinny-dipping nymph clutching the fountain.

Yes, there are flowers, but they'll be very well-behaved, or else strictly staked, growing in a proper, rectangular herbaceous border with a brick wall or a yew hedge running along the back. Or there could be a double border, which is just two borders face-to-face with a path running through the middle, the whole inside a 'room' enclosed by walls or hedges.

Look to stately homes for inspiration. Many of them have features such as formal parterres, with flower beds edged with clipped dwarf hedging, or geometrical herb gardens, divided into segments like an orange, with a sundial in the centre. They may seem to demand a large amount of space, but they can be successfully duplicated on a smaller scale to suit your own plot.

Five ways to make a formal garden

Design	Features	Plants	Materials	Order
Straight lines, square corners, right angles and geometry are the crucial factors in designing a formal garden – it is a style that demands a strong sense of order.	Formal gardens demand a strong architectural feel that can be provided by hard landscaping, such as walls and paths, or features such as statues and follies: the most important word to remember is elegant.	Traditionally, formal gardens are characterized by hedging and topiary. Yew and box are best; there is even a dwarf box for those who desire a formal garden on a smaller scale. Other plants should be suitable for disciplined beds or borders.	From paving to statues to furniture, the materials in a formal garden should be classy and expensive-looking. Synthetic or cheap materials will stand out and ruin the effect.	Good order is key in a formal scheme – hedges will need to be kept clipped, and borders and pathways must be kept tidy and clearly defined. Seating at the end of paths and along borders allows you to survey the order you have created.

Blocks of dahlias and mushrooms of yew make a classic combination at Hinton Ampner, one of my favourite Hampshire gardens.

Formal plants

Whatever else you decide on, you'll need a hedging plant that will stand being closely clipped, and normally the choice is between yew and box, both of which can also be trained as topiary. Go for yew if the site is sunny and the soil well drained; in a shady garden, box is best, though it's also happy in sun if the soil doesn't dry out too badly. If you want dwarf edgings, go for dwarf box (*Buxus sempervirens* 'Suffruticosa') as the other boxes won't stand being clipped this short. Otherwise, use evergreen herbs, like an upright form of rosemary, santolina or one of the dwarf lavenders, such as *Lavandula angustifolia* 'Munstead'.

Other ingredients

Whatever you have, it has to be classy. Paving needs to be York stone or near offer. Statues should be of lead or stone, or you might stretch a point and order a little something in wrought metal. Forget gaudy garden chairs: the sort to go for are classic wooden Lutyens-style benches, or cast aluminium copies of Edwardian ironwork garden seats.

In case you're worrying that it all sounds a bit expensive, that's certainly the impression you want to make but, since quality lasts, a garden like this keeps going for years without needing expensive refurbishment. But you can always cheat. Any competent do-it-yourself fan can make their own wooden seats and tables, and reconstituted stonework looks just like the real thing these days.

Finding formal ingredients

Some larger garden centres have big display areas where you can see a good selection of different types of repro garden furniture, outbuildings and fittings, and most large gardening shows will have a good range of products available on the maker's stalls, but probably the very best place to see all the different ingredients together is the Chelsea Flower Show. The show catalogue lists names and addresses of all the suppliers so you can follow up ideas later.

Making a plan

Once you have some idea of the style of garden you fancy, start to put something down on paper. It's too soon for a shopping list at this stage; the way I always start is by drawing an outline of the garden. This will become the template upon which you try out various ideas, as you build up your dream garden in several stages. There's something hugely intimidating about a blank piece of paper, but once you've drawn in the house and the boundaries, you can fiddle about and see what starts to fall into place.

Drawing the outline

It's worth drawing your garden outline to scale, otherwise when you start filling in some details later, you'll have no idea if the features you want are going to fit.

If you like working with paper and pencil, you'll find squared paper makes life much easier. Choose a scale to fit. One square to the metre usually works for a small garden, but if you own rolling acres you'll soon be off the edge of the page.

Use your computer if you prefer; that's the way I planned the *Ground Force* gardens. You don't need to buy a proper design programme unless you particularly want to; I just use the drawing tools to make straight lines, formal shapes or freehand beds and borders, then I can play about with various ideas and print them off.

From simple sketch to colourful design, what was once a bald and lacklustre patio now becomes an exciting viewpoint for the tiers of bright planting on the slope.

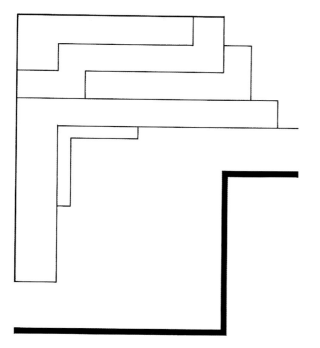

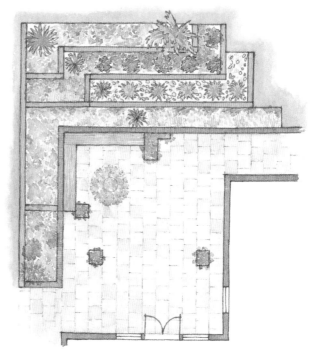

Measuring up

If your plan is to work, the information needs to be accurate in the first place, so measure up very carefully. Landscapers normally use a 30m (100ft) tape that recoils into its own round carrying case, but there's no need to buy one specially. You can make do with an ordinary retractable handyman's tape measure. That's a lot easier than struggling with a school ruler, and it has the big advantage of being flexible. Have an assistant to help; measure your boundaries, then convert them to the right scale and mark them on your plan. If all else fails, you can always just pace the length and width of the garden, then multiply the length of your stride (it's usually about a metre/yard) by the number of paces. That'll probably be good enough for a small garden.

Next comes a bit more measuring, because you need to mark the exact position of the house on your plan, and show where the windows and doors are, so you know where you'll be looking out or going in. Then measure the position of all those things that have to stay put, such as immovable paths, inspection covers, huge trees and tall fences that you can't or don't want to remove, and mark them on your master plan too.

Draw in a small compass rose so you can see which way faces north and south. If there is anything outside your garden that you need to take into consideration, such as superb country views you don't want to lose, a cluster of pylons that you want to hide, or overhanging trees that create heavy shade – make a note on the plan so you remember to take them into account as you work.

Now take a copy of your plan, or lay a big sheet of tracing paper over the top so you don't make a mess of the original, and experiment with some basic shapes. Take your time and have fun – it's nothing to worry about.

Pick of the best

Stick to basic shapes for now and don't be tempted to start filling in minute detail. That will come later. For now, concentrate on making perhaps half a dozen different designs. Pick out the bits you liked best from each and see if they can't be combined in a different way to make something you like even better.

The 'experimenting with ideas' stage is an important one, so take your time. That's why most people choose the winter to design the garden, when there isn't much doing outside and it's very pleasant to sit inside, just thinking and planning. Once you have a basic layout you are reasonably happy with, that's the time to start thinking about specific features, plants and 'hardware'.

Proper measurements will make your plan realistic – you'll then know exactly what you can fit into a given space.

Playing with shapes

Just because your garden is square or rectangular, it doesn't mean that you have to keep it looking that way. It's amazing how something as simple as changing the shape of the lawn can alter your whole perspective on the rest of the garden. So whether you have an existing garden to adapt, or a whole new garden to start from scratch, just play around for a while. It won't commit you to anything, and it might be the start of some good ideas.

There are lots of possibilities to explore, and when one jumps out that makes you feel right, move on to the next stage. So take your basic outline and gradually keep adding the next degree of detail. The picture slowly builds up until you have a finished plan showing everything. You'll find the Master Plan is a great help, whether you are making the garden a bit at a time, or just deciding what to buy at the garden centre. That way you will know where to put it when you get home, because you can fit it into the plan.

Design tips – conjuring up ideas

Don't just sit there staring at a blank sheet of paper waiting for inspiration to strike. Look at photos of good gardens in books and magazines, preferably ones that are roughly the same size, shape and style as the one you are trying to create for yourself. If you've taken pictures of gardens you've visited during the summer, now is the time to dig them out. There's no need to copy someone else's ideas exactly, but if you see something you really like there's no harm in borrowing it as the basis for your own garden. By the time you've added your own personal touches, it'll look quite different. Confidence is hard to come by when you're starting from scratch, so never be afraid to rely on other people's experience.

And if you simply cannot design on paper? You are not a failure. Go out on to the soil and do it there; use lines of sand to mark your shapes, and scuff them out if they don't work. Use canes to indicate prominent trees and bushes. You will not be alone in your preference for designing on the ground – William Robinson ('The father of English gardening') insisted on it. You're in good company. Sometimes I do it myself.

Over the next few pages, I've looked at some simple ideas for laying out the garden shapes you are most likely to encounter. You don't have to copy them, but if you've never done this sort of thing before, it's helpful to have a starting point. Just adapt them as much as you want. And remember to be practical. Choose lawn shapes that are easy to mow, and beds and borders that are large enough to accommodate a decent number of plants. Even in tiny gardens, it is worth remembering the KISS rule – Keep It Simple, Stupid!

Diagonal lawn

If you want a rectangular lawn, there's nothing to say that it has to run parallel with the garden fences. Try laying it diagonally across the garden, but instead of putting it right through the middle, offset it slightly to leave different-sized shapes in the corners.

Two diagonal lawns

You could try for similar effects by using two diagonally placed rectangles that overlap each other – they can be the same size or different, if that fits the space better. It gives a dynamic sense of movement and leaves several planting spaces of interesting shape.

Round lawn

Superimpose a circular lawn on to your garden plan. See what it looks like in the middle – the basis for a formal garden perhaps? Or offset it to one end of the garden, or over to one side. See how the shapes between the edge of the lawn and the boundary round the garden change? Imagine what they'd look like filled with plants, but don't get drawn into fine detail – at this stage it's just a question of opening your mind to ideas.

Two round lawns

Why settle for one round lawn when you can have two? Some of the most stylish modern gardens are based on two overlapping circles. They don't both have to be the same size, and they don't need to overlap equally. Try placing them up and down the garden, then see how it looks if you place them diagonally from corner to corner. Again, notice how the shapes alter between the circles and the edge of the garden, where you'll be putting your planting. See what happens if you draw a quarter circle in one corner and overlap it with a section of a second circle. If you are on a sloping site, one circle could be higher than the other, so you have to step down where they overlap.

Nobody can tell you what you like or don't like – it's instinctive – but you can at least make sure you know all your options. Will it be a diagonal lawn, or two diagonal lawns? A single grass circle or a double one? Only you can decide.

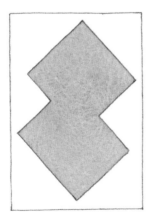
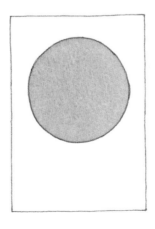
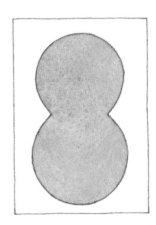

How to... **transfer paper plan to site**

Once you are happy with the shape, size and positioning of your beds, paths and other features on your Master Plan, it's time to see what it looks like for real, out in the garden. You haven't committed yourself yet – there's still time for fine adjustment. Convert the lines on your plan into life-size measurements. You'll find it easier if you write them on the plan as a ready reference. Stick to either metric or imperial measurements – don't mix them up or you'll get in a muddle. (Bear in mind that most building materials, such as paving slabs, are sold in metric nowadays.) It's also a good idea to cut yourself a straight piece of timber exactly one metre long as an instant measuring stick.

What you need

- *some 30cm (1ft) wooden pegs sharpened at one end*
- *plenty of string*
- *cans of landscaper's spray paint or an old plastic lemonade bottle filled with dry sand*
- *tall bamboo canes*

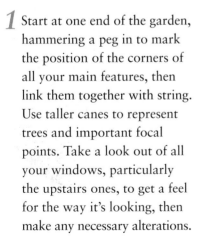

1 Start at one end of the garden, hammering a peg in to mark the position of the corners of all your main features, then link them together with string. Use taller canes to represent trees and important focal points. Take a look out of all your windows, particularly the upstairs ones, to get a feel for the way it's looking, then make any necessary alterations.

2 Use a measuring stick or a tape to add up the dimensions of important features. This way you can work out if they will be large enough to put chairs and tables on, and be able to calculate accurately the amount of materials that will be needed to build them.

3 Once you are happy with the layout, go round spraying builder's marking-out paint or trickling sand directly underneath the strings. With the markings in place, you can take out the pegs and string, leaving the shape of the garden outlined perfectly. Tackle the hard landscaping first – paths and patios – then move on to plant features, such as hedges, beds and lawns.

Regulation rectangles

Ultra-modern designs can look good in small gardens and also be practical. The curving lavender wall masks the ugly shed and is fitted with a seat for soaking up the sun.

A few pages back I showed you how something as simple as changing the shape of the lawn can make a plain rectangular garden look completely different; well, now I'd like to show you some other ways you can make the same shape more interesting, by dividing it up into several smaller areas or 'rooms'.

'That's all very well if you have a huge garden,' I can hear you say. Well, yes if you *do* have a big garden, dividing it up into 'garden rooms' is the best way to pack it full of interest, but you can do the same thing on a small scale in quite a tiny garden. Only here, instead of having tall features to divide it up, you just use shorter ones that you can see over. It's not as radical as it sounds; most of the good small gardens you know will probably have a patch of paving, some borders and a feature of some sort, such as a pond, or a specimen tree with a seat under it. So there are three quite distinct areas for a start, even if they aren't kept apart by real physical barriers.

Because you are only playing about with ideas on paper at the moment, it doesn't matter how your thoughts turn out; nobody is going to see them except you. So experiment with some different basic shapes inside your space – diagonals and circles; the odd lazy 'S', teardrop shapes such as you find in Paisley patterns, and long sweeping curves. Then start to adapt them into beds, borders and lawn, or paving and paths. Don't start thinking about specific plants yet, because we are still working on the big picture.

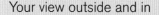

Your view outside and in

Imagine you are looking out from the windows you marked on your plan, and make sure they overlook a good view of the garden. If you have big borders right in front of them, they'll make the room dark and spoil the view. You don't want to be able to see the entire garden from indoors, either. Screen part of it off to give some inducement to explore.

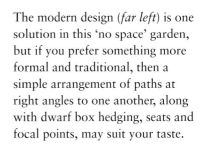

The modern design (*far left*) is one solution in this 'no space' garden, but if you prefer something more formal and traditional, then a simple arrangement of paths at right angles to one another, along with dwarf box hedging, seats and focal points, may suit your taste.

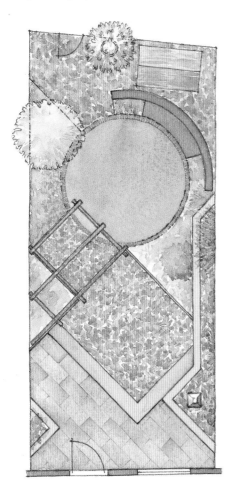

Long and lean

There are more long, lean gardens around than you might think. Mostly they are older, town gardens where, in order to make sure everyone had at least a little bit of road frontage, the original planners carved the building plot up into a lot of thin slices.

By its very nature, the long thin garden draws your eye straight to the far end, where it loses interest. There are several tricks that will remedy this; the idea is to find a way of slowing the eye down by creating some interesting diversions on the way.

One way to do that is to divide the garden up into several smaller and squarer shapes, which each make a 'room' that could have quite a different character. You might have a lawn and flower

This is the plan that was decided upon (*left*) but there is an alternative (*right*) which is every bit as workable. It's all a matter of taste.

Avoid long straight lines

The thing to avoid at all costs is having a path that runs the full length of the garden. It acts like a visual wind-tunnel, carrying your eye straight past everything else to the end of the plot. Stagger your paths so you have to cross the garden from side to side, or cross a diagonal, or walk round a segment of a circle to move from one 'room' to the next. It looks better when you see the garden from the house or the upstairs windows, but when you are out there walking around, it helps you lose your sense of direction and makes you feel that you are wandering around aimlessly instead of being confined inside a regular shape.

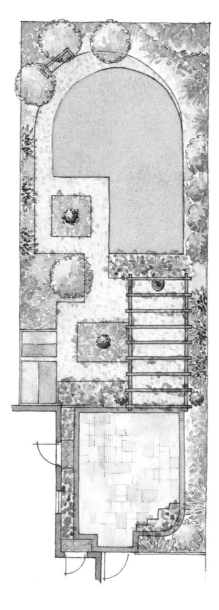

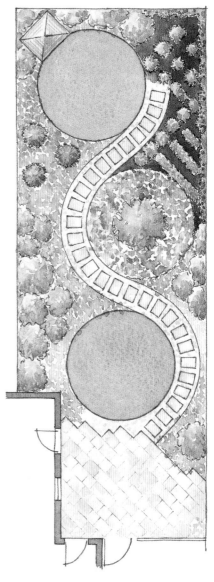

garden in one, a paved seating area with containers in another, and perhaps a formal ornamental vegetable and herb garden in another.

You could base the overall design for the space on a giant 'S' shape, but to make it foreshorten the length of garden slightly don't sit it square in your space; it will be more effective if it is angled so that it runs diagonally from one corner of the garden to the other.

Alternatively, you can go for a more geometrical look based on a series of dynamic diagonals to create a zigzag pattern running down the garden.

The difficulty usually lies in knowing when to stop, and when a design is becoming over elaborate. As a general rule, use strong, hard lines – even if they are curving – and avoid fussy twiddly bits. These will probably irritate you after a while, and can be very difficult to maintain – especially if they make the lawn hard to mow.

This garden (*below*) was completely empty – a blank canvas. In a way this situation is the most daunting – there is nothing to inspire. But once a list of requirements was drawn up – somewhere to sit in the sun, a lawn for toddlers to play on, a few vegetables and herbs, and the accommodation of two small sheds, it started to take shape.

Tricky triangular

Not all gardens are symmetrical, in fact, few are. But the owners of those odd-shaped bits round the edges of building plots often despair of finding a way of organizing their lopsided patch into something that looks like a garden.

If that's your problem, then you are a lot luckier than you think. Irregular shapes can be a lot easier to divide up into separate areas, precisely because you don't have the straitjacket of a formal square or rectangle outline dominating your thoughts and trying to duplicate itself every time you drop your guard.

Just because a garden is asymmetrical and oddly shaped does not mean that it cannot be visually satisfying. Think of it as uniquely challenging!

Once you set it down on paper, an odd shape often dictates how best to divide itself up; circles and diagonals that touch odd-angled boundary walls make all sorts of interesting shapes.

A point at the end of a triangular garden can be squared slightly by lopping off the tip, leaving you with a handy bit of land in which to screen off your shed or compost heaps. Alternatively, you could use the space for a big specimen tree against a background of evergreens, or to plant a bamboo grotto with a bit of garden stonework. They'll all help to disguise the odd shape of the garden and, at the same time, leave you wondering if there isn't something else leading off round the corner. Keep 'em guessing, and the garden will look all the more interesting.

One thing that often looks attractive in a slightly triangular-shaped garden is to have a straight path that runs parallel to one of the sides and going part of the way across the garden. Instead of a plain path, you can substitute a walk-through pergola to cover with climbers or a fruit tunnel.

Once you have taken a bold decision and plotted it in, you start to see a new set of shapes within the garden that suggest all sorts of ideas. So don't worry about dirtying paper; have a go and find out for yourself what works and what doesn't.

The plan (*above left*) is the layout of the garden opposite – it is a languorous feast of sweeping curves. The alternative could have been the layout (*above right*). This design centres around a formal pool and interlocking paths that bisect the garden and its packed formal beds.

2 VERTICAL GARDENING

What's it about?

Vertical gardening is just a handy umbrella term for things that go up, like fences, walls, pergolas and arches, in contrast to things that go along horizontally, like lawns and flower beds. It's a good way of making a flat garden look more three-dimensional, besides giving you extra space to grow plants you might not otherwise have room for. So make more of your verticals – they can practically double your growing space!

How verticals fit into the grand design

Boundaries go round the edge of the garden like the margins round a piece of paper; they are your fences, walls and hedges. They mark the outer extent of your property, giving you an enclosed place to escape from the outside world. They shelter the garden from wind and weather, they provide a background for the garden, and they can also act as your fortifications, keeping intruders out and pets and children in.

Garden structures are also verticals, but they appear more like punctuation marks. Think of sheds, summer-houses and arbours as the full stops at the end of a path, or pergolas as brackets that enclose or frame a chunk of space. Pillars and obelisks are the exclamation marks in your borders, while arches are the page breaks allowing you to step from one chapter of the garden into the next.

As well as being used to lift a garden up off the flat, a climber-covered screen will also act as a divider, which tempts the visitor to explore further, or which masks an ugly shed or garage.

When you begin adding details to your basic plan, start from the outside and work in. Think about all of these taller, more solid features – boundaries and structures – first. They are the things that give your garden its permanent framework and they help you to organize the view into bite-sized bits so that it's not just a solid mass of unbroken greenery from which nothing stands out.

Verticals in small gardens

Tall boundaries are usually a mistake in a small garden. They can make it dark and dingy, and, because you feel hemmed in, they make the space seem even smaller than it really is. It's much better to keep the boundaries lower and lighter, or even partially see-through, by using trellis or open lattice, rustic fences. Add height within the garden using structures and tall plant supports.

Rustic poles and pillars are a great way of growing climbing roses when you don't have a wall, decorative plant supports are perfect for growing a clematis in the middle of a border, and annual climbers are ideal for growing in pots on the patio, trained up an obelisk. Anywhere there is a natural opening – such as over a gate at the side of the house – you can add an arch, which immediately makes room for another two climbers, besides adding extra interest without taking up any space.

Verticals in bigger gardens

Where there is more space to play with, tall features can give the garden more of a sense of mystery. Hedges can be used to divide the space up into a series of outdoor rooms. Instead of being able to look straight to the end of the garden, you have to go outside and walk round to investigate the hidden bits. Don't be ashamed of having a low boredom threshold – pander to it instead.

A pergola or tunnel can turn a straight path into an interesting feature. An arch positioned over the top of a bench turns it into an arbour, and a curved hedge behind a large garden ornament acts like a living frame, creating an instant focal point.

In a bigger garden, you'll also have more room for outbuildings, which not only provide useful storage space, but also add all sorts of new possibilities to your views around the garden.

Problems solved

Vertical gardening can also be a solution to all sorts of problem situations. You can use the principle to turn an ugly chain-link fence into a flowering hedge by covering it with evergreen climbers, disguise a derelict outbuilding by growing ivy over it, or screen off next door's junkyard behind a clematis fence. When it comes to a cover-up, climbers and wall plants are the best things for the job.

Not all forms of vertical gardening need to rely on visible structures – this clematis has swamped its support system to make a cascading dome of flower.

Hedges

The only thing you needed to think about when choosing hedging years ago was cost. In towns, it was invariably privet, while big suburban gardens went mostly for beech or hornbeam that could be bought cheaply as bare-rooted seedlings in winter. Out in the country, they'd have hawthorn because it kept the cows out.

The craze for conifer hedges meant buying more expensive plants growing in pots, as that was the only way they'd transplant well. Nowadays, people who need only a small length of hedge are just as likely to choose pot-grown shrubs from a garden centre to plant as an ornamental screen.

Today's hedges don't only go round the outside of the garden. You are just as likely to meet smaller, more decorative hedges acting as garden dividers or dwarf edgings round beds or paths. And hedging plants may be clipped into frivolous features, such as topiary, 'living architecture', or 'cloud' formations.

Hedging plants come in many forms, which makes them capable of being put to many different uses – from clipped orbs of cotton lavender (*Santolina*), to dwarf kerbs of box (*Buxus*) or towering yew.

How to... **plant a hedge**

By far the cheapest way of making a hedge is to buy bundles of bare-rooted, deciduous hedging plants. These are available only between late autumn and early spring, but small ones cost very little. Stand the plants in a bucket containing a few inches of water for 2–3 hours to rehydrate them when you get them home. If you can't plant them straight away, heel them in by planting them temporarily in a hole or trench somewhere in the garden to keep them fresh.

Alternatively, pot-grown hedging plants can be planted at any time of year when the ground is in a suitable state, but spring or autumn is best. However, they will be considerably more expensive than bare-rooted plants.

What you need

- *enough plants*
  (see spacings below)
- *well-rotted organic matter*
- *general organic fertilizer*
  (in spring)
- *garden line*
- *spade*
- *fork*
- *hose for watering*

1 Prepare the ground thoroughly. Run out a line to mark the position of the hedge, then dig a trench 30cm (12in) deep and 45cm (18in) wide. Spread plenty of well-rotted organic matter along the bottom of it and, if planting in spring, sprinkle a general-purpose fertilizer along its length. Fork this into the bottom of the trench.

2 Space the plants out evenly. For a dwarf or medium-sized hedge, plant a single row spaced 30–60cm (1–2ft) apart. If you want a hedge more than 1.2m (4ft) tall, plant a staggered double row, with the plants 75cm (30in) apart. They will make a thicker, stronger hedge. Adjust the spacing slightly before you plant so that the plants fill the space completely and you don't run out of plants before reaching the end of the row.

3 Plant pot-grown plants as you would normal shrubs, but for bare-rooted plants, dig a hole that is plenty big enough and spread the roots out well in the bottom before covering them with soil. In both cases, water the plants in well, and mulch them with an 8cm (3in) thick layer of well-rotted manure or compost. They will establish all the better for this. After planting, you need to do some trimming (see p.62).

Immediate aftercare

With pot-grown conifers, shrubs and evergreens, just trim the sides slightly and prune the top out of the leader (the main, central shoot). One or more shoots will soon grow to replace it, so it won't stop the hedge growing taller, but it helps encourage bushy growth lower down in the meantime. If you want a tall hedge, it's a good idea to stake the plants for extra stability.

Thinking of having a hedge?

Hedges are 'green', wildlife-friendly and resilient, and they last for many years, but there is a down-side. A new hedge takes several years to reach its full height; it takes up more room round the garden than a fence of similar height, and there is also clipping to think about. Most hedges need trimming once or twice every year. If you choose a fast-growing hedge, it'll reach the required height quickly, but you'll need to clip it much more often to keep the shape. If you live in town or have a small garden, how are you going to get rid of all the clippings? And don't forget that your hedge is going to grow on your neighbour's side too.

It is tempting to leave hedging plants at their full height after planting, but you'll encourage more vigorous growth if you cut them back by up to half their height and then, like this rose hedge (*below*), they will become thicker and more impenetrable.

Bare-rooted deciduous plants need cutting down to about 15cm (6in) from the ground or, if they are already branching from the base, then you only need to shorten them back by one-third. It's tempting not to bother, but it ensures that the hedge fills out from the ground up – otherwise you can be left with a gappy bottom, which you will curse later. As the hedge grows, clip it lightly, little and often during the summer, until it reaches the required size, so that you are continually forming the shape as it grows up.

How to... **clip a hedge**

A hedge up to about 1.5m (5ft) high can be clipped by a person standing on the ground. For taller hedges, use a stepladder or a special hedge-cutting platform, which you can hire. Make sure the ground is firm and level before you start; a wobble could be serious if you're holding a moving hedge-trimmer. With electric trimmers, *always* use a circuit breaker (RCD) to cut off the power instantly should you cut through the flex. When using power tools, *always* wear goggles, long sleeves, long trousers and strong boots. I know it's a bother, but it helps keep you out of the casualty department.

Soft clippings from a hedge that you cut little and often, such as privet, can be put on the compost heap, so long as you mix them with plenty of other ingredients. Bag up woody clippings and take them to a local authority rubbish tip. If you want to compost them, put them through a shredder first and allow a little longer than usual for the material to break down. Don't burn them; they make lots of smoke. Yew clippings can be collected in bulk to use in the manufacture of anti-cancer drugs.

What you need

- *shears or powered hedge-clippers*
- *stepladder or platform (for tall hedges)*
- *posts or stout canes taller than the hedge*
- *ball of string*

1 If the hedge has been left a bit too long since the last cut, and the shape has been badly blurred by a fuzz of new shoots, knock a post or a stout cane in at each end and stretch a taut piece of string along it at the required height. This will act as a visual guide when cutting the top.

2 Trim the sides first, angling them in slightly from bottom to top to give the hedge a 'batter'. This makes the top less likely to splay open, and it stops the top of the hedge shading the bottom, so there's less risk of it going bald at the base. Use a power trimmer in broad sweeps, making sure the blades are kept parallel to the hedge.

3 Cut the top last. You can cut it perfectly flat for a very formal finish, or round it slightly for a more informal look. In areas that have a lot of snow in winter, clipping to a formal point or a high dome allows snow to slide off more easily. This reduces the risk of a weight of snow building up on top and bending the hedge over or splitting it apart.

Which hedging plants?

When you are deciding what sort of hedge to plant, think about how tall you want the hedge to be – not all hedging plants grow tall. Don't choose a tall-growing kind and expect to be able to keep it small and healthy. It won't like it one bit.

Think about how much work it's going to make, too. A slow-growing hedge needs clipping twice a year, but you can get away with just doing it once. A fast-growing hedge needs clipping every six weeks between late spring and early autumn.

Formal clipped hedges

These are the sort of smart, tailored hedges that you see at stately homes and round traditional town or country gardens, that look like a wall of leaves.

Yew (*Taxus baccata*) (**1**) makes a good slow-growing, evergreen hedge in the 1.5–2.4m (5–8ft) range. It looks good all year round, and it's very versatile. You can train it for topiary, clip a hedge with a fancy turret-top, or grow an archway in it. A single row of yew can be clipped into a much narrower hedge than any other, as little as 30cm (12in) wide. A yew hedge doesn't take as long to reach its full height as everyone tells you (mine puts on a good 15cm (6in) a year) and it needs cutting only once a year. It's also less fussy than people think – it does need well-drained soil, but it can be chalky or acid.

Box (*Buxus sempervirens*) (**2**) is ideal if you want a shorter evergreen hedge, say 75cm–1.5m (2–5ft) high. It takes to clipping and training just as well as yew, and it's slow growing, so it doesn't need a lot of cutting. It also stands quite a bit of shade. It doesn't want total gloom though, but in a site that gets about an hour of sun during the day, box will do. The disadvantage is that it has recently begun to fall prey to a disease called box blight, which can kill out great lumps of it. Take a chance if you're desperate for box, but buy from a reputable nursery. Otherwise, go for yew every time.

Beech (*Fagus sylvatica*) (**3**) and **hornbeam** (*Carpinus betulus*) are the traditional, slow-growing, country garden hedges, suitable for growing from 1.5–2.4m (5–8ft) high. They aren't evergreen, but do hang on to their russet-brown dead leaves in winter so you're not left with a wall of bare twigs. You can alternate green beech with purple or copper beech when planting a new hedge, for a piebald look that some people like. Hornbeam is fashionable but duller than beech as its matt leaves do not reflect the light nearly as well.

1 Yew (*Taxus baccata*).

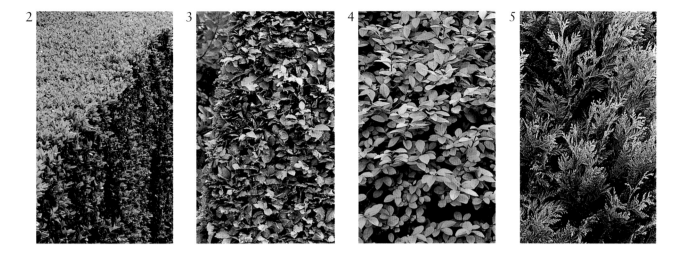

Privet (*Ligustrum ovalifolium*) (**4**) is the hedge everyone loves to hate and it does need a lot of clipping, but it withstands everything from traffic fumes and London clay, to country gales and the odd collision with the ride-on mower, without turning a hair. Privet is great if you want a semi-evergreen hedge about 1.5–2m (5–6ft) high. Only in really severe winters will it lose some of its leaves. *Lonicera nitida* is a good substitute.

Western red cedar (*Thuja plicata*) (**5**) is the nearest thing to the hedge we would all love; an evergreen hedge that grows to about 1.2–1.5cm (4–5ft) and then stops. It needs a couple of light clips a year but, unlike *Leylandii*, it won't go berserk. If you have a reasonably sunny spot with soil that doesn't go boggy in winter, and want a good-looking, reliable conifer hedge, this is a good choice.

2 Box (*Buxus sempervirens*).
3 Beech (*Fagus sylvatica*).
4 Privet (*Ligustrum ovalifolium*).
5 Western red cedar (*Thuja plicata*).

When to clip

Clip slow-growing hedges of beech, hornbeam and thuja twice a year – first in late April/early May, and again in late August/early September.

Clip box in late May or early June on a dull day so that the cut leaves will not scorch. Shears produce a better finish than powered trimmers.

Clip yew once in September when it has stopped growing and it will stay crisp in outline right through the winter.

Clip fast-growing privet and *Lonicera nitida* every six weeks between early May to mid-September.

Remember, don't make the last cut too late, or you'll encourage a late flush of soft young growth just in time for it to get clobbered by an early frost, which doesn't look good.

Informal leafy hedges

The big difference between this sort of hedge and a formal one is that they have big leaves, so you can't clip them with shears without cutting a lot of leaves in half, which then turn brown at the cut edges – it looks awful. This type of hedge is much better pruned with secateurs in late spring so that it looks more natural, rather like a continuous row of shrubs. But even though you don't have to do it every year, don't underestimate how long the job takes to do.

Prunus 'Otto Luyken' (**1**) is a low, dense evergreen, often grown for ground cover, with flowers like white candles in April, but if you want a good low hedge about 60cm (2ft) high, this is it. Prune it to shape after flowering.

Laurel (*Prunus laurocerasus*) (**2**) is bay laurel or cherry laurel, but not to be confused with the culinary bay, *Laurus nobilis*. It's good for a hedge of 1.5–3m (5–10ft) high or more. It will grow as tall as you're ever likely to want to cut it and, if it becomes neglected and overgrown, you can usually get away with cutting it right down to stumps, about 1m (3ft) high, in late spring and training it as a new hedge from scratch.

1 *Prunus* 'Otto Luyken.'
2 Laurel (*Prunus laurocerasus*).
3 Spotted laurel (*Aucuba japonica* 'Crotonifolia').
4 *Elaeagnus* × *ebbingei*.

Restoring an old hedge

If you inherit an old hedge that is in bad condition, don't despair – with a bit of care and attention, you can restore it to its original glory. Don't be too hasty to write it off: restoration may take some time, but it will be less time than growing a new hedge from scratch.

Deciduous hedges, such as hawthorn, beech and hornbeam, can be restored in winter or early spring before any new growth appears. However, evergreen hedges, such as *Lonicera nitida*, yew, holly, escallonia, privet and box, can be restored in late April/early May.

1 Restore one side of the hedge one year, and leave the other for the following year, to avoid giving it too great a check. Cut back the side you are restoring much harder than usual, so that you are cutting into quite thick stems. You can go to within 30cm (1ft) of the centre line of the hedge, but it's not essential to go quite that far if you don't want to.
2 Trim the top and the other side of the hedge as usual.
3 Feed and mulch the hedge well to stimulate new growth. Later in the summer, clip the new shoots lightly to encourage them to branch and thicken out, but make sure you shape the hedge so that it slopes slightly inwards towards the top. Let the hedge grow progressively thicker – the new growth will soon hide the ugly stumps of the severed branches.

Aucuba japonica (3) is the spotted laurel, which comes in plain green, but is usually grown in the gold-spotted or speckled versions. It puts up with appalling conditions, including traffic fumes, pollution and poor soil in dry shade under trees, which makes it a good choice for a city hedge from 1.2–2m (4–6ft) high.

Elaeagnus × *ebbingei* (4) has large, grey-green leaves and tiny, greenish bell flowers hanging down from old twigs well inside the shrub in November, so all you really notice is the scent that seems to come from nowhere. A row of plants makes a good hedge, 2–2.4m (6–8ft) high, especially in seaside areas, since it will put up with salt- and sand-laden gales.

Flowering hedges

Most folk never think of hedges as having flowers, but they all do, even if the flowers are relatively insignificant. Constant clipping often removes flowering shoots from some hedging plants, but others will produce their blooms even when trimmed.

Flowering hedges make colourful garden dividers, but because few keep their leaves in winter, they aren't the best choice for the outer boundary of a garden. Some are suitable for fairly formal, clipped hedges, but most are best grown as a continuous, single or double row of flowering shrubs that needs only light pruning.

1 Hips on *Rosa eglanteria*
(Sweet briar rose).

Roses (1) can make good informal flowering hedges, if you stick to shrub roses; they don't need hard pruning like modern bush roses. *R.* 'Fru Dagmar Hastrup', with single, pink flowers in summer and red hips in late summer and autumn, is good for a hedge about 1.2m (4ft) high, and is good for a windy garden; *R.* 'Buff Beauty' is the same height, with scented cream flowers maturing to manila. No clipping is needed for a shrub rose hedge; just prune out a few old stems in winter. They look a bit bare and twiggy out of season, but the thorns ensure that they still act as a living security fence.

Forsythia (2) tends to be rather untidy when it's grown as a shrub, but if planted as a hedge and allowed to grow about 1.5m (5ft) high, it makes a sheet of sheer yellow in spring and, by clipping it just hard enough to take off the dead flower-heads and roughly re-shape it immediately after flowering, it stays a lot tidier.

Escallonias (3) have a long flowering season – early summer to early autumn. They make good evergreen hedges, 1.5–2m (5–6ft) tall, and are best clipped formally, as soon as the flowers have finished. *Escallonia macrantha* is the one to go for in seaside gardens.

Fuchsia magellanica (4), the hardy fuchsia, makes wonderful hedges in mild climates; it'll make a deciduous or semi-evergreen hedge 1.2–1.5m (4–5ft) high. In colder climates, the plants die down to ground level in winter. Leave the dead stems till late April before cutting them off; they provide a bit of protection for the crowns. Spread a 5cm (2in) layer of bark chippings over the roots for insulation. Either way, you have dangling flowers all through summer and autumn, right up to the first frost.

2 Forsythia.
3 *Escallonia bifida*.
4 *Fuschia magellanica* 'Versicolor'.

Dwarf hedges

Dwarf hedges are a long-lasting way of edging a path, flower bed, or formal herb garden. Most hedge plants grow too big; you need something that can be clipped to 30cm (1ft) high or less. If they are too short to trim with hedging shears or power clippers, use single-handed sheep shears.

Dwarf box (*Buxus sempervirens* 'Suffruticosa') (**5**) is the classic, elegant evergreen edging; plant 10–15cm (4–6in) apart and clip to 15cm (6in) twice a year in the first few years, in late spring and late summer. They are slow growing and easy to root from cuttings if you want to grow your own on the cheap.

Lavender (**6**) looks less formal, but the bigger cultivars get very floppy, so go for one of the dwarf varieties like 'Hidcote', or 'Munstead'. They make a lovely, scented, semi-evergreen dwarf hedge about 30–45cm (12–18in) tall. Clip them over immediately after flowering to trim and deadhead the hedge simultaneously.

Rosemary (**7**) makes a neat herbal hedgelet that almost looks like conifer with its needle-like leaves, but in spring it's smothered in blue flowers. And, on a hot day, you have a heady Mediterranean fragrance. Prune to shape after flowering.

Unconventional hedges

If you prefer a less solid boundary, plant a row of bamboos. *Fargesia murielae* and *F. nitida* are good for this. Let them grow up as a living bamboo screen that looks light and airy, even though it grows to 2–3m (6–10ft). Or plant long, bare willow cuttings in autumn, winter or early spring so that they criss-cross to look like a lattice fence. When they take root and start to grow, clip the new shoots back twice a year for a feature that is a hedge in summer and a rustic fence in winter when it loses its leaves.

5 Dwarf box (*Buxus sempervirens* 'Suffruticosa').

6 *Lavendula angustifolia*.

7 *Rosmarinus officinalis* 'Miss Jessopp's Upright'.

The simplest of timber structures can make a pleasing fence, provided the carpentry is sound.

How high?

Fence panels are very popular with first-time gardeners because they are relatively cheap, easy to put up and, let's be honest, a nice tall fence stops the neighbours from seeing in. If I could say one thing to first-time gardeners, it would be this: don't do it. You'll just make your own garden dark and closed-in; a tall, solid fence has a lot of wind resistance, which makes it prone to being blown down in a gale, flattening everything in its path – and the odds are that neighbours can still see in through the gaps anyway. No, a lower fence looks much better, costs less and lasts longer. If you want a taller fence, go for one with open trellis at the top, which lets more light in but still helps to deflect prying eyes.

Fences

Although hedges have a lot going for them as bird-nesting sites and wildlife havens, when it comes to saving labour, there's a lot to be said for fences. Compared to hedges, they make an instant boundary – there's no waiting for anything to grow – and they take up a lot less space. Whereas a hedge needs about 60–90cm (2–3ft) of space all round the edge of your garden and takes a lot of water and nutrients out of the borders in front of them, a fence occupies next to no space and takes nothing out of the ground.

It's not all plain sailing; there is a bit of maintenance to do when a fence has been up for a few years, and some have quite a limited life. Because fences have a big influence on the garden's character, it's important to choose one that creates the right atmosphere.

Post-and-rail fences (**1**) are the type they put round paddocks out in the country – the rails slot into the posts leaving a lot of open gaps, so though they are good for showing where your boundary is, they don't do much for garden shelter, privacy or security. If you have a country garden, a fence like this makes a grand support for a big climbing rose, and it'll flower right the way along when it's trained out horizontally. You can also use a post-and-rail fence as the foundation for willow or heather panels, or for bamboo screening. Just unroll a roll of bamboo screening along the fence and fix it up to the posts and rails with builder's staples or wire.

Picket fences (**2**) are the type that you often see round old cottages, usually painted white. They look neat and make more effective boundaries than post-and-rail fences because the gaps filter the wind, yet don't make a solid obstruction that is easily blown down. The gaps are too small for animals to get through, but picket fences aren't so good for growing climbers on, as they need regular repainting.

Trellis screens (**3**) are not strong enough to use as garden boundaries, but for dividing space inside the garden they are brilliant, as you can choose a style to match the effect you want to create. There are diamond- or square-lattice panels, curved panels, panels with arched or dished tops, or you can put wooden finials on top of the supporting posts for a more classical look. Trellis panels are also good for making simple garden structures, such as an arch, arbour or open-fronted gazebo. Trellis is great for growing climbers, especially for the lighter, airier kinds, such as annuals, or clematis that can be cut down when you need to treat the timber.

Hazel hurdles (4) look very rustic, so use rustic poles to support them instead of sawn timber. They were originally home-made fences and, since the hazel rods used to make them are thin, the panels dry out and become brittle. They only last about five to ten years. Their life will be prolonged to its maximum if you spray them with preservative using a knapsack sprayer – a brush is impractical. In a cottage garden or wild garden, grow ivy over ageing hurdles and, as the stems 'set', they help to hold everything together, so your fence grows old gracefully and lasts a bit longer.

Willow, bamboo and heather panels (5) are not hugely long-lived either. Plan for maybe ten years, but if you don't need a lot of them and you want bags of style, it's well worth it – and anyway you might fancy something completely different by the time you need to think about replacing them.

Panel fencing (6) lasts about 10–15 years depending on how well it's treated. It is a good, cheap choice and widely available. Panel fences may not be as attractive as other options, but they can be 'improved' by painting or by growing climbers over them.

1 Post-and-rail fence.
2 Picket fence.
3 Trellis screen.
4 Hazel hurdle.
5 Bamboo panel.
6 Panel fencing.

1

2

3

4

5

6

How to... **put up a panel fence**

Panel fences are one of the quickest ways to fence the garden: you should be able to fence a smallish garden easily in a weekend. You can use timber or concrete posts; timber ones often look better, but they will need more maintenance. Concrete posts come ready-equipped with grooves for slotting the panels into and will last forever.

There are many alternatives to interwoven larch panels and they can provide quite a different effect in the garden. Woven willow withies and interwoven hazel hurdles both have a rustic feel. You can prolong their life by treating them with a transparent timber preservative or with linseed oil, but neither material will be as durable as larch. You are looking at a probable life of 8–10 years for alternative panels, whereas larch will last up to twice that long.

1 Measure up carefully so that you order the right number of fence panels and posts. You need one more post than panels. Dig a hole that is as deep as one-third the height of the final fence and position the first post in it. Use a spirit level to check that it is perpendicular, then ram moist concrete (6 parts ballast to 1 part cement) around it.

2 Brace the post and leave overnight for the concrete to harden. Dig the other post holes now, using a gravel board as a measuring guide or 'pinch stick' to mark their positions. The next day run a level string line from the first post along the line of the fence and secure it at the far end. If the ground slopes, this line needn't be at fence height, but all panels can be levelled to it.

3 Fasten the first gravel board to the bottom of the first post with the fixings provided and check that it is level. Use wedges underneath it if the ground is sloping. Any gaps below it can be filled later with soil or gravel. Wonky gravel boards look dreadful, even if the fence above them is level.

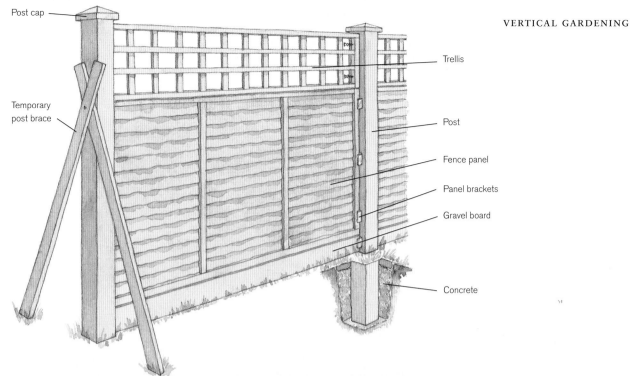

Post cap

Temporary post brace

Trellis

Post

Fence panel

Panel brackets

Gravel board

Concrete

4 Sit the first panel on top of the gravel board and screw it to the first post with the fixings provided. (These are usually U-shaped brackets.) A second pair of hands is very useful and saves on the bad language when the panel topples off the board.

5 Lower the next post into its hole and fasten it to the end of the fence panel. With the spirit level, check it is perpendicular, then tamp concrete around the base to secure it. Continue to the end of the run, cutting the last panel to fit if necessary. Fasten trellis panels in place (if they are required) before cutting off the tops of the posts 2.5cm (1in) above the panel or trellis and securing post cappings to them.

Timber treatment

Wooden fences need treating with preservative every year or two to prolong their life and stop the colour fading. There's no need to stick to traditional wood-coloured preservatives – lurid orange or dreary brown. One of the quickest ways to give a small garden a brand new look is just by changing the colour of exposed woodwork. Pale green, dusky lavender blue, terracotta... you can use it on fences, the shed, trellis or even decking. The most convenient time to treat timber is in winter when plants have died down, but make sure the wood is dry at the time of painting, and that rain is not forecast.

If you want to grow climbers on fences, grow them on trellis panels suspended from the fence by hooks, so the plant can be lifted down and laid flat on the ground when you need to treat the timber.

Walls

Walls are solid and permanent. They cost a lot more than fences and take skill to build – anything over about 1m (3ft) high is really a job for a professional. It shouldn't be higher than that if it's next to a public road, and, if you want one more than 2m (6ft) high, you may need planning consent.

Walls say a lot about the style of your garden. Old red-brick walls suggest antiquity, while pale bricks are more modern. Glass bricks look very contemporary, but are mainly used for designer features inside a garden, rather than as external boundary walls.

Concrete-block walls can be rendered and painted, and sixties-style screen-block walls can be disguised with climbers. You can also build dry-stone walls nowadays from reconstituted stone blocks that you glue together – they are good for building the dwarf walls that surround raised beds.

Colour can be scary in a garden, but exhilarating. And the effects achieved by different colours are startling. The purple wall (*below left*) gives depth to the garden and provides a strong background for the planting. If it were painted yellow (*below right*), it would make the garden appear smaller and overpower the plants.

The shelter effect

Walls are good places to grow slightly tender plants, as they soak up warmth on sunny days and release the heat slowly at night, rather like giant storage radiators, at the same time as providing shelter for plants grown against them.

But, odd though it sounds, less solid boundaries are actually better at sheltering the garden. That's because when wind hits a solid vertical surface, it rushes up over the top, which creates tumbling air the other side. These eddies can mean that the wind is actually stronger than if there were no wall there at all. In a very exposed garden, it's better to use windbreaks made up of about 50 per cent holes, as they let some air pass through. They are less likely to be blown down than a fence, and they don't cause turbulence as a wall does. As a general rule, you can reckon that a permeable barrier will shelter a distance of roughly ten times its height.

Wall shrubs

Wall shrubs are ornamental trees or shrubs that are trained to grow flat against a wall, as an alternative to climbers. They grow a lot slower than climbers and, being naturally twiggy, it's simple to train them out over the area you want to cover, and easy to keep them under control.

The sort of plants that are used as wall shrubs are mostly those that are a touch tender and which benefit from the natural protection of a wall. But wall-training is also a good way to grow shrubs that are naturally untidy, or that normally grow too big to fit into a small garden.

Wall shrubs aren't only for walls – you can grow them against fences or trellis, but if you opt for the more tender kinds, it's only against a wall, with its hot-water-bottle effect in winter, where you'll really see them at their best.

General training and pruning of wall shrubs

Some garden centres sell shrubs that have already been trained flat, ready for planting against a wall – they are usually tied up to a small piece of trellis. With these, it's just a case of untying them from their support and planting them so they stand flat against the wall. As they grow, tie the main stems to trellis or horizontal wires fixed to the wall so that they spread out and cover the required area. In time, sideshoots will grow to fill in the gaps between the main framework of branches. The only real pruning you need to do is to cut off any shoots that stick out from the wall, and remove those that aren't needed to extend the main framework.

Adding height to a low wall

If you have a 1.2m (4ft) wall where you'd rather have one at about eye level, don't try to build it up higher. It won't have adequate foundations and it may not be very stable; top it with trellis instead. Put in some strong posts on your side of the wall and screw the trellis to them. Not only will you now have more room to grow climbers, you've also made the garden more secure – intruders can shin over a low wall very easily, but they are less inclined to tackle trellis since it'll break under their weight, leaving signs of forced entry.

Pre-trained wall shrubs can be expensive, and only a limited range is available, but it's not difficult to train your own. The best way is to start with a rooted cutting, and pinch out the sideshoots that grow where they aren't wanted, leaving only those that make a flat shape. To train your shrub into a fan or espalier shape, tie some ordinary garden canes together to form the outline and fix that to the trellis or wires on your wall. Then plant your young plant at the base and train one stem along each cane.

Training a pot-grown wall shrub

A quicker option, if you're not a perfectionist, is to find an ordinary pot-grown shrub in a garden centre that isn't as bushy as it should be, and simply prune out a few stems to make it a flatter shape so that it's suitable for growing against a wall. The stems will probably still be supple enough to tie in to a framework. You don't have to bother training it into a formal shape at all – if you prefer, you can just leave your wall shrub as a two-dimensional bush tied informally to stiff netting or trellis on the wall.

Trained wall shrubs like this pyracantha often have some wayward stems. These stems should be tied in regularly and any protruding shoots must be cut back to keep the plant close to the wall.

How to... **fix trellis to walls**

Trellis is the best form of support for climbers that climb by means of tendrils of one sort or another. This includes clematis, which need something to wrap its leaf stalks around, and for plants such as sweet peas that hang on using twining tendrils. It's less useful for self-clinging climbers, which use adhesive pads or aerial roots; they prefer sound, flat surfaces to cling to. On pebble-dashed walls, where self-clinging climbers can pull off the rendering in one large sheet, it is worth equipping the wall with trellis which is much more likely to take their weight.

What you need

- *wall plugs*
- *power drill and masonry bit*
- *screwdriver and screws*
- *two timber battens 50 × 25mm (2 × 1in)*
- *trellis panel*

1 Mark the required position of the trellis on the wall and cut battens to fit its width. Drill holes in the battens, then corresponding holes in the wall to take wall plugs. The battens need to be about 30cm (1ft) from the top and the bottom of the trellis.

2 Push the wall plugs into the holes and then screw the two battens to the wall. Paint them with a suitable colour of timber preservative once they are in position.

3 The soil at the base of a wall is often pretty grim, as there'll be footings in the way, so dig your planting hole at least 30cm (1ft) away from it, and do a really good job of soil improvement before planting your climber. Spread the stems out along the bottom of the trellis so the plant starts spreading out right from the very base, otherwise you end up with a distinct fan shape.

Wall shrubs for sunny, south-facing walls

This is too good a spot to waste on anything that you could possibly grow anywhere else, so stick to the real warmth-loving exotics that will make your mouth water.

Cytisus battandieri (**1**), the pineapple broom, is one of the most striking wall shrubs, if you have room for it. It has large, silky leaves and yellow cockades of flowers in July that both look and smell like pineapples. It's big, at least 4.5 × 4.5m (15 × 15ft), and really needs to be trained out over horizontal wires on the south side of a house. I know that's a lot of room for one plant, but it's worth it; it flowers from mid- to late summer, and the foliage looks good, too.

Sophora microphylla **'Sun King'** (**2**) is a relatively new plant and one that I've really enjoyed growing in my garden. It has dark evergreen leaves with tiny leaflets that give it a frothy appearance, and its bright yellow clusters of flowers appear in late winter and early spring. It is tougher than many sophoras: mine is 1.5m (5ft) high and growing in the open. Great for out-of-season brilliance and a good background to other plants when not in flower.

1 *Cytisus battandieri.*
2 *Sophora microphylla* 'Sun King'.
3 *Abutilon vitifolium.*
4 *Ceanothus* 'Puget Blue'.
5 *Fremontodendron californicum.*
6 *Grevillea rosmarinifolia.*

Ceanothus 'Concha'.

Abutilon vitifolium (**3**) is a good choice if you have a tall, narrow, sunny wall, say 3 × 1.5m (10 × 5ft); it's an upright, slightly tender shrub with grey, vine-shaped leaves and big, nodding white or lilac-purple flowers hanging in clusters from early summer to autumn.

Ceanothus (**4**), such as the evergreen *Ceanothus* 'Puget Blue' and *C. thyrsiflorus* var. *repens* are brilliant wall shrubs for a hot, sunny spot; most ceanothus flower for about 6–8 weeks in early summer, when they turn into a fluffy sheet of blue. Once the flowers are over, you can clip the plants quite closely with hedging shears to tidy them up, which also prunes them correctly. Cut off anything that grows beyond its rightful area at the same time. Allow at least 2 × 1m (6 × 3ft), more for the most vigorous varieties.

Fremontodendron californicum (**5**) is a slow-growing evergreen and very good value if you have a small space about 2 × 2m (6 × 6ft), though it will get bigger if it's really happy. The big, yellow, waxy flowers completely cover the stems from May till early autumn. It's a well-behaved plant that won't take over.

Grevillea rosmarinifolia (**6**) is a plant worth the risk if you fancy something really exotic-looking and slightly tender – but I reckon it's tougher than most of the books crack it up to be. Mine has survived some pretty cold spells without turning a hair. It is bushy, with evergreen needles like a delicate rosemary, and reaches 2 × 1m (6 × 3ft). From late autumn through the winter and into early summer, the stem tips are crowded with clusters of tubular pink flowers with spiky stamens sticking out all round – not the time of year that you expect flowers like these at all.

Even in winter on a chilly wall, tough plants like *Cotoneaster horizontalis* can look good when rimed with frost.

1 *Camellia japonica* 'Mercury'.
2 *Crinodendron hookerianum*.
3 *Garrya elliptica*.
4 *Jasminum nudiflorum*.

Wall shrubs for north-facing walls

A north-facing wall is the one most people dread, but there's more you can grow there than you might think.

Camellias (**1**) do very well when they are trained out flat, and in a smallish garden, that's a good way to grow them since they don't take up much room. Ideally, I'd aim to keep a wall-trained camellia pruned so that it fits on a standard trellis panel, 2 × 1m (6 × 3ft), but if there's more room, you can just train it to fit anything up to 2.4 × 2m (8 × 6ft), or more if it's a big cultivar. Being evergreen, it gives you something to look at even when it's not in flower. Camellias need lime-free soil.

Crinodendron hookerianum (**2**) is also ideal for lime-free soil and a mild, sheltered spot; it makes an unusual evergreen with red lantern flowers that hang down from the branches for a couple of months in early and midsummer. It's quite slow growing but it will eventually need a space about 2 × 2.4m (6 × 8ft). It's usually wider than it is tall when grown on a wall.

Garrya elliptica (**3**) is something that's mostly seen as a tree or bushy shrub, but it's a very good wall shrub for a cold, north-facing spot. It's evergreen and has long, grey-green catkins that last all winter. On a wall, it teams very well with variegated ivy, and looks great when illuminated at night.

Jasminum nudiflorum (**4**), winter jasmine, is a star in this situation; a naturally floppy shrub, it needs trellis to prop it up. The yellow, star-shaped flowers are very welcome in winter and early spring. It doesn't have much in the way of leaves, and the green stems can look a bit scruffy, so it's a good idea to team it with some gold-variegated ivy to liven it up. Allow about 2 × 1m (6 × 3ft).

1

2

3

4

Wall shrubs for east-facing walls

East walls are a potential problem. It's tempting to plant early flowers to take advantage of the morning sun, but late frosts can really wreck flowers that are defrosted too fast on a sunny morning – it's safer to stick to shrubs that flower later in the year.

Cotoneaster horizontalis (5) has masses of tiny white flowers in June, berries from late summer and well into winter if the birds don't spot them, and those herringbone-shaped stems pile up well against a wall. It's semi-evergreen, but even if it sheds its leaves in winter, it has a great-looking skeleton. Allow about 1×2m (3×6ft).

Chaenomeles speciosa (6), the flowering quince, looks best trained on a wall; it makes such a scruffy shrub. You can espalier it, and it looks very cottagey with its main branches tied to horizontal wires or trellis. The spring flowers may be white, pink or red and there are many fine cultivars available; 2×1.2m (6×4ft) should do it.

Euonymus fortunei (7) can be grown as a small, evergreen, free-standing shrub but, if you plant it against a wall, it flattens out and scrambles up; it doesn't need much training at all. The gold-variegated 'Emerald 'n' Gold' and 'Blondy' bring splashes of colour to uninspiring spots. It'll grow to 5×1m (15×3ft) against a wall, but you can cut it back to whatever size you want.

Pyracantha (8) is a beautiful wall shrub as an espalier, and festooned around doors and windows. Even without fancy training, it's good just tied to horizontal wires or trellis. Clip the plants just after the flowers fade, removing all this year's new growth, but not the faded flowers, which produce berries. In autumn and winter, you'll have a wall of orange, red or yellow bunches against a backdrop of evergreen leaves. Allow 2×1.5m (6×5ft) or more.

5 *Cotoneaster horizontalis.*
6 *Chaenomeles speciosa.*
7 *Euonymus fortunei*
   'Emerald 'n' Gold'.
8 *Pyracantha.*

Wall shrubs for west-facing walls

A west wall is the second best place for wall plants in any garden. Because it's not as hot and dry as a south wall, it's a good place for sun-lovers that like more moisture at root level, but there are some seriously splendid contenders for the space. Any of these can also be grown on a south wall, as long as the soil is rich and moist.

Abeliophyllum distichum (1) isn't well known, but it's a wonderful shrub for a sunny wall, with white, almond-scented flowers on bare stems in late winter and early spring. It's slow growing and quite small, so you only need to allow about 1.5 × 1m (5 × 3ft).

Magnolia grandiflora (2) is the evergreen shrub that puts on a big summer show on a huge wall. Think of rhododendron leaves and a giant magnolia flower, but in late summer. This will eventually cover the complete side of a four-storey house, so it's not one to take on lightly, but if you have lime-free soil and a good set of ladders so you can keep the stems tied in, you're in business. You can keep it to two storeys by pruning – and it does take time to grow. The variety 'Exmouth' flowers at an early age.

1 *Abeliophyllum distichum.*
2 *Magnolia grandiflora.*
3 *Azara serrata.*
4 *Carpenteria californica.*
5 *Itea ilicifolia.*
6 *Phygelius capensis* 'Sensation'.

Azara serrata (3) is pleasingly out-of-the-ordinary and produces large clusters of fluffy yellow flowers in May and June which are followed, in good summers, by small white berries. It has oval, serrated, evergreen leaves, and it grows to around 4 × 3m (12 × 10ft). Grow *Clematis texensis* through it for late summer colour.

Carpenteria californica (4) looks like a giant cistus with huge, fragile, single white flowers in midsummer and is perfect for creating an exotic look. As wall shrubs go, this one isn't too big – it'll cover a wall up to 2 × 2m (6 × 6ft). Yes, it's slightly tender, but in a sheltered, sunny spot with well-drained soil, it should be fine.

Itea ilicifolia (5), sweetspire, is another shrub you don't often see. This is what you'd call sophisticated rather than startling, with evergreen, holly-shaped leaves and, in late summer, 30cm (1ft) long strands of greenish flowers that look like giant catkins from a distance. Very classy. It's slow to get going, but eventually makes about 2.4 × 2m (8 × 6ft) against a wall.

Phygelius capensis (6), the Cape figwort, grows as a shrub in sunny borders, but it does even better up against a wall, where it will grow 1.5–2m × 1m (5–6 × 3ft) across. It has rich red flowers with a dash of yellow at the throat and will flower itself silly from July until late September or early October. In a cold northern garden, this is often about the only way to grow it reliably, but I'd recommend it anywhere. It's often tougher than you'd think.

Itea ilicifolia provides a double whammy – evergreen foliage and long pale green tassles of flower.

Garden structures

Arches, pergolas and outbuildings aren't essential by any means, but they are brilliant for giving the garden character – and fast. Style-wise you can choose from rustic twigs or trellis and smart-formal or even classical. Victorian and Edwardian designs are always popular, and I suppose it won't be long before we start to see contemporary interpretations.

Any structure of this sort is good for adding height to a flat garden, and for giving you somewhere to grow climbers that you might not otherwise have room for. Think carefully where to place these structures. An arch looks natural where two boundaries meet, making it obvious that you are coming to the end of one part of the garden and are about to enter another. A summer-house or gazebo stands out like a sore thumb parked in the middle of the lawn, but tucked into a corner, half hidden by planting, it acts as a natural focal point for its own 'garden within a garden'. And for lifting the back of a border, pillars and obelisks are brilliant.

A well-furnished pergola is an irresistible invitation to explore.

Simple obelisks made of timber or steel can be used to add instant height to a border and to support climbing plants, such as clematis and sweet peas.

Pillars and obelisks

These are the most basic kind of garden structures. Pillars are straightforward poles, usually pushed in to the back of a border, allowing you to grow a few climbers there instead of the traditional evergreen hedge. Rows of pillars that are linked by thick swags of rope, with climbing or rambler roses trained out along them, are known as colonnades or catenaries.

Obelisks are shorter, more decorative uprights, maybe made of wrought iron or willow or hazel twigs, and they can be pushed into a border – probably nearer the front – or used in containers.

Both are meant for growing climbers, but due to the size restriction, you need to stick to smaller climbers that won't just rush up to the top and then dangle over. Smaller clematis and annual climbers are your best bet here.

Arches and their offspring

If you knock four pillars in to make a square and join the tops together with timbers, you have turned them into an arch. You can make your own out of rustic poles or sawn timber, or buy arches ready made from various materials, including metal. Either way, if you cover the sides and top with netting or trellis, you'll make them even more climber-friendly.

A row of arches makes a tunnel, which is a trendy feature to put over a long straight path. Cover it with a mixture of different climbers, or one or two really huge kinds, such as Virginia

Mixing climbers together

You don't have to limit yourself to one climber per upright; you can grow two or even three in the same space. This extends the flowering season of your structure, if you choose plants that peak one after the other. Or use evergreen foliage plants, such as ivy, to add winter interest to summer-flowering climbers when they've lost their leaves. If you plant them all in the same spot, you should improve the soil over a larger area than you would just for one. Pruning can be a problem when you have several climbers intertwined, so take care to team only those kinds that can all be left to grow without any pruning, or which all need hard pruning, so you don't have to bother working out which stem belongs to which.

An arch (*above*) is an effective way of marking a change in mood between sections of the garden; an arbour (*above right*) is a calming place to sit; and a summer-house (*opposite*) is a welcome retreat.

Persuading climbers to climb

Self-clingers need help to start with because you can't persuade the existing growth to hang on. Only new growth will produce the aerial roots it needs in order to climb. When planting a self-clinger, such as ivy or climbing hydrangea (see p.90), cut the new plant back hard so that the new growth starts to grip to the upright surface right from the base of the plant. Otherwise, lay the stems down horizontally along the base of the wall and new sideshoots will grow up from there and cling on.

creeper (*Parthenocissus quinquefolia*). Some people train cordon fruit trees over the 'ribs' to make a fruit tunnel, and others choose laburnum so that its flowers hang down into the space beneath.

A pergola is really just a traditional, formal tunnel with a square top instead of an arched one. A pergola is meant to go over a path or paving, so you might have one running down or across the garden. They are also often found in their lean-to form against the back of a house. You can make a Mediterranean version by using rustic branches for the roof struts and growing grape vines over the top. Alternatively, keep it traditional and grow something like a wisteria, or a collection of different clematis, one up each 'leg'. These are the sort of structures that are meant to be almost hidden under climbers, so go as heavy on them as you like – scramblers and twiners welcome.

Arbours and gazebos

Think of these as big arches with seats underneath. The difference, if you want to be quite correct about it, is that an arbour is supposed to have an evergreen hedge planted round three sides for shelter, with a climber growing over the top as a 'living roof'. A gazebo, on the other hand, is more open-plan, made of trellis, and with climbers growing all over. It has an open door and maybe 'windows' through which to gaze out at the view. Climbers are a big part of the equation, and all your twiners and scramblers will do just fine here too.

Summer-houses

A summer-house is simply a solid gazebo – a good-looking garden building with a proper roof, walls, doors and glass windows. It will form part of the view when you are looking at it from a distance, and gives you somewhere to sit and enjoy the garden when the weather is a touch iffy for taking tea on the lawn. It's also a safe, dry place to store your garden seats and croquet set.

When it comes to growing climbers over it, the effect needs to be slightly restrained, so you need to choose non-rampant types or your glamorous building will be swamped in foliage. And if you grow the self-clinging climbers, the woodwork may be wrecked, so I'd go for a discreet clematis or some annual morning glories growing on some netting or trellis on one side. If you want an economy summer-house, you can always decorate the shed with window-boxes and trellis, and glamorize the inside. If you do prefer a more natural look and want to grow plants over it, choose small, slow climbers so thatyour summe-house won't be swamped. The 'climbing blueberry' (*Billardiera longiflora*) is an evergreen with light airy foliage reaching 2–3m (6–10ft), with green bell-shaped summer flowers followed by purple grape-sized fruit. Team it with *Ampelopsis glandulosa* var. *brevipedunculata* 'Elegans', which has mini grape leaves in pink, cream and white with pink tendrils. Neither needs any proper pruning; just cut out any bits that die back at the end of winter.

Matching plant to place

Small, slow-growing climbers will never muster enough oomph to cover a complete pergola, though they'll be good for pillars or in containers, shinning up an obelisk.

Big climbers, such as Clematis armandii, *can't be kept small enough to grow on a single trellis panel in a tiny garden – if you prune them too hard you'll never see any flowers. Grow them in less disciplined situations, like over a pergola, on a long fence, or over a large outbuilding.*

Real whoppers, such as Virginia creeper, can also be grown up through trees, but don't risk that with real sun-loving species like passionflower, or they won't get enough light to trigger flowering.

How to... **build a pergola**

The very simplest way to build a pergola is to buy a kit from the garden centre, which comes complete with all the timber cut to length and pre-notched or with metal brackets included so you just slot everything into place. Otherwise, be prepared for a spot of DIY. The big advantage here is that you can design and build your pergola to any shape and size, even adding overhangs which are a great decorative feature of pergolas and gives you somewhere to put hanging baskets. But, most importantly, remember to allow enough headroom – aim for around 2.5m (7½ft).

Pergolas are great for framing views and for encouraging the visitor to explore. They make a sort of 3-D invitation. For this reason they are often best positioned near the house rather than at the far end of the garden where much of the invitation effect is lost. Traditional pergolas may be directly attached to the house and may have sloping rafters, in which case make sure that at the lowest height they still offer ample headroom.

What you need

For the frame

- *10 × 10cm (4 × 4in) timbers for the uprights – spaced about 2m (6ft) apart. Lengths of 3m (9½ft) will allow them to be buried for 60cm (2ft) while allowing 2.5m (7½ft) headroom.*
- *15 × 5cm (6 × 2in) timbers the length of the pergola for the two main rails.*

    (If the pergola is to be built against a house wall, you will need posts only on one side. The other end of the rafters will be supported by a wall plate, made from 15 × 5cm (6 × 2in) timber bolted to the wall.)

For the rafters

- *15 × 5cm (6 × 2in) timbers, one at each end and the others at roughly 90cm (3ft) intervals along the length of the pergola. Each rafter needs to be the full width of the pergola, plus an extra 30cm (1ft) at each end to allow for a well-proportioned overhang.*

- *wood screws and bolts*
- *power drill, saw and fixing tools, spirit level, set square*
- *digging tools and concrete*
- *timber preservative*
- *canes and string*
- *you'll also need several helpers for holding things in place*

1 Mark out the position of the pergola and calculate how much timber you will need. When you are confident you have all your materials, mark out the position of the holes using canes and string and check that they are square with a set square. Dig holes 60cm (2ft) deep and 30cm (1ft) across for each post.

2 Position the vertical posts in the holes and check that they are a) in exactly the right spot, b) perpendicular and c) at the correct height. If the pergola is being built against a wall, fasten the timber wall plate to the masonry with anchor bolts once you have checked that it is level.

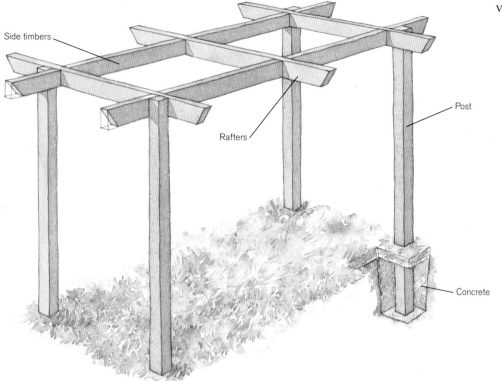

Side timbers

Rafters

Post

Concrete

3 Get a helper to hold the post and maintain its level while stiff concrete is shovelled around the base. Pressure-treated timber will last much longer than untreated timber, even if it is treated with preservative after construction.

4 Tamp the concrete into place with a wooden rammer. Make the finished level a few inches below the soil surface so that it can be dressed with soil or gravel once construction is complete. Allow a day or two before the rafters are fixed in position so that the concrete has time to harden.

5 Bolt the two long timbers down the sides of the pergola at the top of the posts, and then position the rafters. Exclude these on a small pergola, as here, as the rafters can be placed directly on the posts in a criss-cross fashion. Cut a square notch into the top and bottom timbers so that the two marry together as a simple joint. Secure with screws and apply timber preservative.

A mixture of *Clematis* 'Prince Charles' and *Rosa* 'Kiftsgate' growing over a colonnade, where swags of rope are used to link timber poles.

Climbers

Unlike wall shrubs, which are relatively easy to keep to the shape and size you want by annual pruning, large, fast-growing climbers tend to head off on their own and can quickly get out of control. When you're choosing a climber, you do need to take into account practical considerations, such as sun or shade and soil type, but the thing you really must look at is how big it can grow. With climbers, big usually equals fast, and while hard pruning can keep them in check, it may also reduce their flowering capabilities.

Climbers for a north- or east-facing wall

Climbers that will grow happily on a north- or east-facing wall will also grow on other aspects as well, but on a north wall they will often 'lean' forwards to try and find more light, so be prepared for a bit more tying up than usual.

Berberidopsis corallina (**1**) is a distinctly choice and unusual climber that you don't often see. If you have acid soil that doesn't dry out badly and a fairly mild, sheltered garden, give it a go. It's evergreen and reasonably slow growing, to 7.5 × 2m (25 × 6ft) eventually, with attractive long, heart-shaped leaves and bunches of red flowers dangling like rows of red beads in late summer. Give it something to twine through, like netting or trellis. It's not easily pleased, but if you have the right place for it, I can promise you, it's sensational.

Hydrangea anomala subsp. *petiolaris* (**2**) is a climbing hydrangea that is a good go-anywhere plant with large, white, lace-cap flowers in July and golden leaf tints in autumn. You don't need to bother holding it up, since it clings to the wall with its aerial roots, but, like ivy, it's not for anywhere with dodgy mortar. Slow to establish and start flowering (give it four years before panicking), it needs generous mulching, feeding and watering to get it going. It will eventually reach 12 × 2.4m (40 × 8ft).

Akebia quinata (**3**) is a semi-evergreen climber with rounded green leaves that are tinged with purple when the weather turns colder in winter. The early spring flowers are a dusky maroon and spicily aromatic, and sausage-shaped purple seed pods follow them. Akebia will scramble its way up a wire-covered wall or through a tree to a height of 10m (30ft) but can be kept smaller by pruning. Give it a try if you fancy something refreshingly different and don't mind visitors asking 'What's that?'

Schizophragma integrifolium (4) is a sort of flashy cousin of the climbing hydrangea, with July flowers that can be up to 30cm (1ft) across and long, decorative bracts. Like the climbing hydrangea, it is perfectly happy on a north-facing wall, although it usually flowers even better in sunnier spots. It will eventually grow 12m (40ft) or more high but can be restricted by pruning when grown against a wall. It is often slow to start, so be patient. The rewards are great, eventually. It isn't a particularly well-known plant, so don't expect to find it easily.

Parthenocissus henryana (5), the Chinese Virginia creeper, is a cousin of the Virginia creeper; the latter grows far too big, and too fast, for most gardens. It'll make 21m (70ft) or more, and only really looks its best for six weeks in autumn, when the leaves colour up, just before they fall off. No, for most gardens, the Chinese version is much better. It is smaller, at $10 \times 2m$ ($32 \times 6ft$), but it can be pruned hard in winter. It is more colourful generally, as the five-lobed leaves are tinged pink with silvery midribs all summer, and it looks slightly variegated, then the whole lot turns scarlet in autumn.

More climbers for north walls

Clematis – *C. alpina* and *C. macropetala* cultivars (blue or white); *C.* 'Comtesse de Bouchaud' (pink); *C.* 'Marie Boisselot' (white); *C.* 'Nelly Moser' (light and dark pink).

Roses – *Rosa* 'Albéric Barbier' (cream rambler); *R.* 'Bleu Magenta' (grape-purple rambler); *R.* 'Danse du Feu' (red climber); *R.* 'Madame Alfred Carrière' (scented white climber); *R.* 'Souvenir du Docteur Jamain' (claret-red climber, best trained flat against a north wall).

1 *Berberidopsis corallina.*
2 *Hydrangea anomala* subsp. *petiolaris.*
3 *Akebia quinata.*
4 *Schizophragma integrifolium.*
5 *Parthenocissus henryana.*

Climbers for south- or west-facing walls

The soil is not all that brilliant at the foot of a wall, thanks to the builders' rubble and footings down there, but when it's also hot and sunny, then conditions are particularly tough for plants. Prepare the soil very well if you want to grow climbers. Make a bed at least 60–90cm (2–3ft) wide along the base of the wall – remove the old soil entirely, if necessary. Dig out a trench 45cm (18in) deep and fill it with a mixture of topsoil and well-rotted organic matter. If you grow mildew-prone climbers, such as roses, clematis or honeysuckle, in a hot dry spot, keep them well watered in dry spells to avoid bringing on an attack.

Actinidia kolomikta (1) is grown for its foliage, but you need patience because the leaves don't develop their spectacular pink and white tips until the plant is several years old. You need a reasonable space to grow it, as it makes 4.5 × 3m (15 × 10ft) or more. Once it is established, it has tiny but well-scented cream flowers in July.

Vitis vinifera (2), the domestic grape vine, makes a very attractive climber with a couple of very useful bonuses up its sleeve. One is that you'll have a harvest of edible grapes. The plants you'll most often see offered for sale are the sour sort for making wine but, if you buy from a specialist nursery, you'll find some decent dessert kinds like *V.* 'Fragola'. *V.* 'Brant' has bright orange autumn tints and edible grapes, and *V. v.* 'Purpurea' has purple leaves and small, sweet, purple grapes. The other big plus with grape vines is that they stand hard annual pruning to keep them within bounds – chop last summer's young growth back to a single permanent woody main stem about 1.5m (5ft) high. Do this in mid-winter when they are dormant, or the stems bleed badly, which can kill the plant.

Wisteria (3) is probably the first climber most people think of, and it causes the most heartache if you buy a duff one. Always choose a grafted plant, which should flower within three years. Train the main stems out over a wall, tying them to horizontal wires supported by vine eyes, and prune regularly to build up flowering spurs. Don't let them run rampant. There are two species that are commonly grown, both twiners capable of growing about 9 × 2.4m (30 × 8ft) or more, with dangling bunches of scented flowers in purplish shades or white. *W. floribunda*, the Japanese wisteria, flowers in June; Chinese wisteria (*W. sinensis*) flowers a month earlier. Both come in a range of named cultivars with flowers in various colours. If you've set your heart on a wisteria and don't have a big enough wall, grow it up a pole in a pot and train it as a standard. It'll flower a lot sooner and it's an easy way to keep it to a manageable size.

1 *Actinidia kolomikta.*
2 *Vitis* 'Brant'.

Pruning wisteria

Once you have your basic shape trained out over the wall, go over the plant every year in July and cut back all those long, whippy tendrils of new shoots to within 15cm (6in) of where they start from.

If the climber has grown as far as you want it to go, this is also the time to 'stop' the new growth at the end of the main framework of branches so that they don't grow any longer. Just cut the ends off.

In January, shorten all sideshoots to finger length. This is quite straightforward, but it can be time-consuming when you come to tackle a full-grown specimen.

Solanum crispum 'Glasnevin' (4), the Chilean potato vine, will eventually cover the side of a house, say 6 × 6m (20 × 20ft). Its great claim to fame is the purple and yellow 'potato' flowers that it carries from July to September. You almost expect to find the border beneath packed with King Edwards, but no such luck.

Passiflora caerulea (5), passionflower, looks almost tropical with its 5cm (2in) wide, lavender and white, rosette-shaped flowers that keep coming all summer. After a hot summer, it bears yellow, egg-shaped fruits that aren't worth eating, though they won't poison you. In winter, it may keep its leaves if the weather is mild, but usually looks scruffy. In a cold area, it can be killed off almost back to ground level. Either way, it needs tidying up in spring, just enough to cut back stems that have died back. Over a summer, you can expect it to cover about 3 × 2m (10 × 6ft). It needs trellis or netting to climb on, as it clings with tendrils. The white-flowered form, 'Constance Elliot' is scented, though more tender – probably best grown in a pot and moved into the conservatory in winter.

3 *Wisteria floribunda* 'Alba'.
4 *Solanum crispum* 'Glasnevin'.
5 *Passiflora caerulea*.

Climbers for scent

You only have to flip through a nursery catalogue to see that there are supposed to be lots of scented climbers – but the trouble is, in the sort of places you grow climbers you can't often get close enough to the flowers to have a decent sniff, so they have to be pretty strong to 'carry'. Aside from roses (see pages 103 and 105), these are my top three.

***Jasminum officinale* 'Grandiflora'** (1) is the jasmine of old cottage gardens, but the perfume is big in aromatherapy circles, so it won't seem out of place in a more modern garden either. It's a big twiner, reaching 6–7.5 ¥ 2m (20–25 ¥ 6ft), with sweet-scented white flowers lasting from June to September.

Lonicera (2), honeysuckle, isn't always as strongly scented as you'd expect from its reputation. One of the best for general garden use is a cultivated form of the wild woodbine, *Lonicera periclymenum* 'Serotina', the late Dutch honeysuckle, a twiner with clusters of small, curved-trumpet flowers that are purplish outside and yellow/cream/buff shades inside. Unlike some supposedly smarter cultivars, this one flowers constantly from July to October and it'll grow to about 6m (20ft) long. You can concertina its stems round a pillar, train it on to a trellis panel, or let it run up into a tree.

Trachelospermum jasminoides (3) has to be the ultimate scented climber, if you're lucky enough to live in a mild spot. It's got everything – it's an evergreen twiner with masses of strongly jasmine-scented white flowers in July and August. Okay, so it doesn't flower quite as long as real jasmine, but the flowers are more spectacular, and because it's evergreen, you aren't left with a lot of bare stems to look at in winter. Perfect for a pergola, arch or gazebo. It grows to 8m (25ft).

1 *Jasminum officinale.*
2 *Lonicera periclymenum* 'Serotina'.
3 *Trachelospermum jasminoides.*

Clematis

By growing a mixture of large-flowered hybrids and species clematis, it's just about possible to have a clematis in flower every day of the year. Large-flowered hybrids are the familiar ones, with flowers that are often striped like grandad's pyjamas; the species often have flowers more like nodding bells or small, open bowls. What they all have in common is that they like to be grown where their roots are in cool shade, but where their stems and flowers can grow out into the light. In a sunny spot, surround clematis roots with low plants, pebbles or pieces of tile to keep them cool.

Watch out for... clematis wilt

The only serious problem with clematis is clematis wilt, which mainly affects the large-flowered hybrids. Young plants are the most often affected, but older ones aren't immune. Affected plants collapse suddenly, as if they need watering badly, and the leaves start to dry out. If you are sure that the plant isn't simply short of water, cut all the stems off close to the ground and dispose of them (don't put them on the compost heap).

Keep the roots cool and moist, and feed occasionally with a dilute liquid feed and new growth should appear – though this may not occur until the following year. Wilt can sometimes affect the same plant several times, but repeat the treatment and it'll usually recover and grow normally. It's not really a good idea to plant a new clematis where one has already died of wilt, even though, in theory, the disease isn't spread through the soil.

If you want an alternative to large-flowered hybrids for growing where clematis wilt is a problem, go for any of the *Clematis viticella* or *C. texensis* cultivars, as they are not affected.

Planting clematis

Unlike most plants, clematis need to be planted deeply. Dig a planting hole about twice the usual depth and plant so that the top of the root ball is buried 10–15cm (4–6in) below the surface of the soil. This is so that if the stem of the plant is damaged – by careless hoeing or mowing, or an attack of clematis wilt – there will be plenty of buds below ground from which new shoots can emerge, so the plant regrows instead of being killed.

Clematis are very heavy feeders and need moisture at the roots, so they like lots of organic matter. If you want to grow one up a wall, where the ground is usually poor and dry, dig a very large planting hole and fork in lots of well-rotted organic matter, then plant so the roots are 30cm (12in) from the wall.

Pruning clematis

People worry about which clematis to prune or not. The easy answer is to keep the label when you buy a new plant, because the pruning instructions are written on the back. If you have an existing clematis and don't know the name, leave it alone and see when it flowers.

As a general rule, the ones that flower from June onwards, continuously through the summer, need pruning hard every year. The time to do it is any time during the winter up to the end of February, before the plants start growing again. Simply cut the whole plant back to about 30cm (1ft) above the ground and remove all the debris, leaving the trellis clean.

The kinds that flower in May or June, and then again in September, can be pruned more lightly. Just shorten the main stems back to a fat pair of buds, about 1m (3ft) above the ground. Do this in late winter.

Clematis texensis and its hybrids can be cut back almost to ground level in late winter. Most of the other species don't need any pruning. If they get too big or untidy, you can either cut them back just enough to tidy them up after flowering (if they finish flowering before the end of June), or in winter if they flower later. *Clematis montana*, on the other hand, will eventually resemble what a friend of mine calls a 'disembowelled mattress'. The plant is adept at covering sheds and garages, but like many vigorous climbers it doesn't know when to stop. Pruning can be a daunting thought, and so is usually avoided. But if you feel you have to tackle it, do the job immediately after flowering in late spring. Cut it back as hard as you like, but be prepared to have a lean show of flowers the following year. Subsequently the plant will make a full recovery.

Layering clematis

Clematis don't root well from cuttings, so the easiest way to propagate more plants is by layering. You can do it at any time of year, but late spring is usually best.

Look for a strong young shoot that originates close to the base of the plant. Improve the soil at the foot of the plant by forking in lots of well-rotted organic matter, then bend the shoot down and bury 10–12cm (4–5in) of the middle section, between two sets of leaves, in the prepared ground, holding it down with stones or a wire 'hairpin'. The length isn't critical, just make sure that the tip of the shoot sticks out of the ground.

Expect a layered shoot to take a year or so to root properly; you can tell because the new plant starts to grow strongly. Wait till it's a reasonable size and then dig it up in spring or autumn, sever it from its mum and replant it.

The layered stem of a clematis is conveniently held in contact with the ground by a large pebble.

How to... **grow a clematis in a tub**

Clematis make brilliant climbers for tubs, and this is a superb way of growing them when you don't have much wall space, if you expect to move house, or you simply like to move your various garden 'ingredients' round, rather like rearranging the furniture indoors. Although clematis normally have a very informal feel to them, by growing in containers like square Versailles planters with obelisks to match, you can turn them into a formal feature: stand a pair either side of a front door, or run a row along the side of a path or up each side of a flight of wide steps.

Clematis are very greedy feeders and drinkers and at the first sign of drought they will suffer. For this reason they need to be cosseted a bit when grown in tubs. Some varieties are more suitable than others for this kind of cultivation. Try early flowerers, such as C. *alpina* and C. *macropetala*, and the spectacular C. *florida* var. *sieboldiana*, plus the large-flowered 'Barbara Dibley', 'Miss Bateman', 'Elsa Späth', 'Nelly Moser' and 'The President'.

> ### What you need
>
> - *tub or pot 38–45cm (15–18in) in diameter*
> - *one clematis – choose a small cultivar with a long, continuous flowering season*
> - *an obelisk, the feet of which fit inside the pot*
> - *John Innes No. 3 potting compost*
> - *a bucketful of smooth stones*
> - *drainage material*

1 Place a layer of broken clay pots or bits of polystyrene plant tray in the bottom of the tub, covering the drainage holes, and just cover them with potting compost. Take the clematis out of its pot and stand it in the centre, after teasing out a few of the biggest roots if they have made a solid ball.

2 Fill the tub with compost to within 2.5cm (1in) of the rim. Firm lightly, water well, and then cover with a mulch of pebbles.

3 Stand the obelisk over the plant and firm the feet down around the inside edge of the tub. Untie the clematis and spread its stems out around the base of the obelisk; weave them very gently through the framework and tie them in place. Keep the plant well watered and apply diluted liquid tomato feed weekly from May to September.

1 *Clematis montana* seen here growing along a washing line.

Clematis species

There are about two hundred species of clematis and at least twice as many cultivars that have been bred from them. In general, the species don't flower for such long periods, but the flowers are often more delicately lovely and, in some, appear at times of the year when not much else is happening. These are some of my favourites.

Clematis montana (1) is another large species, and one that most people know. It grows to 6–9 × 1.5m (20–30 × 5ft), with lots of small white flowers in May and June. *C. montana* var. *rubens* has pink flowers and bronzy foliage. There are also larger-flowered, white forms, such as *C. m.* 'Alexander'; and several scented forms, such as *C. m.* var. *rubens* 'Elizabeth', with pink flowers. *C. montana* cultivars are no trouble at all to grow, don't need pruning and are good for any aspect that gets a fair bit of sun. But because they are so big, they aren't the best kinds for growing on trellis; use them for covering a wall or large fence, or grow one up through a fair-sized tree. Complete butchery immediately after flowering is the way to renovate one that has got totally out of hand.

C. alpina cultivars (2) are small plants, and fill a space of about 2 × 1m (6 × 3ft). They have nodding, blue or white bell flowers in April and May. Alpinas enjoy a cool spot and are good for growing on a north wall, though any aspect is fine. They are easy and don't need any pruning.

C. cirrhosa 'Freckles' (3) is a winter-flowering star. It's an evergreen species that flowers from December to March, with nodding, cup-shaped, cream flowers speckled with red. It always reminds me of a bird's egg. It grows slowly at first and won't flower well until it's several years old. It reaches maybe 6m (20ft), but doesn't need pruning, so it's good for growing through a tree or large shrub, in a sheltered spot close to the house. In a cold area, it's good for an unheated conservatory.

C. florida var. sieboldiana (4) (also known as *C. florida* 'Sieboldii') grows only to about 2m × 60cm (6 × 2ft), so it's ideal if you have one small piece of trellis to cover, and it is also brilliant for containers. The flowers are a decent size and look like giant passionflowers in purple and creamy white; they are produced throughout the summer. It needs a warm sheltered spot, and doesn't need pruning. If you like this one, you'll also enjoy its close cousin, *Clematis florida* var. *flore-pleno,* which has enormous white, double, rosette-like flowers.

C. texensis cultivars (**5**) have 5cm (2in) long, elongated, bell-shaped, red or pink flowers from July to October, on stems reaching about 3m (10ft). They like any aspect except a north-facing one. With these, hard pruning is a good idea – you can cut them back to the ground each winter.

C. viticella cultivars (**6**) come in many colours and some look like large-flowered hybrids, but their blooms are only about half the size; they are produced in large numbers from July to September. Plants grow 3–6m (10–20ft) long and can be pruned or not, as you prefer. They enjoy any aspect except a north-facing one. They are a good choice in a garden where hybrid clematis are affected by clematis wilt, as viticellas don't suffer from it.

C. armandii (**7**) is a monster evergreen species that will fill a space to 9 × 2m (30 × 6ft). It has architectural evergreen leaves and scented white flowers in March and April. *C. armandii* needs a sheltered spot facing south or west and, again, doesn't need pruning. The pink form 'Apple Blossom' is harder to find, but worth seeking out. The leaves are poisonous to dogs – be careful.

2 *Clematis alpina* 'Pamela Jackman'.
3 *C. cirrhosa* 'Freckles'.
4 *C. florida* var. *sieboldiana*.
5 *C. texensis*.
6 *C. viticella* 'Polish Spirit'.
7 *C. armandii*.

Clematis, the large-flowered hybrids

Large-flowered clematis hybrids are the most popular kinds, with flowers the size of saucers. They are great for growing up trellis, or through small trees or large shrubs and, with a few exceptions, they mostly grow to the 2.4–3.6m (8–12ft) size range. If you want a bigger plant, go for *Clematis* 'Jackmanii', or one of the other 'Jackmanii' cultivars; they can reach 4.5–6m (15–20ft). Large-flowered clematis hybrids fall into two groups, depending on when they flower, and it's worth knowing which are which because then you will know which ones to prune and which to leave alone.

All-summer flowering

Plants in this group flower continuously from June to September. As a general rule, these are the ones you can prune hard.

Clematis 'Niobe' (1) has single, rich, deep red-velvet flowers.

C. 'Comtesse de Bouchaud' (2) has single, mauve-pink flowers.

C. 'Jackmanii' (3) has single, purple flowers that have a really rich, velvety texture.

1 *Clematis* 'Niobe'.
2 C. 'Comtesse de Bouchaud'.
3 C. 'Jackmanii Superba'.

4

4 C. 'Perle d'Azur'.
5 C. 'Duchess of Edinburgh'.
6 C. 'Nelly Moser'.

Early- and late-flowering clematis

These have a couple of bursts of flower. The first is in May or June, then they stop for the summer before putting on another late burst of bloom in September. They generally don't need hard pruning, otherwise you'll be cutting off the growth that should carry the second batch of flowers.

C. 'Perle d'Azur' (4) is incredibly generous with its single lavender-blue flowers, which are produced from early summer to early autumn. It can cope with sunny or shady walls and can be pruned quite hard in late winter.

C. 'Duchess of Edinburgh' (5) produces very double, white flowers in the first summer flush that look like first-prize rosettes, and then, in September, it produces single white flowers. It does best with little or no pruning.

C. 'Nelly Moser' (6) has pale and dark pink striped flowers and, again, like many of the striped kinds, appreciates a little shade to avoid the bleaching effects of sunlight. It does well in an east-, west- or north-facing spot. In some years, it will flower right into November until it's stopped by the frosts.

5

6

Climbing roses

Roses are *the* traditional climbers for covering walls, pergolas and arbours, but few cultivars have a truly continuous flowering season, so team them with honeysuckle or clematis to fill the gaps.

Climbing roses need a permanent framework of stems to cover the designated area; the flowers are borne on sideshoots that are pruned back annually. They are good for training on walls, fences or trellis, up pillars or over arches. Choose one that fits the space available, so that you won't constantly be chopping it back to size.

Pruning climbing roses

When you first plant a climbing rose, it's essential to space the main stems so that they cover the space evenly. Fix them in place by tying them to horizontal wires, trellis or wall nails. Tie new shoots in to fill in the framework so that you cover the space with a network of stems, 20–30cm (8–12in) apart. Anything you don't need is cut off. The rose will flower on short stems growing from the framework. As the flowers fade, remove them, leaving behind 8–10cm (3–4in) of stem. This does two jobs at once: deadheading and summer pruning, so the plant stays tidy. With old climbers, cut an occasional old, unproductive stem back to a junction with a young stem, which can be trained in its place – do that in winter.

Training a climbing rose on a pergola

If you let a rose run straight to the top of a pergola post, all the flowers appear at the top of the stems, where you can't see them. Roses flower best on stems that are as nearly horizontal as possible, so if the stems spiral round a post, they'll flower all the way up.

At the side of a post, dig a planting hole three times bigger than the pot that the rose came in. Add lots of well-rotted compost and mix in a handful of rose fertilizer. Plant the rose with the bud union (the bulge where the cultivar joins the rootstock) about 2.5cm (1in) below the soil surface. Water and mulch generously.

Cut off any dead, weak or sticky-out stems, leaving the most strongly upright ones. Gently wind them round the post, and tie firmly in place with garden twine. As the shoots grow, continue winding them in while they're still flexible, keeping them fairly close together, like a coiled spring. When they reach the top of the post, let them run along the pergola top, but keep them tied down. Prune exactly as for a normal climber. If they're on a pillar, cut the top off flush with the top of the post. Do this each year in winter.

Climbing roses are pruned quite lightly immediately after flowering, the flowered shoots being pruned back to leave finger-long stems.

When growing roses up a pergola, tie in the flexible stems in spiral fashion as they extend.

Climbing roses

There are many varieties to choose from, but here are four – in a range of colours – that will seldom let you down.

Rosa 'Compassion' (**1**) is a medium-sized climber for walls and fences and has highly perfumed, peach-and-apricot flowers. It needs very little pruning, once it's trained. Allow 2.4 × 2m (8 × 6ft).

R. 'Danse du Feu' (**2**) is a very free-flowering climber with scarlet flowers in two flushes each season; good for a north-facing wall or a spot in light shade. Give it about 3 × 2.4m (10 × 8ft).

R. 'Golden Showers' (**3**) has scented yellow flowers from early summer to autumn. It needs heavy feeding. Roughly 2.4 × 2.4m (8 × 8ft).

R. 'Madame Alfred Carrière' (**4**) is an old climber with scented, pink-flushed, white flowers. Good for a north wall; 3.6 × 3m (12 × 10ft).

R. Swan Lake (**5**) is one of the best white-flowered climbers. It makes quite a small plant with unusually weatherproof flowers. It's good for growing on pillars and posts, or on a wall. 2.4 × 2m (8 × 6ft).

Roses for scent

R. 'Albertine' (rambler with pale pink flowers); R. 'Gloire de Dijon' (old climbing rose, with large, buff-peach flowers); R. 'Alchymist' (climber, with egg-yolk yellow flowers); R. 'Wedding Day' (huge rambler with single, white flowers); R. 'Madame Grégoire Staechelin' (climber with large, frilly pink flowers); R. 'Zéphirine Drouhin' (climber with almost thornless stems and mauve-pink flowers, good for arches); R. 'Crimson Shower' (rambler with red-crimson flowers).

1 *Rosa* 'Compassion'.
2 *R.* 'Danse du Feu'.
3 *R.* 'Golden Showers'.
4 *R.* 'Madame Alfred Carrière'.
5 *R.* Swan Lake.

Rambler roses

Ramblers are vigorous roses that flower on long canes, almost like blackberries, with large clusters of fairly small flowers at the tips. They are less disciplined than climbing roses, and the bigger cultivars are best allowed to scramble up trees, through shrubs, along fences or over outbuildings. Not all ramblers are huge, uncontrollable monsters, though; there are lots of smaller cultivars that are more suitable for covering modest structures.

Pruning ramblers

Prune ramblers after they finish flowering. Some cultivars have one flush of flower that is over by midsummer, but others have two flushes of flower, so wait till autumn, when the second flush is finished, before pruning. (If you inherit an unnamed rambler, leave it unpruned till autumn in the first year so that you can see whether it flowers once or twice.) To prune, cut back all the stems that carried flowers to just above an unflowered shoot. That removes a lot of this year's growth and makes the plant look much tidier, but leaves all the stems that will carry next year's flowers. The new, vigorous, unflowered shoots are the ones to leave.

Rambling roses are pruned after flowering. Remove the older, flowered stems as close to the base as possible and train in young, vigorous, unflowered shoots, which will carry next year's flowers.

Rambling roses

These varieties are a fairly well-behaved bunch, but there is one monster that you can let rip through an old tree or over a shed.

Rosa **'Albéric Barbier'** (**1**) is medium-sized by rambler standards, at about 4.5 × 3.6m (15 × 12ft). Yellow buds open and mature to rich cream. It's good for pillars, on rustic poles at the back of a border.

Watch out for... blackspot, mildew and rust

Some roses are notoriously affected by fungal diseases, others are more resistant. The traditional remedy is to spray thoroughly every two weeks from late spring to early autumn with a rose fungicide that tackles all the three main rose diseases – some brands include a greenfly killer as well.

In my garden, I prefer not to spray, and that means making sure that the roses are never under stress (shortage of water is the fastest route to mildew and blackspot). Organically enriched soil and thick surface mulches are a great help. I also plant disease-resistant cultivars when I can, and keep all my plants well fed.

R. **'Albertine'** (**2**) is another medium-sized rose, about 4.5 × 3.6m (15 × 12ft), with copper-pink flowers. It's good for walls and trellis.

R. **'Bleu Magenta'** (**3**) is a good choice for a north wall or light shade, with grape-purple flowers and few thorns; 3 × 2.4m (10 × 8ft).

R. **'Kiftsgate'** (**4**) is huge, reaching 9 × 3m (30 × 10ft) or more. The large, fragrant white flowers are like those of 'Wedding Day' and 'Rambling Rector', which are both about the same size; they are the best for growing up large trees or on post-and-rail fences and are all vigorous enough to cover old buildings – like the gasworks.

1 *Rosa* 'Albéric Barbier'.
2 *R.* 'Albertine'.
3 *R.* 'Bleu Magenta'.
4 *R.* 'Kiftsgate'

3 PATIO GARDENING

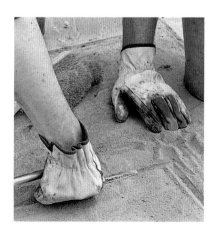

Perfect patios

The ideal patio is a cross between a living room and a garden – a sheltered suntrap where you have privacy to eat, entertain or simply sit and enjoy fine weather in a holiday atmosphere with all mod cons.

When planning your patio, think about what you will be using it for. Deciding on where to put patio furniture and fittings is a bit like arranging furniture inside a small living room. Start with the biggest items first, such as seats and tables, then add decorations such as pots and plants, where they won't be in the way. If you will be using the patio mainly as a dining area, make sure there's room for seats and tables conveniently near to the barbecue. The barbecue needs to be placed fairly near to the house, and with nothing in your way when you walk from there to the table, patio doors or the kitchen – you don't want to be tripping over steps or beds of plants when you are carrying food or drinks.

If you are including a table, make sure that there's enough room for walking around it easily without knocking into plants. If you have a garden hose, be sure to site it so that it has a clear run to your outdoor tap without catching on furniture or knocking pots over. Hang a hose reel on the wall so that it's easy to tidy away.

If you don't have a shed or garage for storing patio paraphernalia when it's not in use, a 'garden chest' on the patio makes a handy place to keep folding chairs, cushions or barbecue gear, besides hosepipes and spare pots. But however elaborate it becomes, a patio or deck isn't finished without plants.

You can create whatever atmosphere you want on a patio. Here the choice is for a calm and secluded haven, surrounded by plants.

Siting

Most patios are built at the back of the house so that you can walk straight from the living room into the garden and vice versa, without getting mucky feet. Nowadays, the original French windows have largely been replaced by sliding patio doors that can make the patio seem like an extension of the living room when they're wide open in warm weather.

But you don't have to have a 'standard' patio layout. If the back of the house doesn't happen to face the right direction to catch the sun, it's perfectly acceptable to build a patio at the bottom of the garden to be sure of your suntrap. Alternatively, if you prefer to sit in the shade, you can add awnings or a pergola and wall fountain to turn a too-sunny patio into a cooler and shadier haven where you can sit outside without risk of sunburn.

For a more contemporary look, you might forgo the usual paving and plump for the wooden equivalent – decking – instead. It's easy to construct, durable and relatively cheap.

Planning

A patio is one of the most expensive garden features to build and – since everything is stuck down – one of the hardest to change, so it's worth taking a bit of trouble to get it right. Start by planning it out on squared paper or on your computer.

Choose a shape, size and materials that complement the style of your house and its construction. The shape need not be formal and rectangular or completely flat – you can build a patio on the diagonal, or include steps and a change of level. You might want to build in a water feature or barbecue. And you might like to surround part of it with a dwarf wall to separate it slightly from the rest of the garden, or incorporate screening to give you some privacy from the neighbours.

It's a good idea to avoid having large areas of identical pavers, which can look boring, even if you choose an expensive type. Be adventurous. Leave out occasional slabs to make internal beds in which you can grow plants, or fill them with gravel, pebbles, slate chippings or smaller slabs to make contrasting textures. Leave some soil beds at the foot of a wall, as that makes it much easier to grow climbers later.

If you don't have much time for watering lots of small, portable containers (and potted plants need a lot of water in hot, dry weather) think about building raised beds. They hold a much bigger quantity of soil and they don't take as much watering as pots and hanging baskets.

Brick patios

It requires more skill to lay a brick patio than one constructed of slabs, but the overall effect can be very pleasing and suitably intricate in a small area. You can lay the bricks (frostproof engineering bricks are best) on a wet or damp mortar mix laid over firmed scalpings. Allow the mortar to set before you infill with dry grouting (wet grouting can stain the bricks). You can lay in the traditional bonds in staggered rows, or in herringbone fashion. Panels of brickwork are very useful for breaking up long runs of paving.

Patio furniture is instrumental in creating atmosphere – here traditional furniture imparts a homely feel.

Including lighting in a garden creates a whole new world after dark, especially if the lights are positioned to highlight focal points or works of art, like this bonsai tree.

Patio furnishing

Patios have moved on from being simple paved areas decorated with pots into what are, in some cases, fully furnished outdoor 'rooms', complete with sophisticated cooking, eating and leisure facilities. You can even install an outdoor Jacuzzi, put in outdoor lighting, and bring out the portable patio heaters.

Garden lighting

A patio is the first place to think about outdoor lighting. Security lights are fine in their place, but they do nothing for the after-dark ambience. Something more subdued is what's needed. Arrange several small globe lights round the edge of the patio, on the wall or just above your table – much the same as you'd have wall lights and table lamps indoors. Include a couple of lights around your barbecue so that you can see what you are doing. And use marker lights to illuminate steps or low beds with a weak pool of light – this sort of lighting looks good and helps to avoid accidents.

Then there are the more ornamental effects. Use a spotlight to highlight something special, maybe a giant urn or a climber on the wall. Or you could uplight a tree or sidelight an architectural plant to cast dramatic shadows. If you have a built-in water feature, consider underwater lights – they will help bring water to life after dark.

Building a slab patio

A lot of people prefer to 'get a man in', but building a patio is a job that keen DIY fans can do for themselves, given time. There are a few golden rules to remember when laying a patio, and positioning it is very important. Always make sure that you leave at least 15cm (6in) between the damp-proof course of the house and the surface of the patio. Also make sure that the patio slopes very slightly away from the house, so that rainwater runs away freely; you need a slope or fall of 1cm per metre (½in per yard).

The patio will need foundations and for this you should dig out to twice the depth of the paving slabs to allow for the mortar bed that you'll set them in. The bedding mortar should be made by mixing 4 parts sharp sand to 2 parts soft sand to 1 part cement. Alternatively, you can save yourself the bother and buy bags of ready-made mortar mix that just needs water added. Make the mixture slightly stiff. For filling cracks between slabs, the recipe for jointing mortar is a dry mix of 3 parts soft sand to 1 part cement.

Top paving and path materials

Slabs	Gravel	Cobble setts	Bark	Slate
Settle for grey or buff sandstone which shows off plants well, or, if you love colours, dusky pink sandstone from India. Pressure-hose the surface in winter to prevent slipping.	The cheapest hard surface in the garden, and the easiest to lay. Chippings come in assorted shades, and 'washed pea shingle' is the buff stuff that most drives are made of.	Setts are available in man-made stone or granite. They can be laid on the square or in concentric circles and are very attractive to look at – especially as feature panels in paving.	An inexpensive and practical material, ideal for non-sloping paths and areas under swings or climbing frames, where it provides soft landings for lively children.	Very fashionable. Slate 'paddles' (smooth, flat slate pebbles) make a great mulch and are surprisingly easy to walk on when laid loose on top of scalpings to make a path.

How to... **lay a patio**

If you have decided to go ahead and lay the patio yourself, follow this method. It is applicable to most types of paving. You can brighten up the paving with some fancy finishes – you could miss out one or more paving slabs to make a 'panel' with a contrasting surface. Good surfaces include gravel, loose pebbles or slate paddles (water-worn slate fragments) and they can be laid over the existing soil. Alternatively, for a cobbled panel, spread bedding mortar (see p.111) to within about 1cm (½in) of the surface, select even-sized cobblestones and gently press them to about half their depth, then lay a straight plank over the top and tap gently with a rubber hammer to make sure all the stones are submerged to the same depth.

If you want a soil bed, you may have to remove some earth if it's poor quality and replace it with good topsoil from elsewhere in the garden. Alternatively, you could use John Innes potting compost.

1 When you've marked out the area with pegs and string and checked that it is the right shape (both visually and from a practical point of view) excavate the area to a depth of 15cm (6in) using a spade. Avoid loosening the soil beneath that depth. If you are laying paving stones up to your house, the ground will need to be excavated to a depth of 15cm (6in) plus the depth of two bricks below the damp proof course of the building.

2 Spread a layer of 'scalpings' over the area and firm it with a powered compactor. Aim for a finished depth of 10cm (4in). Hammering wooden pegs into the ground so that they indicate the finished depth of the scalpings will make sure you maintain an even covering. Aim for a slight fall away from the house so that water runs off the finished patio and away from the building. Use a spirit level and a longboard to achieve this.

3 Lay out the slabs in their final positions. This is important if you are using random sizes of paving. Fitting the jigsaw together before you lay the slabs on mortar will avoid mistakes later. Aim for a pleasing pattern, with different-sized slabs next to one another. Start laying against the house wall (or from a fence or wall if the patio is elsewhere in the garden) and work outwards. Leave 1cm (½in) gaps between the slabs to allow for grouting.

If you want a bed at the edge of your patio, improve the soil by adding compost or topsoil, but make sure that the surface remains at least one brick below the damp proof course.

Lay slabs on a 10cm (4in) bed of firmed scalpings, topped by 5–8cm (2–3in) of bedding mortar. Make sure that they slope away from the house to drain away rainfall.

Occasional slabs can be left out to allow for planting pockets or different textured materials such as gravel or slate paddles.

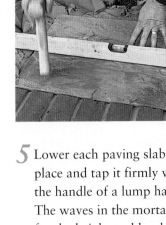

4 Lift a few slabs to one side, remembering where they were positioned. Mix a barrow-load of bedding mortar at a time. Make it reasonably sloppy so that it can be easily worked with a builder's trowel. You are aiming for a bed between 5 and 8cm (2 and 3in) deep which will be fine for domestic traffic. Use the point of the trowel to texture the surface of the mortar into 'waves'.

5 Lower each paving slab in to place and tap it firmly with the handle of a lump hammer. The waves in the mortar allow for the height and level of the slab to be adjusted. Use a spirit level to make sure that the slight fall away from the house is maintained, and that the slabs are positioned evenly within this fall. Keep off the newly laid paving for at least 24 hours to allow the mortar to harden.

6 Once the slabs are set, fill in the gaps between them with the moist grouting mixture. Firm it into place with your fingers (gloves prevent cement from dessicating your hands!) and then rub it smooth with a grouting 'iron'. The mixture will take up water from the soil and scalpings below by capillary action, and eventually set hard. Sweep away any excess with a hand brush and then over the entire area with a soft broom.

Building decking

Decking often looks more stylish than slabs in a contemporary garden, and it lends itself better to angular or geometrical shapes; there's lots of potential. It looks good as a stand-alone feature in the garden – a deck can be built overhanging a pond, or can be raised up above ground to create a platform.

Decking is also the easiest way of making a level surface on sloping ground. You can have 'banisters' and built-in bench seats, or make a square wooden platform just above ground level and surround it with plants, grasses, a patch of wild garden, or pebbles and cobbles. You can easily incorporate all sorts of other timber features with decking, such as trellis, pergola poles or bamboo screens to add even more design opportunities.

Whatever its detractors may say, a well-built deck in the right place can look simply stunning and is wonderfully practical.

Decks are much easier to build than patios, they last a lot longer than some people would have you believe, and they aren't that difficult when it comes to maintenance. They are certainly no more labour intensive to maintain than wooden fences or a shed. A blast with a pressure hose will quickly remove any slippery algae.

Decks don't have to be huge or elaborate. Sometimes good decks come in small packages – like this recycled cable reel.

Since none of the timber actually touches the ground – it all sits up on wooden legs or brick piers – there's plenty of air circulation underneath. This reduces the risk of wood rotting, as it inevitably does if it touches the soil, and good air circulation helps ensure that it doesn't remain wet for long.

Pressure-treated timber has already been treated with preservative to prevent rotting, and this method ensures that the preservative penetrates the wood deeply. But it is still a good idea to paint the finished deck with two coats of timber preservative. You can either go for a natural wood colour, such as pine or cedar, or use a coloured product to paint your deck a stylish shade such as dusky lavender, or perhaps a more subdued and weathered-looking pale grey. If you re-apply it every year, the colour remains pristine and you will ensure the maximum life for the timber.

If you are worried about losing things down the gaps, then make sure the gaps are narrow – 5mm (¼in) is ample – or raise the deck sufficiently to make sure that you can rake them out. If you are worried about vermin nesting under the deck – don't. Provided the ground is cleaned and mulched to start with, and there is good air circulation, there is no reason for them to make a home there.

Cheat's decking

Where you already have a firm, level surface like a path or patio, you can cheat by laying ready-made decking squares, using the existing hard surface for foundations. Left loose, decking squares are liable to skate about when you walk on them, so nail them down to rows of horizontal planks to act as under-decking battens or fit them inside a retaining wooden frame. Choose heavy-duty, solid decking squares; the thin, lightweight kinds are best used as temporary stepping-stones in gravel paths, grass or borders.

How to... make decking

First, draw up a detailed plan first on paper to calculate how much timber and other materials you need. If possible, adjust the dimensions of your planned deck to fit in with floorboard widths (plus gaps between) and standard lengths available from DIY stores. This minimizes cutting of planks to fit. When spacing the concrete foundation pads, note that the boards should overlap the joists by 5cm (2in) all round. If you want a deck longer than one plank, stagger the joints in successive rows. And if using the more expensive hardwoods, make sure they're from a sustainable forestry.

1 Roughly level the site with a spade. Remove big weeds, but leave the soil firm. Lay out the joists 45cm (18in) apart and mark the spots for the posts to support them: one at each corner, then at 1.5m (5ft) intervals around the deck. Dig a hole 30cm (1ft) square and deep for each post, and sit half a concrete building block firmly in the base. Sit the post on the block and fill around it with stiff, damp concrete, ramming it thoroughly. Use a spirit level to ensure it's straight. Leave two days to set. Spread an 8cm (3in) layer of gravel over the site on a weed-suppressing mat if necessary.

2 Attach the joists that will form the rim of the deck. Fasten them to the outside of the posts at the required height with galvanized bolts and check that they are level. You can leave the posts long and link them with swags of rope later, or cut them off flush with the joists for a plain area of decking. Once the outer framework is in position, further joists are added on the inside at 45cm (18in) intervals. Attach them to the outer timbers with joist hangers or screws. To maintain stability, spacers or 'noggins' of timber should be secured between the joists at staggered intervals of 1–2m (4–6ft).

3 Lay the decking boards on top of the framework: placing them at 45 degrees to the joists looks more pleasing than at right angles. Cut some spacers (thin slivers of wood) so that the decking planks can be held 5mm (¼in) apart to allow for drainage. The planks should overlap the framework by at least 5cm (2in). Fix them to the joists with countersunk screws. Stagger the joints for a better appearance. Draw a line to mark the final edge, then cut all the boards in one go so that the 5cm (2in) overhang is maintained. Paint the deck (if required) with a preservative, but keep the colour muted.

What you need

- *pressure-treated softwood timber – hardwood is even better but expensive*
- *10 × 10cm (4 × 4in) posts for the uprights*
- *15 × 5cm (6 × 2in) joists to support the decking boards*
- *10 × 2.5cm (4 × 1in) grooved boards for the deck floor*
- *galvanized bolts, joist hangers and countersunk screws*
- *concrete for foundations; 6 parts ballast to 1 part cement*
- *spade, power drill/screwdriver, spanners and saw*
- *set square, tape measure and spirit level*
- *pre-cast concrete blocks to sit in the support post holes*
- *gravel or weed-suppressing mat*

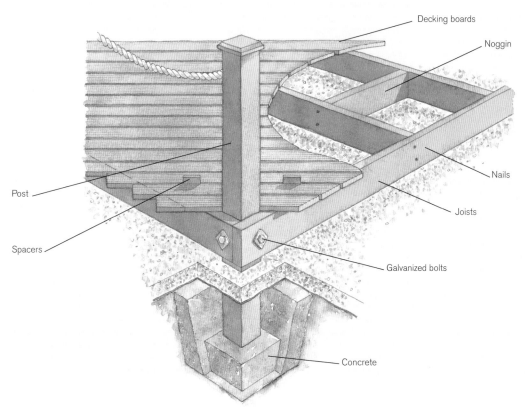

Decking boards

Noggin

Nails

Joists

Galvanized bolts

Concrete

Post

Spacers

Filling in the gaps

A good way to give a large patio character is to grow plants in the gaps between some of the paving slabs. The secret of getting plants to grow between slabs is advance preparation. You can't just chip out a hole in solid mortar, force the unfortunate plant in, and hope it'll survive. When laying the patio, make sure there's some decent topsoil underneath the parts you want to plant up, and just bed those slabs onto blobs of mortar instead of laying them on a continuous bed of it. Leave wide gaps between your paving, and put small plants in, then fill what's left of the crack with gravel. If you are thinking of planting into cracks in existing paving, you need to lift the slabs first and improve the soil underneath, then re-lay the slabs on blobs of bedding mortar. If the gaps are too small to put plants in, use 'plugs' (tiny plants grown in cell-packs a bit like egg boxes), or sprinkle suitable seeds in soil-filled gaps instead.

However careful you are though, plants will sometimes be stepped on. That won't bother the tough, wiry kinds as long as you don't make a habit of it. A patio is usually in a hot, sunny spot, so choose plants that can stand the conditions; the following are good choices.

1 *Alchemilla mollis.*
2 *Armeria maritima.*
3 *Dianthus gratianopolitanus* red.
4 *Parahebe catarractae* 'Miss Wilmott'.
5 *Thymus serpyllum.*
6 *Anthemis punctata* subsp. *cupaniana.*

Alchemilla mollis (1), lady's mantle, if grown anywhere in the garden, will most likely self-sow its seedlings into the gaps in your paving, where they will come up and look good with their fan-shaped evergreen leaves and sprays of airy, lime-green flowers that form mounds about 30 × 30cm (12 × 12in). You can plant small plants, but they aren't as tough as self-sown ones.

Armeria maritima (2), thrift, grows wild at the seaside, making 10–15cm (4–6in) tufts of tough, grassy, evergreen leaves with wiry stems and round pink flowers on top, a bit like nautical chives – a good tough one for growing in cracks between paving.

Dianthus species (3), including some of the British native pinks, grow wild in dry, rocky places, such as Cheddar Gorge and on rocky coasts, so the maiden pink (*Dianthus deltoides)* and its cultivars, and Cheddar pink (*Dianthus gratianopolitanus*) will be quite at home in paving or gravel. They look like slim-line versions of garden pinks with fine, almost needle-like, grey-green leaves and miniature pink flowers, in single or double versions. They have no scent that you'd notice, which is a pity. If you must have perfume, though, there are a few of the alpine pinks with a wonderful clove scent that might do the trick – try the red-flowered *D.* 'Hidcote' or the dark-eyed, pale pink *D.* 'Little Jock'.

Parahebe catarractae (4) is another plant I'd particularly recommend. You should find it in a garden centre with a good rock plant department. It's a small, mound-shaped, bushy shrub, about 30cm (12in) high and 45cm (18in) across, that's covered with small blue flowers, just like speedwell, for most of the summer. Delicious.

Thymus serpyllum (5), wild thyme, and its cultivars make good springy, evergreen mats about 5cm (2in) deep and, when fully grown, may be 60–90cm (2–3ft) across. They release a wonderful fragrance when walked on. In summer, the mats are dotted with pink flowers and bees in roughly equal numbers.

Anthemis punctata subsp. cupaniana (6) is one of the many rock plants that would do well in this situation, as it is one of the low, mound-forming, evergreen, drought-resistant kinds that are the ones to look out for at the garden centre. It has silvery green, chrysanthemum-like leaves and big, white, solid-looking daisy flowers with yellow centres, like fried eggs stuck all over the mounds, which grow to perhaps 30cm (1ft) high by 60cm (2ft) across in time.

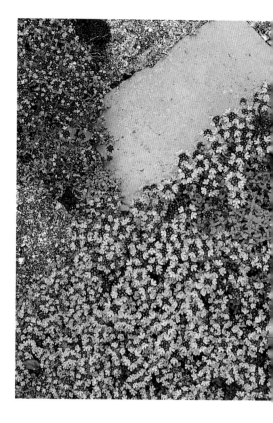

There's something really satisfying about positioning carpeting plants around paving slabs – visually it always works a treat.

Plants for patio beds

Where you've made a proper bed in the patio, or left a gap in decking to grow a plant through, you can afford to go for plants that grow taller, look more architectural, or which simply don't stand for being stepped on. Treat a bed such as this like a big container – the plants will need feeding and watering, even though they are growing in the ground. Drought-tolerant evergreens are the labour-saving option here too; once established, you can virtually forget them.

Drought-tolerant plants (**1**) include rock plants, such as *Sedum acre* and *S. spathulifolium*, and both of these do very well in dry conditions. Sempervivums do too; they start out as fat rosettes 2.5–5cm (1–2in) across, and grow in clusters but, in summer, they suddenly send up a thick spike studded with pink, red or greenish yellow flowers about 30cm (12in) high.

For a more traditional flower-border look, drought-loving perennials, such as *Sedum spectabile*, artemisias and eryngiums (the sea hollies), would cope well, but for solid flowers all summer it has to be alstroemeria. Don't go for the old-fashioned ones; new strains come in various heights from 25–90cm (10–36in). Look out for cultivars with 'Princess' in their name; they flower the whole summer, as long as you remember to keep tugging out the dead flower stems. Do it just as though you were pulling sticks of rhubarb; they come out quite cleanly, leaving the show to go on.

Although phormiums (New Zealand flax) are not grasses, their sword-like leaves have a similarly architectural effect and they are quite tough provided they are not left in cold, wet earth over winter.

Grasses (**2**) are good for a contemporary look. If it's hot, sunny and dry and you won't remember to water, the one I'd stick with is the blue fescue, *Festuca glauca*. There are several even bluer cultivars, such as 'Elijah Blue' – you can't go wrong with them. Some of the evergreen grasses and sedges prefer some moisture in the soil, so grow these only if you can provide suitable conditions.

Another grass-like plant is the black-leaved lily turf, *Ophiopogon planiscapus* 'Nigrescens'. It is a bit of an oddity and isn't everyone's cup of tea but, in the right spot, it is very eye-catching. The narrow, strap-shaped evergreen leaves are about 15cm (6in) high, and they spread to make a thinnish patch that looks good interplanted with dwarf bulbs, such as crocus, hardy cyclamen and colchicums. Plant a carpet of them in a bed in a contemporary patio or deck to make a surrealist 'lawn' that Salvador Dali would have envied.

Spiky phormiums (New Zealand flax) in a glazed pot, and pink nerines alongside *Miscanthus sinensis* 'Zebrinus' are set off well by the chunky sleepers of this solid timber patio.

1 *Eryngium alpinum.*
2 *Ophiopogon planiscapus* 'Nigrescens'.
3 *Juniperus communis* 'Compressa'.
4 *Hebe* 'Watson's Pink'.

Conifers (3) go well with the sorts of grasses that don't like to go short of moisture, but the only one that puts up with hot, dry conditions without being browned-off is the juniper. Any of the junipers would be happy here, and you can make an attractive cameo from a group of spreading, upright and bushy ones. If I could only have one it would have to be *Juniperus communis* 'Compressa', the dwarf 'Noah's Ark juniper', which grows into a perfect flame shape about 75cm (30in) tall.

Hebes (4) are brilliant evergreens with fluffy bottlebrush flowers; they're good for anywhere hot and sunny with good drainage. They flower from early to late summer and some keep on right into autumn. I'd go for *Hebe* 'Gauntlettii' for its tight-packed tubes of pink-purple flowers that last till October, if the weather is kind, or 'Great Orme', with feathery pink bottlebrushes; both come in at just over 1m (3ft). 'Watson's Pink' is a bright pink summer bloomer well worth having. In windy areas (where the big-leaved hebes may scorch), or in contemporary gardens, the starker, khaki-green mounds of the whipcord type, *Hebe ochracea* 'James Stirling', might suit better.

Paths and steps

This cobbled path at Barleywood might not be the smoothest surface to walk on, but it looks good in all weathers – especially when rain gives it a high gloss.

However attractively you lay out your front garden, the postman and other regular callers will always take the quickest way to the front door even if that means taking a short cut through a flower bed. That's why you need two kinds of path – the direct kind that takes people straight to the places they need to go, and the slowly meandering variety for ambling round enjoying the garden.

When designing a garden, it pays to anticipate where people will take the shortest possible route. That's the place to put hard-wearing paths with smooth, level surfaces – make sure they are wide enough for a removal man shifting a sofa. Leave your romantic, rambling paths – made of gravel, bark chippings or broken tiles – for a walk through the flowers, which is where you want to encourage people to slow down.

If you have a sloping path that needs steps at the steepest parts, they should follow the same rule. Always construct steps with risers (the face of the step) of even heights, and with treads that are wide enough to accommodate your feet. Serious steps that are used for access should be built of solid materials, with non-slip surfaces and maybe handrails to make sure they stay safe in all weathers. The sort of steps you use occasionally, or that are more decorative than useful, can afford to be made of less formal materials, such as railway sleepers or long logs, which can be sunk into the soil and backfilled with earth or hardcore, topped with gravel.

Proper paths

If you want a paved path, lay slabs in place on top of the soil so you can see where they need to go, then mark round the edge with the spade and move the slabs offside. Skim off the top 5cm (2in) or so of soil from the marked-out area, leaving the ground beneath undisturbed. This gives a firm base that also acts as a mould. Make up a barrow-load of bedding mortar, using the same recipe as for laying a patio (see page 111), and lay your slabs a few at a time till you reach the other end. Don't make too much mortar at a time because it'll start to set before you can use it.

You can make a serious gravel path by excavating the shape to a depth of 8–10cm (3–4in). Then bang in wooden pegs and nail wooden shuttering to them, or set twist-topped tiles on edge along each side of the path. Then spread a layer of broken rubble or hardcore and firm and level it with the head of a sledgehammer. Rake 5cm (2in) of gravel over the top. You need a proper edge to a gravel path to stop the stuff walking out into the grass or borders.

In this cottage garden (*opposite*) we used paving slabs set in shingle to make the going easier under foot but still informal.

Frivolous paths

The sorts of paths that you use for wandering slowly around the garden don't need the same sort of base as serious paths by any means. There's no reason why you shouldn't simply excavate your path to 2.5–5cm (1–2in) deep, put wooden shuttering in the sides, nailed to short, wooden holding pegs, and fill the depression with gravel. That way you can plant scented things, such as wild thyme (*Thymus serpyllum*), into the gravel.

If you like a firmer feeling underfoot, you could sink an irregular line of pavers into the gravel to make stepping-stones. Bed them onto blobs of bedding mortar to keep them firm. Alternatively, you could set bricks on to a firm, level, excavated soil base, so they are packed tightly together in the traditional herringbone fashion. They need to be buried to about half their depth in the soil to fix them firmly and the edge bricks are best mortared in to keep the whole lot in place.

You could also make a bed of mortar (recipe as before) and press small, rounded pebbles in to make a cobblestone path – like the one I made at Barleywood leading up to my tree fern grove. The construction is 'serious' but I defy anyone to walk quickly on it – you really have to slow down and enjoy the garden!

Marker lights

A row of small, low-voltage lights is quite bright enough to mark the position of a path for when you come home after dark in winter, and it's an especially good idea on steps. If you don't want the bother of organizing an electricity supply, solar-powered lights are very easy to use. You just push them in wherever they are needed. They charge up during the day and come on automatically after dark, unless you turn them off using the manual over-ride that most models have. Mind you, don't expect a lot of light from them – think of them as candles rather than lamps.

How to... **build a gravel path**

There's something special about a gravel path. Its very crunchiness makes it attractive, and there's the added advantage that you can hear people coming – even uninvited guests. But gravel is also an affable material – it goes with all kinds of plants. It can look smart in an urban setting, or suitably 'cottagey' in rural areas. But I suppose the greatest attraction of gravel is its relative cheapness and ease of use. You don't have to be a master mason to rake out a load of gravel, but you do need to do your groundwork properly if the path is to be durable, smart and well-drained. Gravel and lawnmowers do not mix, or if they do, the outcome is often costly, so always provide a barrier between path and grass.

Once your gravel path is in place, an occasional raking is all that is needed to keep it looking good, and maybe a top-up every couple of years to replace gravel that has been trodden in or simply walked away in the treads of people's shoes.

What you need

- 10cm × 2.5cm (4in × 1in) pressure-treated timber for the edges and 5cm (2in) square, 30cm- (1ft-) long pegs
- spade, fork and rake
- scalpings (stone, gravel and dust mixture from builders' merchants)
- compressing machine (on hire)
- club hammer, screws and powered screwdriver
- gravel (the rounded buff kind sold as 'washed pea shingle')

1 Mark out the path and excavate the soil to a depth of 10cm (4in), removing turf, weeds etc. Put the edging boards in place as markers and hammer the pegs in to hold them, keeping them vertical. When all the pegs are in place, fasten the boards to them with galvanized screws. The finished pegs should sit 2.5cm (1in) below the top edge of the boards.

2 Spread a generous layer of scalpings over the surface of the soil and rake roughly level. Make several passes with the whacker plate to firm and level them, adding more scalpings to even out any dips. You can run right up to the edge of the boards so that the scalpings are flattened all the way across the path to a level about 3cm (1½in) below the top edge of the boards.

3 Add gravel or shingle to a depth of around 2.5cm (1in) and rake level. If laid any deeper, the gravel will be difficult to walk on. The finished gravel level should be about 1cm (½in) below the top of the boards. You will end up with a path that looks good and is instantly accessible. Weeds seldom spring up through the scalpings, and any that do are easily pulled out.

Steps

If you want a flight of steps on a long slope, you need a builder. It's a serious construction project that must have proper foundations to be safe and sound. But if you only want two or three steps leading up to the patio, or to make small changes of level within the garden, then you can quite easily do it yourself.

If you have a naturally sloping garden, it's quite simple to use a spade to chop out two or three wide, shallow steps where you need them, leaving the soil beneath very compact. Make sure that they are level, and that each riser is the same height, then put a good layer of bedding mortar on top and set paving slabs in place.

Alternatively, you could lay a railway sleeper to make the riser for your step. Hammer a long metal peg in front of the sleeper, one close to each end, to make sure there is no chance of it slipping, and fill the tread with 2.5cm (1in) of gravel to make it non-slip. To give your feet something to grip on a very shallow slope, you can do the same thing using long, thin logs with wooden pegs knocked in front of them. Clearly you'd have to check these over regularly, because the steps will become unstable if the wood rots – they're fine for a woodland walk though.

Steeper steps need more support. Cut the steps out as before and use bricks and masonry mortar to make a low 'wall' for each riser. When they've set, fill any gaps with more masonry mortar. Trowel 2.5cm (1in) or so of bedding mortar over the tread and lay paving slabs on top. Give them several days to dry before you use them. Check steps regularly and repair loose slabs immediately.

Coping with a slope

Rather than make a single run of steps straight up a steep slope, which is tiresome to walk up, you could cut a longer, shallow path across the slope, like a hairpin bend on a mountain road. It makes walking much easier, especially when you have a barrow or mower to shift up the garden. If necessary, you can put in the odd step without having to do major construction. Don't use loose gravel on a sloping path; you'll slither on it and it will all end up in a heap at the bottom. Wet bark chips make a slope slippery too. Add a rustic handrail on the steepest bits.

For the garden do-it-yourselfer, timber is often easier to work with than stone, and old railway sleepers make particularly good steps.

Container gardening

These days it's not enough to have a few geraniums in tubs on your patio; you need style. That means not only picking the right plants to suit the spot, but also choosing containers and other inanimate objects that fit your theme. It's almost like recreating a theatrical stage set in your back garden.

Changing the pots in a doorstep display to add seasonal brightness makes sure that the display is never taken for granted.

Traditional style
The traditional patio look is for bedding plants everywhere – in tubs, pots and troughs, window-boxes and hanging baskets. Old favourites, such as lobelias, petunias, fuchsias and pelargoniums, are guaranteed good performers, and it's fun to try some of the new patio plants that come out every year. A traditional display is a patchwork of summer colour and you can plan a new colour scheme each year if you want, but I warn you, it's a lot of work. If you don't have much time for daily watering, put in a drip-feed watering system and let the timer take the strain. It'll cost a few quid, but it's worth it for peace of mind. There's still all the feeding and deadheading to be done so that the show doesn't grind to a halt halfway through summer.

Contemporary style
The minimalist look is handy because you use less to say more. Not only do you need fewer plants and pots, there's a lot less watering to do. Forget bedding plants – cut down the chores by using a few architectural all-year-rounders, such as phormium, bamboo or *Fatsia japonica* in striking containers. Keep an eye on the glossy magazines; they always reflect the latest trends.

Cottage garden style

The chintzy, cluttered, chocolate-box look of an old-fashioned country garden can be carried through onto a patio using containers of hardy annual flowers, such as nasturtiums, miniature sunflowers and the short-growing, knee-high sweet peas. Add a piece of potted topiary to give it a modern cutting edge that still looks in character. If you are a plant fanatic, you could use stone troughs filled with a mixture of drought-tolerant alpines like sedums, sempervivums and alpine pinks.

Tropical style

Tropical exotics are very fashionable right now and, if you are going for genuinely tender plants, you'll need a heated greenhouse to keep things such as cannas, potted tree ferns, outdoor palms and bananas safely through the winter. Cacti and succulents also do well outside in summer if you fancy a desert-island-castaway touch – big aloes and agaves look great against a background of giant leaves. If you have a hot, sunny wall or pergola, I think it's worth risking a slightly tender climber, such as *Campsis* × *tagliabuana* 'Madame Galen' or *Trachelospermum jasminoides* (see page 94) whose flowers have a decidedly tropical perfume. In a hot spot, they'll both be reasonably hardy. A tinkling fountain goes well with this look.

Often a single architectural plant, like this agave, is all that is needed to make a focal point against a stark background.

Oriental style

A genuine oriental garden looks a bit – well, it has to be said – staid to most western eyes, but you can get into the mood with pots of Japanese maples, bamboos and a cloud-trimmed conifer. Add a pebble pool and some paving surrounded by gravel and large, smooth, round stones. Plant clumps of *Sisyrinchium striatum* and wandflower (*Dierama pulcherrima*) to grow through the gravel for a splash of colour. Oriental gardens look very stylish all year round and there's comparatively little work involved.

Mediterranean style

At its simplest, you can bring in a hint of the Mediterranean by using the plain, old clay pots that you found round the back of the shed, planted with scarlet, single-flowered pelargoniums. Stand them on shelves above plain paving – old bricks and planks will do the trick. Alternatively, you can go upmarket with posh pots or your citrus plants, olive trees and bougainvillea collection.

Use terracotta flooring tiles underfoot (outdoor ones, or they'll flake after frost). Don't forget that if you want to use truly tender plants, you'll need a greenhouse or a conservatory to protect them from frost through the winter.

How to... **plant bulbs in containers**

What you need

- *John Innes No. 2 potting compost*
- *bulbs*
- *deep tub, 30–45cm (12–18in) in diameter, with pot feet or bricks to stand it on*
- *gravel or broken clay pot 'crocks' for drainage*

The best way to be sure of a really good show of bulbs in containers is to pack as many as possible into the available space. And the best way to do that is to plant them in layers like a club sandwich. This technique is mostly used in autumn to plant spring bulbs, the most popular sort for containers, but you can also use it in spring to plant tubs of lilies, which are great for summer scent and colour on a patio.

For a spring display you can use several layers of the same variety of daffodil or narcissus or you can do as shown below and plant larger bulbs such as daffodils and narcissi in the bottom layers, and smaller bulbs such as muscari and crocuses higher up.

1 Stand the container on pot feet or bricks where you want the bulbs to flower, because it'll be too heavy to move later. Fill the bottom 2.5cm (1in) of the tub with crocks so that surplus water will drain away quickly. Cover the drainage material with 5cm (2in) or so of compost and plant your first layer of bulbs. Space them just far enough apart so they don't quite touch each other or the sides of the container. Press them gently down into the compost so they stand up.

2 Cover the first layer of bulbs carefully with more compost, using just enough to bury the tips, then plant a second layer of bulbs. If there's room, repeat the process with a third layer of bulbs, and again cover them with compost.

3 Finish off with a layer of bedding plants such as dwarf wallflowers, winter-flowering pansies or forget-me-nots to go with spring-flowering bulbs. Use something trailing, such as lobelias, to go with summer bulbs. Just water lightly until you can see the bulb leaves appearing – if you keep the compost too wet, too early on, the bulbs will just sit in water and rot.

Top of the pots

There are so many plants you could grow in pots on patios that it's almost impossible to pick out a few real favourites. I've chosen a mixture of traditional and modern to suit most styles of patio, but nowadays, it's fair to say that almost anything goes in containers – even if only temporarily.

Patio plants

The term patio plants is simply marketing-speak for a wide range of short, bushy plants with a long flowering season that are good for growing in containers. You'll sometimes meet patio plants for autumn, winter or spring use, but the term usually means summer-flowering, half-hardy annuals and tender perennials that are treated as annuals. These don't withstand frost, and can't be put outside until mid- or late May, but if they are kept well dead-headed, fed and watered all summer, you can expect all the best kinds to keep flowering until they are killed by the first proper frost in the autumn. Real troupers. Some can be kept under cover in winter to use again next year.

Some don't like it hot

Don't assume that all house plants will enjoy a baking on your patio. Those that naturally grow in shady tropical rainforests will not appreciate being moved into an environment that is closer to the Arizona desert.

All kinds of plants can be mixed together on a patio provided that they enjoy the prevailing conditions.

The eryngium (on the left of the picture) is a sun-worshipper while the caladium (on the right) prefers shade and shows its displeasure by turning crisp on a sun-baked patio.

Argyranthemums (1) are a good choice for summer containers. Also known as the marguerite, they have daisy flowers and foliage like a cut-leaved chrysanthemum. The best known is probably the single yellow 'Jamaica Primrose', but argyranthemums also come in pink, and white and with double or single flowers. Daisies go with everything; they're as much at home with fuchsias as lobelias.

Helichrysum petiolare (2) is a great foliage plant for containers. There are several – the grey-leaved species, the brighter 'Limelight' with pale gold leaves, and 'Variegatum' with cream-edged, green leaves. The woolly foliage tells you that this is a plant that tolerates sun and drought, so it makes a good partner for pelargoniums and other sun lovers, though it thrives in most container conditions. It roots easily from cuttings and is no trouble to keep though winter.

Brachyscome (3), the Swan River daisy, has small, blue daisy flowers and goes flat out all summer. It looks good with fuchsias that have a blue or purple 'skirt', and the ferny foliage doesn't mask the flowers. It's difficult to overwinter, but cheap to buy or grow from seed.

1 *Argyranthemum* 'Jamaica Primrose'.
2 *Helichrysum petiolare* 'Variegatum'.
3 *Brachyscome multifida* 'Blue Mist'.
4 Diascia.
5 *Pelargonium* 'Lord Bute'.
6 *Fuchsia* 'Alice Hoffman'.

Diascias (4) are relative newcomers, with spikes of small, mask-shaped pink flowers and, as long as the compost doesn't dry out badly, they keep on flowering all summer. You can treat the ones sold as patio plants as annuals and buy new ones each year, or take softwood cuttings (see page 299) and keep young plants growing in a bright, frost-free place during the winter.

Pelargoniums (5) are the best known of the lot, often called geraniums. Zonal pelargoniums are the bushy, upright kind, named for the darker zone that patterns the leaves of some cultivars. Ivy-leaved pelargoniums are the trailing ones with ivy-like leaves. Cascade pelargoniums are a prolific, ivy-leaved strain with very narrow petals and so many flowers that the plants are almost entirely hidden by them. All pelargoniums are very free-flowering, sun-loving and fairly drought-proof – they won't keel over if you forget to water occasionally. They root well from cuttings and are easy to keep through the winter provided you don't overwater them.

Fuchsias (6) are reliable and easy to grow. Trailers are naturals for hanging baskets or around the edge of a big container, where they sprawl elegantly down and hide the edges. Bush fuchsias are good for the centre of a tub, or for training as standards. You often see them with pelargoniums, but fuchsias actually prefer cooler, moister conditions and light, dappled shade. They are easy to grow from cuttings, and no trouble to keep through the winter – just cut them back hard and take cuttings from them in spring.

Petunias (7) are great for a slightly shady, wind-sheltered spot. The Surfinias are one of the most reliably long-flowering plants for containers. The scent is brilliant; you'll notice it most in a porch or gazebo, where it's not wafted away on the breeze. Regular dead-heading is vital, but the flowers are huge, so it's quick to do. New strains of petunias with much smaller, more bell-shaped flowers are excellent for containers, especially in windier spots. Don't bother to root cuttings – they're too prone to viruses; buy new plants at the start of each summer, or grow your petunias from seed.

Trailing verbena (8) has been around for a long time but it's only become a container essential since named cultivars have been promoted as patio plants. It was 'Sissinghurst Pink' and a few other good performers that got the ball rolling, but there are lots of different varieties available in a good range of colours. It's easier to buy new ones each year than to overwinter them – you don't need many.

7 Petunia.
8 Verbena.

7

8

Container plants for summer scent

Scented flowers are a definite plus for containers. Choose those with a long flowering season or that have aromatic leaves, so you really feel the benefit all summer.

Position aromatic foliage plants close to a patio or sitting area and their fragrances will be released whenever the plants are brushed against.

Aloysia triphylla (**1**), lemon verbena, is the lemoniest scented plant I know, and great for containers. It's a tender bush with intensely scented leaves and insignificant white flowers. It reaches about 75 × 45cm (30 × 18in) in a container on its own over the summer – it'll be smaller in a container with other plants. Easy from cuttings; keep it in a frost-free greenhouse in winter, and enjoy brushing past it.

Salvia rutilans (**2**), pineapple sage, doesn't look a bit like herb sage. It has large, pointed-oval leaves and spikes of long, red, pipe-cleaner flowers. It enjoys the heat and, when bruised, the leaves have a strong and sweet pineapple scent. It needs a heated greenhouse in winter, and is easy to grow from cuttings.

Heliotropium arborescens (**3**), heliotrope, is a good plant for a sunny container, with large, wrinkled leaves, and big heads of tiny lavender- or violet-blue flowers that smell strongly of hot cherry pie. It'll reach 30cm (1ft) high by as much across during summer, but is happy crammed into a tub between other plants. Grow from cuttings or seed, or keep plants in a frost-free greenhouse in winter.

Scented-leaved pelargoniums (4) are old favourites. There are different cultivars that smell of anything from oranges and lemons to roses or spice if you bruise the leaves gently. Don't expect a fragrant version of the zonal pelargonium; they look nothing like them, though they grow to about the same size. A few have bright flowers, but most are unremarkable; small and off-white. Keep them in a frost-free greenhouse in winter; propagate from cuttings.

Matthiola bicornis* subsp. *bicornis (5), night-scented stock, is my first choice where there isn't much room, but – as you'd expect – it's only scented at night. The flowers aren't exciting – light mauve, pale pink and off-white 'stars' dotted on skinny plants, 15cm (6in) tall. Shoe-horn a clump in between more spectacular plants, or sow seeds straight into the container – they are only annuals.

Mentha* x *piperita* f. *citrata (6), Eau-de-Cologne mint, has attractive, round leaves that smell like scent out of a bottle, and lavender flowers. Mix it with herbs or cottage-style flowers – it grows about 45cm (18in) high. *Mentha spicata*, spearmint, is twice as tall but very minty and a pot will stop it spreading. They are hardy, so leave them in the garden over the winter.

1 *Aloysia triphylla*.
2 *Salvia rutilans*.
3 *Heliotropium arborescens* 'Marine'.
4 *Pelargonium* 'Lady Plymouth'.
5 *Matthiola bicornis* subsp. *bicornis*.
6 *Mentha × piperata* f. *citrata*.

Container plants for autumn and winter

There's more scope for winter containers than ever. There are a few good winter-flowering bedding plants that would suit, but you can also grow evergreens and winter shrubs in containers just for a single winter before planting them out in the garden – twice the value for your money!

Keeping patio plants through the winter

Even though you can't leave tender plants outside in winter because they'll be killed by frost, quite a few patio plants can be used again next year.

Dig the old plants up in autumn before there's a frost, cut the tops down to about 15cm (6in) and put them in pots in a greenhouse or conservatory with just enough heat to keep the frost out. You can replant them outside again in late spring after the last frost, usually around mid- to late May.

Otherwise, root shoot-tip cuttings in late summer, and keep them in a frost-free greenhouse, or on a windowsill indoors for the winter. Young plants produced this way usually look better and flower more profusely than old ones. They also take up much less room than the old plants.

Evergreen shrubs (1) are invaluable for temporary use in tubs; you can plant conifers, box and *Viburnum tinus*, but the ones that I reckon make the best show are skimmias. *Skimmia japonica* 'Rubella' has triangular bunches of rosy pink buds that open in spring to masses of small, star-shaped flowers – it's a male form. *Skimmia japonica* 'Veitchii' is a female plant that carries big red berries in winter. You need both, so plant one of each in the same pot; it will look like one plant and produce buds *and* berries. They are slow growing, so can stay in the pot for several years. The secret weapon of the winter containers is a little thing called checkerberry (*Gaultheria procumbens*). It's a short, spreading evergreen with lots of red berries that last for months. Although it prefers acid soil, it'll survive in normal potting compost for a few months. Try it in hanging baskets with ivies, or in tubs with winter-flowering heathers.

Winter-flowering heathers (*Erica carnea* cultivars) (2) are an excellent choice for winter containers; they are compact, flower from November to March, and are very wind resistant, so if you have an exposed patio they won't shrivel up like your average winter bedding. Ericaceous compost isn't essential for this group of heathers, as they are fairly lime-tolerant. The plants go well with ornamental cabbages and kales and with all those evergreen shrubs I've described (and more besides). With these combinations, you can make colourful winter tubs.

Universal pansies (3) have been the biggest advance in winter bedding over the last quarter century or so, and they're great for containers. None of the other winter-flowering pansies go on so relentlessly in all but the most atrocious weather. Look after them well and grow them where the compost won't freeze solid or become waterlogged, and they flower from early autumn until you have to pull them out in May to make way for summer plants. Keep an eye open for the brand new Panola – a cross between a pansy and a viola – which has the universal pansy's ability to recover after bad weather, but the greater flower production of the viola.

Ivies (4) are very versatile and, if you track down a specialist nursery, you'll find a much wider range than you see in your average garden centre – lots of colourful, variegated forms and unusual leaf shapes, including maple-shape, curly, ferny and bird's-foot cultivars. They make classy winter container plants on their own, but they're also good mixers – use them as leafy fringes around tubs of evergreens and trailers for window-boxes and hanging baskets with winter bedding – they're good fillers for gaps anywhere really.

1 *Skimmia japonica* 'Rubella'.
2 *Erica carnea* 'Springwood Pink'.
3 Pansies.
4 Ivy.

1 *Fritillaria meleagris*.
2 *Pulmonaria officinalis* 'Sissinghurst White'.
3 *Primula vulgaris*.
4 *Viburnum tinus*.

Container plants for spring

Once spring comes round, garden centres miraculously fill up with small flowers for planting colourful seasonal containers – you'll be spoilt for choice.

Bulbs and tubers (1) are now sold in spring in pots just as they are coming into flower, for the benefit of people who forgot to plant bulbs in autumn, and those who have not the patience to wait. It's an expensive way of buying them, but the big advantage is it's instant. You can pick several pots at exactly the same stage of development so you don't end up with a lopsided-looking container, as you might if the flowers don't all come out at once. You'll find various kinds of tulips, grape hyacinths (*Muscari*) and snake's-head fritillaries (*Fritillaria meleagris*) sold in pots in spring, but my favourites are dwarf daffs – not too top-heavy for tubs, and small enough to plant in window-boxes if you want to. The double forms of *Ranunculus asiaticus* are better known as turban buttercups. They are not available until spring is fairly well under way, but if you are looking for something a bit different and instantly glamorous, this is probably it. They come in a good range of colours and the flowers do look just like turbans on stalks.

Perennials (2) can be grown in containers first, particularly early spring perennials, and then planted out in the garden, but if you want one good one, go for pulmonarias. Most are compact, with red, blue or white flowers out at the same time on the same plant, and some, such as *Pulmonaria saccharata*, have spotty leaves that go well with almost any neighbour. They're good for filling the gaps around the edge of a tub of spring bulbs.

2

3

4

Spring bedding plants don't last long – usually a few weeks, compared to months for the summer sort. Since it is so short-term, there's no need to do a 'proper' job of planting containers. Don't bother emptying the old compost out. Just sink each plant, still in its pot, to its rim in the container, then, when the flowers are over, you can lift it out and drop another one into its place. That way, it's quick and easy to maintain the display until it's time to make a fresh start – when you'll be planting your summer bedding plants.

Primulas (3) – coloured primroses, cultivars and hybrids of the wild primrose (*Primula vulgaris*) – are some of the earliest spring flowers, appearing soon after Christmas. The weather then is too unreliable to plant them outside safely, so unless you live somewhere very mild, put them in your porch or somewhere equally sheltered. By March or early April, it's fine to plant them out. The Polyanthus Group primulas are a bit later flowering, usually coinciding with the main rush of spring bulbs in the garden. Years ago, we used to plant them in autumn for formal spring bedding but, frankly, I prefer the idea of buying them in flower in spring and planting them in containers to give a burst of instant colour.

Shrubs (4) can look wonderful, even if temporarily, in a tub and one of the best for this has to be a viburnum. *Viburnum tinus* gives you a good run for your money, as the buds look good against the evergreen leaves all winter, and then open out to small white flowers in spring so you have two seasons' worth from the same plant. But if you want a real cracker, then look out for *V. carlesii*. It doesn't flower until late spring, when the leaves are already out. The flowers are pretty – a pale, peachy pink – but the scent is one of the best you'll meet in any garden. It'll reach 2 × 2m (6 × 6ft) in time, but a 'baby' in a tub can be moved to wherever you want some concentrated perfume.

I love grouping small pots of spring-flowering bulbs like this. Here are *Narcissus* 'Tête à tête', *Crocus chrysanthus* 'Snow Bunting', *Hyacinthus* 'Carnegie' and *Hyacinthus* 'Blue Magic'.

Once they've reached a decent size of container, patio plants need not be potted on each year, but can be given a shot in the arm each spring if old compost is removed from the top of the pot and replaced with a fresh topdressing of new compost that contains slow-release feed.

Container plants for all year round

When you're too busy to bother replanting containers every season, and don't have time for the constant attention that bedding plants need, then choose long-lived plants, such as hardy shrubs and perennials, that can stay in the same pots for years.

All-year-round plants can stay put for years without being repotted, as long as you topdress them every spring and mix slow-release feed into the new compost that you use to replace the old stuff you trowel off. Even if the plants you choose are capable of reaching a fair size in time, the pot acts like a corset, stopping them from growing too big. Most all-year-round shrubs will need a 38–45cm (15–18in) pot to do well; fill it with John Innes No. 3 potting compost and put some drainage material in the bottom. In winter, let the compost freeze solid or the plants will dry out (they can't use frozen water): move them into a greenhouse, conservatory or even the shed if a long spell of hard weather is predicted.

Bamboos (**1**) are very cool for pots and look ace, even though, in theory, a lot of species grow too tall and top-heavy. Any bamboo will do well in a container, but if you want coloured canes rather than a thicket of leaves, the ones to go for are the wonderful golden-stemmed bamboo (*Phyllostachys aureosulcata* var. *aureocaulis*), and the black bamboo (*Phyllostachys nigra*). Don't be fooled by the name; black bamboo has bright green stems to start with that turn black only when they are two or three years old, but the plant is still spectacular. They'll both reach 3m (10ft) feet or so, eventually, so give them a large enough tub.

Topiary (**2**) is very fashionable, and box (*Buxus sempervirens*) is the best for the job. The garden centre will sell you the finished article, at a price, or you can train your own designs. Work free-hand if you are feeling confident, or buy metal wire 'templates' that you pop into the pot over the top of a small plant, and just clip round the outside when it grows through – easy.

Patio roses (**3**) are the all-year-round answer to bedding plants. These roses are one of the few shrubs that flower for as long as summer bedding, from June to September or October – and they don't grow much bigger than a lot of bedding plants. Most cultivars make about 30–45 × 30cm (12–18 × 12in). Prune them as you would normal bush roses in spring.

Subtropical plants (**4**) are frequently featuring in gardens now as people find themselves pining for palms. The best two for our climate are the Chusan palm (*Trachycarpus fortunei*) – that's the one with windmill-shaped leaves you see growing everywhere in Cornwall – and the dwarf fan palm (*Chamaerops humilis*) which has, well, fan-shaped leaves. They are both slow growing, evergreen and will take ages to reach much more than 1.2–2m (4–6 ft), but the fan palm is the bushier of the two. Unless you live in a mild, sheltered area, both can be a touch iffy in winter – even if they aren't actually killed the leaves can look very brown and battered – so they are best moved under cover when the weather gets rough.

Herbaceous perennials (5) don't really count as year-round plants, since they die down every winter, but I'd make an exception for hostas because if ever a perennial was designed for tub- or pot-living, this is it. There are lots of cultivars, with big, round, blue, elephant-ear leaves, or elegant, yellow- or cream-variegated, heart shapes, growing in clumps about 30cm (1ft) or more high.
A good colony growing in a wide wooden tub looks stunningly traditional, but grow them in a big, modern-looking ceramic pot and they suddenly take on a contemporary flavour. They're good for growing in light shade, though they put up with sun if you can keep them moist enough – the trick is to grow them in something without drainage holes in the bottom and keep them well topped up.

1 *Phyllostachys nigra.*
2 *Buxus sempervirens.*
3 *Rosa* 'Flower Power'.
4 *Trachycarpus fortunei.*
5 Hosta.

The year-round patio

The patio isn't a five-month wonder; there is life after summer is over. Even if it's too cold to sit out there, you'll still want to be able to enjoy it from the warmth indoors. And, with luck, you might even get some of those clement early spring days when you can sit out there and bask in anticipation of the summer to come.

With just a single container (see below) you can ring the changes and make sure of a bright display in every season. Some plants, such as phormium (New Zealand flax) and ivy can be permanent residents, and temporary occupants can be added and subtracted as they come in and out of flower. Alternatively, in a large tub, you can plant a taller evergreen shrub, such as *Viburnum tinus* (see p. 137), or a small, coloured-stemmed dogwood like *Cornus alba* 'Sibirica' to form your centrepiece.

Create an evergreen framework to give the patio a basic winter structure, then add a few winter tubs to act as focal points. Don't just think in terms of winter bedding, because there are lots of shrubs with evergreen leaves and other kinds of winter interest that you can plant for one season only, before planting them out in the garden. Double the value for money!

The ivy, hebe and phormium (New Zealand flax) are the permanent residents in this metal planter, but the seasonal display changes with the seasons. In spring (*far left*) daffodils and hyacinths provide the colour, followed in summer (*second left*) by petunias, verbena and grey-leafed senecio. In autumn (*second right*) dwarf perennial asters bring their colour to the picture along with an ornamental cabbage, and in winter (*far right*) pansies and heathers change the scheme yet again.

Plant a formal row of evergreen edging plants such as dwarf box (*Buxus sempervirens* 'Suffruticosa'), santolina or rosemary around the edge of internal beds, plus the perimeter if you fancy a formal look. Stand a matching pair of trimmed bay trees (*Laurus nobilis*) either side of the patio doors to make a glamorous entrance and exit.

Line a wire-framed hanging basket with a green-fibre mat, or a similar very open-textured liner that won't hold much water, fill it with potting compost and plant it with ivies or other evergreen foliage plants. Add winter-flowering pansies if you have a very sheltered spot, but remember that evergreens will stand up to winter conditions far better than flowers. Hang the baskets up in your most sheltered places, such as under the eaves or in a corner.

Each winter give the patio a good going over. Clean the paving off with a stiff broom and hot, soapy water, or a pressure washer, to get rid of decomposing leaves and moss. Weed the gaps between slabs, and wash down the sort of furniture that is left outside in winter. Re-paint it or treat it to a lick of timber preservative if it needs perking up. While it's quiet in the garden, take the opportunity to clean any unused pots so that they're all ready for planting in the seasons to come.

4 BEDS AND BORDERS

Placing plants

Beds and borders are your plant features. For plant enthusiasts, these are the most important part of the garden around which everything else revolves, but in contemporary and low-maintenance gardens, they often take second place to 'hard landscaping' and bold, architectural features. That may be why some dyed-in-the-wool gardeners have a problem with decking, gravel and blue paint.

As a general rule, the more beds and borders you have, the more work it will take to maintain the garden, but a lot depends on the type of plants you grow – bedding plants and perennials need more attention than an area of shrubs, naturalized bulbs and ground-cover plants. Somewhere along the line there is a compromise – a happy balance. And you do want to be a gardener, don't you?

Borders go round things – maybe the edge of the garden, along the edge of a path, or round outbuildings. Beds are entirely surrounded by something else, such as lawn, paving or gravel.

These dahlias at Hinton Ampner in Hampshire, are grown in traditional formal flowerbeds surrounded by clipped yew hedges.

Formal beds and borders use a lot of straight lines; they have geometric shapes, maybe round, square or octagonal for a formal bed. Formal borders are normally rectangular. They may contain one particular type of plant, such as herbs, annual bedding, dahlias, or herbaceous flowers, though you can have mixed planting in formal borders. Double borders are a great feature of formal gardens: they are simply two rectangular borders facing each other with a paved or gravel path or swathe of fine turf running between the two.

Informal borders are curved to create a more natural, casual style, while island beds are often teardrop-shaped, or landscaped to fit into natural contours in the ground, like an island in a sea of lawn. The casual style suits mixed planting schemes especially well, so you can mix small trees, shrubs, evergreens, perennials, bulbs and flowers to give year-round interest, which makes good use of a small space.

Most domestic gardens have a more relaxed arrangement of informal flowerbeds stuffed with a mixture of plants.

Design rules

Many people end up reshaping their beds and borders for years without ever being happy with the result. It'll save a lot of work later if you can manage to avoid most of the common mistakes from the start and if you can first plan your beds on paper (see page 45).

Define your edges

If you are going for a formal look, make sure straight edges are really straight and circles really round. In an informal garden, curves should be gentle and generous; violent bends and sharp angles look over-fussy – besides being a pain to mow round.

Stick to a sensible size

Beds and borders should be in proportion to the size of the garden. Don't make borders too narrow, or put in lots of fussy little beds. A few big ones usually look much better and they are less effort to look after since there are fewer lawn edges to trim. But don't make them too big either – you are much more likely to keep beds and borders hoed regularly if you can reach all the soil without standing on it. That's one reason why island beds are so popular.

Deep borders are not only spectacular because of their generous proportions, they also allow more room for plants to grow. Gentle, sweeping curves along the front of the border are easy on the eye, and the path makes cultivation easy, while preventing the plants flopping on to the lawn.

Give hedges a wide berth

If you want to save work, avoid making narrow traditional borders with a hedge along the back, because they *are* hard work. A hedge makes a perfect depot for weeds, such as bindweed, and slugs and snails. It takes all the water and nutrients out of the soil and, when the hedge needs cutting, you find it's a struggle to avoid stepping on your plants. If you must make a border in front of a hedge, leave a path along the back especially for the purpose – which means giving up a lot of space. Borders are best running alongside paths, or in front of fences or walls, otherwise go for a free-standing island bed instead.

Soil preparation checklist

• Get rid of weeds – it's fine to turn in annual weeds without any seed-heads, but dig out perennial weeds and, if there are persistent perennial weeds, such as couch grass or bindweed, take time to eradicate them properly first. Use a glyphosate-based weedkiller, which kills the roots as well as the tops; alternatively hoe or use a flame gun regularly until the weeds stop growing back.

• Improve the soil structure – dig in as much well-rotted organic matter as you can. On heavy clay soil, use gritty horticultural sand as well – up to a barrowful per sq. metre/yard. I know it sounds a lot. It is a lot. But it works.

• Final preparation: sprinkle a general-purpose organic fertilizer over the soil shortly before planting, and rake it in, breaking down clods to produce a crumb-like tilth. Gather up any big stones (ignore smaller ones), roots or rubbish as you go. If planting in autumn or winter, just break down the clods for now – wait till spring to apply fertilizer.

Plan your beds and borders

When deciding on a plan, work from the back to the front for the borders and from the centre out to the edges for island beds. That way you'll be sure you have your framework plants where you want them – making a long-term background for the smaller plants at the front and those with more temporary effects.

Before you start to plant

First, prepare your soil – you can do it at any time of year as long as the ground is neither boggy, nor frozen, nor bone dry – then draw up your planting plan (see p. 148). When you've chosen and bought your plants, stand them roughly in position – in their pots – so that you can make last-minute changes before planting. If you change your mind later, you can always dig them up and move them.

Preparing a planting plan

This is the bit plant buffs can't wait to get to, when you actually start thinking about precisely what you are going to grow.

The way to go about it is to decide on the framework planting first – those plants that create the year-round 'bones' of the garden, trees and evergreens, followed by deciduous flowering shrubs. Leave the flowers till last, as they tend to be smaller plants that have a more temporary effect on the look of the garden.

Don't worry if you aren't a plant expert, or you don't have any design experience. It's much easier to work with abstract shapes for now and put names to them later. Work out roughly the shapes and sizes of plants that you need – some grow tall and upright, some are wide and weeping, and others are low and spreading and form carpets.

I always like to arrange plants as a series of triangles, putting contrasting shapes, textures and sizes together. Your triangles should be different sizes, and they should overlap each other by varying amounts. They won't look completely triangular once they are filled out in plants, but it's a good way to start and it avoids creating the 'tray of scones' look.

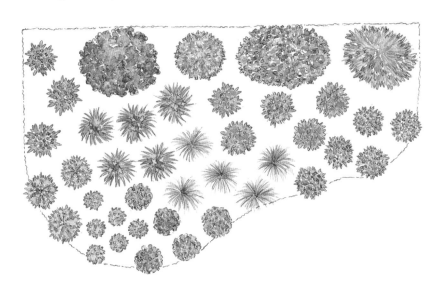

Converting your plan into real, live plants

When you are deciding which plants will suit your plan, you need to know what shape they are, what size you can expect them to reach in five years, what growing conditions they need, and what they do – do they have big foliage, masses of flowers – if so, what colour and when? You also need to know what category of plant you are looking for.

Tips for the plantaholic

Keen plantspeople, whose main interest lies in finding room for the particular plants they want to grow, will find the same technique works for them – they just need to go about things the other way round.

Start by considering the shapes, sizes and general requirements of the plants you want to grow, mark them in on your plan and design everything else round them. Your 'key' plants will look a lot better if you use this approach, than if you just cram them in anywhere there is room. This is what all too often happens, and that's why so many plantspeople's gardens contain great plants that you can't really appreciate because they don't do each other any favours. Planning is vital whatever your style.

Sketch out a rough planting plan showing not only how the plants are positioned to make an attractive picture, but also how many will be needed in each 'drift'.

It all sounds so daunting, doesn't it? But take your time, do your research and it will become a fascinating pleasure. Think of it as a puzzle for which only you can find the answer. If you start working it out in autumn, you're bound to have it sorted by planting time in spring! Who's rushing?

From a design point of view, there are three kinds of plants. The stars are the architectural specimens that need to be focal points or centrepieces. Then there are the domed, upright or bushy shapes that make up the main contents of the triangular shapes in your beds and borders. This group also includes more distinctive, upright spikes and spires. Finally, there are the everyday fillers – plants that may not be individually exciting, but which are essential for showing off the stars. They make your various triangles hang together, or fill out the shapes in contemporary gardens. These are the dumplings of the border.

Horticulturally speaking, plants are grouped into trees, shrubs, evergreens, perennials, alpines, bulbs and so forth. Knowing the type of plant usually gives you a rough idea of shapes and sizes, and whether they keep their leaves in winter, or disappear underground entirely at certain times of year.

The labels on the plants at the garden centre will give you most of the basic information about size and growing conditions, but you can do a lot of research at home using reference books.

Still in their pots, arrange your plants in triangles or groups of odd numbers so that the look of the bed is just right before you start digging.

Trees

Use trees in your framework planting, around the edge of the garden, at the back of mixed borders, or towards the centre of larger island beds. Especially striking or architectural species also make good specimen plants or focal points to grow in the lawn. Trees are there to add height, interesting shapes, and seasonal features, such as striking foliage, flowers or fruit. There's lots of choice. Unless otherwise stated, the ones I've included here are happy in most reasonable garden conditions.

The best time to plant new trees, whether they are bare-rooted or container-grown, is between autumn and late winter or very early spring, when they're still dormant. If you do it then, they're most likely to get plenty of rainfall to help them establish. They will still need watering in dry spells; I think lack of water is the biggest single reason for failure of new trees, so go to it! A mulch of about 1m (3ft) across at the root zone will help keep in the soil moisture and keep down competing weeds, but keep it clear of the immediate trunk. In theory, you can plant container-grown trees any time the soil is workable, that is not too dry, too wet or frozen – but the later in spring you plant, the more watering you'll have to do if they are to establish properly.

The Judas tree (*Cercis siliquastrum*) smothers its branches with rose-pink, pea-shaped flowers that open in spring before the leaves appear. The leaves are kidney-shaped and take on stunning autumn tints before they fall. It grows slowly to 3 × 3m (20 × 20ft).

Trees for small gardens

Yes, size does matter in a small garden. But just as important is that, in a small space, you want good value from your plants, and that means several features of interest. The trees on the following pages fit the bill.

Crab apples (1) are real three-in-one trees. They have white or pink blossom in spring, small yellow, orange, red or purplish fruit in late summer and autumn, and, in winter, the bare trees reveal their attractive shape. *Malus* × *schiedeckeri* 'Red Jade' is an architectural, weeping form, about 3.6 × 5.4m (12 × 18ft). It's very free with its pink and white flowers in late spring and the red, cherry-sized fruits can hang on the tree until March. M. × *zumi* 'Golden Hornet' is a more upright shape, around 4.5 × 3m (15 × 10ft); it's good for the back of a border and its wonderful golden fruits hang on the tree until after Christmas.

***Gleditsia triacanthos* 'Rubylace'** (2) is a cracker, if foliage is your main priority. It's a purple-leaved form of the honey locust, with frondy foliage on prickly stems and a loose, domed shape. The leaves change to bronzy green from midsummer onwards. Don't be alarmed by the ultimate height of 9 × 3m (30 × 10ft); it takes ages to get there. Use it as a specimen tree or plant it in a border.

***Cornus controversa* 'Variegata'** (3) is sometimes called the 'table dogwood' because its branches are arranged in flattened tiers. It's a beautiful small tree, to 8m (25ft) in time, but if you find the right space for it in a small garden it will not outgrow its welcome. The cow-parsley-like heads of creamy white flowers open in May, but it is the foliage that takes the breath away – the leaves are slightly twisted, and a wonderful mixture of creamy white and green. In winter they fall to reveal deep plum-purple stems. I love this tree; it always reminds me of a wedding cake!

1 *Malus* × *zumi* 'Golden Hornet'.
2 *Gleditsia triacanthos* 'Rubylace'.
3 *Cornus controversa* 'Variegata'.

Rule of thumb

Don't be put off planting trees because of bad publicity surrounding a few that have caused problems close to buildings. If you stick to decorative garden trees, you can plant them as close to the house as the height they can be expected to grow. Remember that, as a general rule, the spread of the tree is even more important than its height. The sky's the limit when it comes to height, but wide-spreading trees cast a lot of shade, and it's the big, fast-growing, thirsty woodland or forest species that cause problems close to houses, especially if they are growing on the sort of clay that shrinks badly when it dries out. Avoid at all costs willows, poplars and sycamore – the prime causes of shifting foundations. If you are worried about existing large trees, the local authority tree officer should be able to advise you.

Fruiting and berrying trees

These are good for attracting birds to the garden, but some have an edible bonus that we can enjoy ourselves.

Morus nigra (**1**), the black mulberry, grows into a craggy, domed tree, with large, heart-shaped leaves and edible fruits that look like big, dark red loganberries. They ripen in late summer and taste wonderful eaten raw, straight from the tree. You know they are ripe when they feel soft and come off at a touch, but they make a filthy mess of your clothes – the juice stains horribly. If the fruit is your main reason for growing it, look out for a named cultivar, which will start cropping within a few years; unnamed plants can keep you waiting ten years or more. Allow 4.5 × 4.5m (15 × 15ft).

Sorbus hupehensis (**2**) is a form of mountain ash which is good for the back of a border. The bunches of white, pink-tinged berries stand out well against a blue sky. In a wildlife garden go for the plain *Sorbus aucuparia*, whose red berries are among the first fruits to ripen in late summer. Also look out for *S. aucuparia* 'Aspleniifolia', which has finely divided, ferny-looking leaves and an upright-conical habit. Allow about 6 × 2.4m (20 × 8ft). All rowans have good autumn colours and are happy on acid soils. On thin chalky ones, they tend to be short-lived.

Mespilus germanica (**3**), the medlar, is a most attractive medium-sized, dome-shaped tree, roughly 5.5 × 6m (18 × 20ft), with large, white 'pear-blossom' in spring and big, long, oval leaves that turn gold in autumn. The 5cm (2in) diameter, greeny-brown fruits hang on the tree after the leaves have fallen, looking just like round, carved wooden ornaments. You can eat them, but you're supposed to let medlars 'blet', or almost rot, before they are fit to eat or make into jelly. It may have been a medieval favourite but thanks, I think I'll pass on that one and just enjoy it as a garden tree.

1 *Morus nigra.*
2 *Sorbus hupehensis.*
3 *Mespilus germanica.*

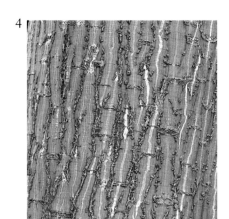

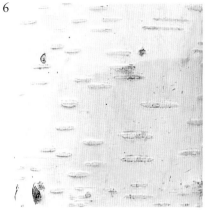

Trees with attractive bark

In winter, when the leaves have fallen, trees with exceptional bark are the ones that stand out most in the garden. Even if you don't have acres to play with, it's worth trying to find room for a small one.

Acer capillipes (4) is one of the snake-bark maples, so called because of the wavy, grey-green stripes running up and down the trunk. The leaves are three-pointed maple leaves that turn bright red in autumn and, in spring, the young shoots are bright red too, so there are plenty of seasonal attractions. It makes a dome-shaped tree that eventually gets to the larger side of medium, but it's slow growing, so anticipate 4.5 × 4.5m (15 × 15ft).

***Eucalyptus* species** (5) include many with very striking, flaking bark that leaves peculiar stripy, piebald and python-skin patterns, and the best of these is probably *Eucalyptus pauciflora* subsp. *niphophila*, the snow gum. The older, thicker trees are the ones that have the most characteristic bark patterns, so leave them unpollarded. This means you'll have quite a large tree, as it grows fast and reaches maybe 6 × 4.5m (20 × 15ft) or more, but it doesn't cast much shade. Older trees often lean over and grow into angular architectural shapes, which makes them good as 'character' specimen trees.

***Betula* species** (6) make good, small to medium-sized garden trees, but if I was only allowed one it would have to be *Betula utilis* var. *jacquemontii*, Jacquemont's birch. It has the typical open, spreading birch form and, like other birches, doesn't cast a lot of shade. What's special about it is the peeling bark that is dazzling white: I wash mine twice a year! In theory it can grow quite tall but, in gardens, it'll take a long time to grow to more than 10 × 4.5m (30 × 15ft).

4 *Acer capillipes.*
5 *Eucalyptus pauciflora* subsp. *niphophila.*
6 *Betula utilis* var. *jacquemontii.*

Tree sizes

It's hard to give the ultimate size of trees accurately because size varies according to growing conditions. The sizes given are roughly what to expect of a tree within 10–15 years. If trees outgrow their place, you can cut them down and use the space for something else, or call in a tree surgeon to reduce and thin the crown. Preventing a potentially big tree from getting bigger needs professional pruning before it becomes a problem. If it's tackled regularly, this also stops the roots spreading further – a good thing if it's close to a house. Trees are to be loved, but they do have a finite life. Try to recognize when that life is at an end. Thank the tree, cut it down and plant another. Gardening is about renewal, not mindless preservation.

Flowering trees

Everyone goes mad over lilac and cherry blossom in spring, but these are not always the best flowering trees to go for – in a windy situation, the flowers last no time at all and, if the weather is wet at flowering time the petals turn brown, so you might only see them at their best one year in three. Don't let me put you off if you like them, but don't say I didn't warn you.

Buddleja alternifolia (**1**) is a relative of the butterfly bush (*Buddleja davidii*). Left to itself it makes a big, untidy shrub; it's much better trained on a single stem to make a tree. It then grows into a rounded mushroom sort of shape, and has clusters of scented lavender flowers arranged along semi-trailing stems in early summer. It'll make about 3.6 × 2.4m (12 × 8ft), which makes it suitable for most small gardens. Best at the back of a border.

***Prunus* × *subhirtella* 'Autumnalis'** (**2**) is an altogether better bet. Okay, the flowers are smaller than most cherries, but there are lots of them and they are more weather resistant – white, and produced in batches from autumn till spring whenever the weather is mild. The tree is graceful, dome-shaped, and eventually reaches 7.5 × 6m (25 × 20ft). Its cousins, of similar size, are all well worth growing. 'Autumnalis Rosea' has pink flowers, and there is a weeping form with double flowers, 'Pendula Rosea Plena', which is a real cracker.

Genista aetnensis (**3**), Mount Etna broom, is a tree you don't often see. Think of a broom bush, but growing on a trunk and with its branches weeping down. In midsummer, the whole tree looks as if it's been powdered with gold dust as the yellow pea-flowers come out, and if you get close enough, you'll find it's pleasantly scented. Not something for a cold situation, but good in a warm, sunny, sheltered, southern garden. It reaches about 7.5 × 7.5m (25 × 25ft), casts virtually no shade, and is a brilliant specimen on a lawn.

1 *Buddleja alternifolia.*
2 *Prunus* × *subhirtella* 'Autumnalis'.
3 *Genista aetnensis.*

Evergreen shrubs

Since they keep their leaves in winter, evergreens form a year-round backbone to the garden. The majority are ideal for outlining the shape of beds and borders, but some of the large-leaved kinds are architectural plants that can stand alone as specimens.

Evergreens are generally easy to grow in any reasonable garden soil, in sun or light shade, though some kinds, such as camellias and rhododendrons need lime-free, or acid soil. They don't need regular pruning, but if they do become too big, then simply cut out a few complete branches in early spring to improve the shape – avoid snipping little bits all over the place. Don't plant too many evergreens in your garden. If you do, the scene will become unchanging and a little like a cemetery. That said, evergreens are available in lots of colours other than deep funereal green.

Some shrubs, especially evergreens such as camellias and rhododendrons, are difficult to root from cuttings, so if you want to raise new plants, layering is the most reliable means of doing it. It's also a good way to beef up a sparse specimen quickly; instead of severing the rooted layers to dig up and plant elsewhere, just leave them where they are, round the edge of the parent plant, so that it looks thicker. Layering can be done at any time in autumn or spring; August often gives the best results with rhododendrons.

Layering a shrub

Choose healthy young shoots growing round the edge of the plant that can easily be bent down to the ground. Fork plenty of organic matter in to improve the soil at the point the chosen shoots touch the ground; work in some gritty sand if the ground is heavy clay.

Use a knife to make a shallow sloping cut 2.5–5cm (1–2in) long, no more than a third of the way through the stem, and about 10–15cm (4–6in) from the tip. Dust the cut surfaces with hormone rooting powder and twist the stem slightly so the wound stays open, or else lodge a match-stick in it. Bend the shoot down to the ground, lay the wounded part flat into a shallow, 2.5cm (1in) deep trench in the improved soil. Hold it down with wire hoops, pressing one over the stem either side of the wound.

Bury the stem, but leave at least 5cm (2in) of the tip of the shoot above ground. Water the layer, and repeat in dry spells. Layers should be rooted a year later, but leave them where they are until the young plant has started to grow new shoots before cutting its 'umbilical cord'. Then wait another few months before moving it. The best times to dig up and move rooted layers of evergreens are April or September. If you have layered deciduous shrubs, move them in March or October.

Architectural evergreens

Any of these can be grown in a border, but they are also good specimens if you want year-round character in a special spot.

Phormium tenax (**1**), New Zealand flax, is valuable for its modernistic, spiky shape, strappy leaves, and in some cultivars, loud colour schemes – purple, pink or peachy stripes. Don't just think of them for contemporary gardens; they look good in mixed borders and in tubs too. They need a sunny spot with reasonable drainage. Phormiums grow slowly to make clumps about 2m (6ft) high and 1.2–2m (4–6ft) wide. Although grown for foliage, mature plants produce spikes of waxy, cream bells in a hot summer. If hammered by frost in bad winters, they usually regrow from the base.

Fatsia japonica (**2**) is one of the best-known architectural evergreens, especially with flower arrangers. It's a bushy shrub that grows into a 1.5–2m (5–6ft) mound, with shiny, fig-shaped leaves that, on a big specimen can be almost 30cm (1ft) across. Although foliage is the main reason for growing it, fatsia flowers in November, with clusters of cream flowers followed by black berries, very like those of ivy. Late insects love it and so do the birds that live on them.

Viburnum rhytidophyllum (**3**) has dark green, wrinkly, long, oval leaves with beige, felty backs and, in winter, the whole plant is dotted with clusters of matching beige-felted buds that open in spring to tiny white flowers. Given time, it grows into a huge, mound-shaped plant 4.5 × 4.5m (15 × 15ft), but you can keep it smaller by pruning.

1 *Phormium* 'Sundowner'.
2 *Fatsia japonica.*
3 *Viburnum rhytidophyllum.*

Large, flowering evergreens

Flowering evergreens are dual-purpose shrubs, with good flowers of their own, but the larger kinds also make a good background for other plants when they are planted at the back of a border.

Mahonias (4) are essential evergreens, not just for architectural foliage, but for the winter or early spring flowers that, in some, are scented of lily-of-the-valley. If I could have only one, it would be *Mahonia × media* 'Lionel Fortescue'. It flowers in mild spells from autumn right through to spring, it's well scented, and makes a rather upright, spiky shape, about 2.1 × 1m (7 × 3ft) in five years. It can get much bigger, but when it develops middle-aged spread, you can prune to keep it a suitable size, just after flowering. Cut it back quite hard, to around knee height, and it will regrow happily.

Arbutus unedo (5), the strawberry tree, is an architectural gem. It has warm, red-brown, self-shredding bark, and clusters of white, urn-shaped flowers in autumn. It fruits at the same time – the fruits are from last year's flowers. The round, red 'strawberries' actually look more like lychees and, yes, you can eat them, but they're totally tasteless, so I wouldn't bother. *A. unedo* makes a big, bushy shrub or small tree, depending whether it's grown on one or several stems. It reaches 2.4 × 1.5m (8 × 5ft) in ten years, more eventually.

Ceanothus (6) are among the most spectacular flowering evergreens and are well known for their fluffy blue flowers of spring or summer. But *Ceanothus* 'Autumnal Blue' flowers constantly from midsummer to autumn. The flowers are the colour of a deep blue summer sky. It's a rather upright shrub, growing about 3 × 2m (10 × 6ft), and needs a warm, sunny spot with good drainage. In a border, don't put anything too tall in front of it to cut out the light. Alternatively, plant it on a sunny, south-facing wall and clip it lightly each spring to keep it flat.

4 *Mahonia lomariifolia.*
5 *Arbutus unedo* f. *rubra.*
6 *Ceanothus* 'Autumnal Blue'.

Small, flowering evergreens

The small, flowering evergreens are useful for the front of a border. Alternate them with perennials or deciduous shrubs and the area doesn't suddenly turn totally bare when winter comes round. Pop a few clumps of short-growing spring bulbs in between them in autumn, and you have the basis of a good all-year-round feature.

Sarcococca hookeriana* var. *digyna (**1**), Christmas box, is less upfront, but more unusual. The name is a bit misleading because it doesn't usually flower till late winter or early spring, and then what you notice first is the scent. The flowers are spindly and fragile-looking, white with a hint of mauve, and lined up along the stems. The plant looks like a series of 1m (3ft) suckers that spread out slowly. Okay, not the most spectacular plant, but it does its stuff at a sparse time of year and it's a lot better than it sounds.

Cistus (**2**), the sun rose, flowers all summer and has large, single flowers, like crumpled poppies in white or shades of pink. All cistus need lots of sun and well-drained soil. *Cistus × hybridus*, with white flowers, and the aptly named 'Silver Pink' grow into neat mounds, 1 × 1m (3 × 3ft), and are the best for rock or gravel gardens, banks and the front of sunny borders. Other species grow into 2m (6ft) mounds; they tend to be untidy, so I'd stick to the shorter, more squat jobs myself.

Hebes (**3**) have fluffy spikes of bottlebrush flowers and a very long season, from June or July to October. They need similar conditions to the sun rose, and the two look good together. There's a wide range in garden centres these days, but old favourites, such as *Hebe* 'Autumn Glory' (violet-purple) will make dome-shaped bushes about 1.2m (4ft) tall and across, and *H. pinguifolia* 'Sutherlandii' makes upright grey-leafed domes topped with white flowers in summer.

1 *Sarcococca hookeriana* var. *digyna*.
2 *Cistus × hybridus*.
3 *Hebe pinguifolia* 'Sutherlandii'.

1

2

3

Lime-hating evergreens

If you garden on acid soil, then you can go in for all the lime-hating shrubs that, elsewhere, the rest of us can only grow in tubs of ericaceous compost. Rhododendrons, camellias and pieris are the 'big three'. They all like dappled shade or weak sun and a sheltered site with plenty of organic matter in the ground so it doesn't dry out badly in summer. I always like to see them growing with 'bark trees' such as birches, *Acer griseum* and *Arbutus unedo*, and character shrubs, such as Japanese maples, all of which are happy in rhododendron-growing conditions as well as in normal gardens.

Rhododendrons (4) flower mostly in May, with a little overlap either side. They range in size from the tiny miniature ones that aren't much bigger than the indoor azaleas that you grow in pots at Christmas, to real whoppers that are big trees in the wild. For most gardens, the bushy hybrids that reach about 2 × 2.4m (6 × 8ft) in ten years are the ones to go for. They come in most colours. Some of the best rhodies for small gardens or tubs are *Rhododendron yakushimanum* hybrids, such as 'Sneezy' (pink) and 'Grumpy' (creamy pink); they make tight, dome shapes 1.2 × 1.2m (4 × 4ft).

Camellias (5) flower from mid-March to early May, with pink or white flowers, some of which look almost like waterlilies. They'll put up with near-neutral soil, though it's a good idea to give them a shot of feed containing sequestered iron each spring, so the leaves don't go yellow. There are dozens of popular cultivars; the semi-double, pink *Camellia × williamsii* 'Donation' is still one of the best. The flowers tend to fall as they fade, rather than staying on the bush and turning brown, as is the case with varieties of *C. japonica*. Camellias need shelter to protect the fragile flowers, and east-facing sites should be avoided. Give those with white flowers extra shelter; the petals turn brown at the least excuse if exposed to bad weather.

Pieris (6) is the plant people often think of as an outdoor poinsettia. The dome-shaped plants have strings of white bells at the tips of some shoots in spring, and the rest have bright red or pink new foliage; the two don't always coincide. For the rest of the year, they look a tad ordinary unless you grow a variegated one, such as *P.* 'Flaming Silver', which has white-edged leaves. Most are slow growing and, at ten years of age, have usually reached about 2 × 1.2m (6 × 4ft) or thereabouts. Given enough time, in acidic woodland, where conditions suit them perfectly, they can get quite big. If you need to prune them, do so after the flowers are over and the spring leaf colours have faded back to green. They need shelter from drying winds and frost which can turn new growth brown.

4 *Rhododendron yakushimanum* 'Ken Janeck'.
5 *Camellia × williamsii* 'Donation'.
6 *Pieris japonica* 'Pink Delight'.

Deciduous shrubs

Flowering deciduous shrubs add seasonal highlights to a border; most kinds are only at their best for about six weeks of the year, so you need to achieve a balance between these and the plants that provide all-year-round interest, particularly as these plants lose their leaves in winter. Many of them are faster growing than evergreens and some need regular pruning to keep them tidy.

Unless specific growing conditions are stated, you can safely assume that woody plants are happy in any reasonable garden soil that has been properly prepared, enriched with a reasonable amount of organic matter and isn't waterlogged in winter.

Spring in the shade garden at Barleywood, where deciduous shrubs such as viburnum and amelanchier come into their own before the leaf canopy of the oak is at its summer density.

Shrubs for spring flowers

Spring is the peak season for the most popular shrubs: berberis, viburnums, forsythia, kerria and *Daphne mezereum*, but if you want three real troupers, these are the ones I wouldn't be without.

Ribes sanguineum (**1**), the flowering currant, is an old-fashioned, cottage-garden shrub with a bushy, upright shape, at around 1.5 × 1.5m (5 × 5ft), and with deep pink, bunch-of-grapes flowers in April. The buffalo currant (*Ribes odoratum*) is bigger, 2 × 1.5m (6 × 5ft), with scented yellow flowers and leaves that take on purple autumn tints. Both are un-fussy jobs for sun or light shade.

Magnolia stellata (**2**), the star magnolia, is the one with the white, waterlily-like flowers that open just ahead of the leaves. It makes a rounded bush about 1.5 × 1.5m (5 × 5ft). Grow it in a bed or border, or as a stand-alone shrub in the lawn. Very similar, but bigger all round and with pale pink flowers is *Magnolia × loebneri* 'Leonard Messel'. Like most magnolias, these hate being moved once they are established. They need a sheltered site in sun or light shade, but unlike the bigger tree magnolias, they aren't fussy about the soil as long as it's reasonably well drained. Don't disturb the thick, fleshy roots at planting time; you'll slow down establishment.

Spiraeas (**3**) that are spring-flowering have a foam of tiny white flowers splashed all over the plants. They're good for separating colours that clash in a border and look great with evergreen foliage and carpets of spring bulbs. *Spiraea* 'Arguta', bridal wreath, is an old favourite – a slightly untidy, bushy dome, 2 × 2m (6 × 6ft), flowering in April. It's indispensable for flower arrangers. In smaller gardens, go for *S. nipponica* 'Snowmound' – a compact 1-m (3-ft) dome with arching sprays of close-packed white flowers in June.

1 *Ribes sanguineum* 'Porky Pink'.
2 *Magnolia stellata*.
3 *Spiraea* 'Arguta'.

Shrubs for summer flowers

Most gardeners turn to border perennials for summer colour, forgetting that there are plenty of good flowering shrubs that will add brightness further back in the border.

Hydrangeas (**1**) are old stalwarts, good anywhere where the soil is reasonably moist, in sun or in light shade under trees. The dome-shaped bushes average out around 1.2–1.5m (4–5ft) tall by as much across, though they'll grow bigger in the right spot. The hefty, rounded heads of pink, white or blue flowers are at their best in late summer, then dry out on the plant and fade attractively. The flowers come in two types – mopheads, whose domed heads are filled with flowers, and lacecaps, which have a fringe of flowers round an open centre. Don't deadhead hydrangeas when the flowers are over; leave it till spring as the umbrella of dead flowers protects the young shoots. But if you are going to prune hydrangeas, do it properly – so many people don't and wonder why they never have any flowers. It's one of the most regular problems that crops up in my postbag.

Kolkwitzia amabilis (**2**), the beauty bush, looks its best in June and early July when it is covered in yellow-spotted, pink, foxglove-like flowers. You'll need plenty of room for it as it grows into a loose, twiggy, dome shape about 2.4 × 2.4m (8 × 8ft). When buying, ask for the cultivar 'Pink Cloud' and, if possible, buy it in flower. A lot of people are disappointed when they end up with a poor-flowering form. This is an excellent shrub through which to grow a late-flowering clematis; it's big enough to take one, and it does need a little colour later in the year.

Pruning hydrangeas

You don't have to prune hydrangeas at all, but it's a good way of giving them a spring tidy and deadhead in one. Young plants rarely need anything more than light deadheading, taking off no more than the remains of the old flower.

Large, elderly hydrangeas often need thinning out. Start by cutting out one or two of the oldest stems completely, as low down in the plant as you can. Then take out any long or ungainly looking stems that stick out and spoil the symmetrical shape.

Finally, go over the whole plant deadheading it, only instead of just removing the dead head, follow the stem down to the next non-flowered side shoot and cut just above it. If the dead heads have disappeared during the winter, you can usually see where they have been by the bare bit of shoot at the top of the stem. Shoots with leaves right to the tip have not flowered and, if you cut those back, you will be removing the coming year's flower-buds.

1 *Hydrangea* 'Nigra'.
2 *Kolkwitzia amabilis.*
3 *Lavatera.*
4 *Hibiscus syriacus* 'Diana'.

Lavatera (3) is brilliant for the back of a sunny, well-drained border. It looks like a hollyhock with 2m (6ft) stems, greyish leaves, and large, rose pink flowers. 'Barnsley' has paler pink flowers with a red 'eye'. The plants will flower from midsummer to autumn, but they aren't long lived and quickly look tatty. The secret is to cut the whole plant back hard in spring to get rid of the old stems and encourage some new, young, free-flowering ones. Replace older, worn out plants from cuttings every two or three years.

Hibiscus syriacus (4), a hardy hibiscus, is a spectacular shrub. All it needs is a sunny, sheltered spot with well-drained soil. It grows slowly to make an upright shape, 1.5 × 1m (5 × 3ft), and throughout late summer and early autumn, it is covered in flowers like those of the familiar subtropical hibiscus, but not quite so big, maybe 5cm (2in) across. 'Oiseau Bleu' (pale blue) and 'Woodbridge' (mauve-pink) are the most popular. 'Diana' is the best white-flowered single. I'd give the double-flowered cultivars a miss, unless you grow them in pots in the conservatory – they sound attractive, but the flowers get bashed to bits outside.

Blue hydrangeas

To get the truest colours, blue hydrangeas need acid soil, pH 4–5; and pink or red ones need a soil pH of 6–7; get it wrong and most change to a washed-out mauve. White ones stay whitest at pH 6.5–7.5. Check with a soil-testing kit to see which colours will grow best for you. If you don't have the right soil for blue cultivars, you can feed the plants with blueing compound (Aluminium sulphate) to acidify the soil, though you need to keep treating them regularly. You can improve red or pink flower colours by watering them several times a year with a handful of garden lime dissolved in a watering can full of water. Otherwise grow blue hydrangeas in pots of ericaceous compost and they will show their true colours.

5 *Potentilla* 'Limelight'.
6 *Buddleja davidii* 'Black Knight'.

Potentillas (5) are brilliant fillers for the front of a border, or grow them on a bank, in a rock garden, or in tubs. They are tidy, dome-shaped plants with ferny foliage studded with masses of small flowers in orange, red, yellow or pink. They have an incredibly long flowering season, from mid-May to mid-October, and although they like sun, they'll 'do' for light shade between bigger shrubs – red-flowered cultivars are actually best grown in light shade as it stops the flower colour fading.

Buddleja davidii (6), the butterfly bush, is easily identified, as from midsummer to autumn, its cone-shaped, purple, mauve or bluish flowers are covered with butterflies. There is a variegated cultivar, 'Harlequin', which you either love or hate, but the old favourite is the deep purple-flowered 'Black Knight'. Buddleias usually grow about 3–3.6 × 2.4m (10–12 × 8ft). If that's too big for you, look for 'Nanho Petite Indigo'; it only reaches 2 × 1.2m (6 × 4ft).

Pruning buddleias

The butterfly bush (*Buddleja davidii*) grows at an alarming rate, and if you don't prune it each year it becomes tall and leggy and looks very scruffy. Prune it in two stages each year.

In autumn, after the last flowers are over, cut off the top third of the shrub. Don't worry about pruning above a bud, because all you are doing is 'shortening the sail' so the thing won't get too badly bashed about in the wind – buddleias are quite brittle.

The real pruning is done in spring, around mid-March. Simply cut back last year's cane-like stems to within 2.5cm (1in) of their base, just above where they grow from the trunk. To tame an overgrown buddleia, cut the whole shrub back to a stump about 60cm (2ft) above ground in March New shoots will grow even out of quite thick, old trunks, so you won't kill it.

Shrubs for autumn colour

By the time summer is over, borders are often left with an end-of-term feeling, so it's worth looking out for a few slightly unusual shrubs to add a splash of late colour to your garden palette.

***Callicarpa bodinieri* var. *giraldii* 'Profusion'** (1), beauty berry, has great autumn colour. The leaves turn pink, red and purple before they fall, leaving the shrub thickly clad in clusters of small violet berries that you probably missed earlier. It will grow to about 2 × 2m (6 × 6ft), which may make it a bit big for a lot of gardens where an 'autumn special' is a bit of a luxury, but do grow it if you can, it's a cracker.

Hydrangea quercifolia (2) is the oak-leaved hydrangea, which has large white cones of lacecap flowers in late summer, and oakleaf-shaped leaves that turn bronze-red in autumn. It grows about 1.5 × 1.5m (5 × 5ft). Prune it the same as for other hydrangeas (see page 162). If you like the oak-leaved hydrangea, you'll probably like cultivars of other hydrangea species, such as *H. paniculata* 'Grandiflora' and *H. arborescens* 'Annabelle'. Both flower in late summer with massive white flower-heads that keep going well into autumn, when the leaves turn golden yellow.

Clerodendrum trichotomum* var. *fargesii (3) is an unusual large shrub or small tree, about 2.4 × 2.4m (8 × 8ft), which saves its whole show for the back end of the year. It flowers in late August, with sprays of maroon buds that open to a starburst of small, white flowers. Soon after, the maroon calyces part to reveal the bright turquoise berries that they enclose. The foliage has a slightly acrid scent when bruised, so it's best put where you won't touch it – it needs lots of sun, shelter and well-drained soil. You might have to seek it out, but it really is worth the effort.

1 *Callicarpa bodinieri* var. *giraldii* 'Profusion'.
2 *Hydrangea arborescens* 'Annabelle'.
3 *Clerodendrum trichotomum* var. *fargesii*.

Shrubs for winter interest

Once winter comes round, there are very few shrubs worth getting excited about, so don't miss out on the few that are.

***Cornus alba* 'Sibirica'** (**1**), the red-stemmed dogwood, is a plant you can't take your eyes off in winter. The bare stems are that shade they used to call sealing-wax red. Those of *Cornus sanguinea* 'Midwinter Fire' are a stunning mix of cochineal red and orange. These dogwoods are brilliant for a boggy or even wet spot, but are equally happy in normal garden conditions, in sun or light shade, and grow about 1.5 × 1.2m (5 × 4ft). Cut out all the oldest stems annually in March to trigger lots of young shoots, which have the brightest-coloured bark. Manure them well to keep up their strength.

Hamamelis* × *intermedia (**2**), the witch hazels, come top of my winter must-have list. They are rather upright then spreading, open bushes that grow 2.4 × 2m (8 × 6ft), and flower in mild spells from leaf-fall in autumn until April. There are hybrids with red, orange or yellow flowers, but the one I'd recommend is *H.* × *intermedia* 'Pallida', which has the biggest, pale yellow, spidery flowers of any of them, coupled with golden autumn foliage tints. The flowers are strongly perfumed on a warm spring day, but if the weather is cold, huff on them and you'll fool them into releasing their scent. If you fancy a witch hazel but don't have room down the garden, try growing one in a pot – I've had one for several years and it's still doing beautifully. The yellow-flowered ones have golden autumn colour, and the orange and red ones have ruddy leaf tints. Nifty.

1 *Cornus alba* 'Sibirica'.
2 *Hamamelis* × *intermedia* 'Pallida'.
3 *Corylus avellana* 'Contorta'.
4 *Daphne cneorum*.
5 *Philadelphus*.
6 *Viburnum farreri*.

***Corylus avellana* 'Contorta'** (**3**) is a real winter stunner. It has wildly twisted stems that you only see properly when the leaves have fallen. In early spring, there are long yellow catkins dangling from them. Slow growing, it gets to about 2.4 × 2.4m (8 × 8ft).

Scented shrubs

Shrubs with scented flowers add oomph to whatever else is looking good at the time. Plant them in a sheltered spot so that the fragrance doesn't blow away; the warmer and more still the air is, the more powerfully the scent will build up.

Daphne cneorum (4) is a low-growing evergreen shrub with oval leaves which smothers itself in rose-pink flowers in late spring. The delightful fragrance will stop you in your tracks. Plant it on a bank or a traditional rock garden where it can tumble down the slope. It is happy in any well-drained soil, even those that are chalky. The variety 'Eximia' is particularly fine. Size 15cm (6in) by 1m (3ft).

Philadelphus (5), the mock orange, has very fragrant white flowers in June and July. They come as small as the 75cm × 1.5m (30in × 5ft) 'Manteau d'Hermine', with strongly scented double flowers, but *P.* 'Belle Etoile', at 1.2 × 1.5m (4 × 5ft), and *P. coronarius*, which comes in at 2.4 × 2m (8 × 6ft) are arguably the strongest scented. If you want a philadelphus that looks good when the flowers are over, the ones you want are *P. coronarius* 'Variegatus', with cream and green leaves, or the acid-yellow-leaved *P. coronarius* 'Aureus'. Don't give this one too sun-baked a spot or it will scorch.

Viburnums (6) with good scent come in two waves. The early batch includes *Viburnum farreri* (white to palest pink) and *V. × bodnantense* 'Dawn' (bright pink), which bloom from autumn, through mild spells in winter, to early spring. *V. carlesii* 'Aurora' (pale pink), *V. × juddii* (very pale pink), and *V. × carlcephalum* (white) all flower from mid- to late spring. Most grow to about 2 × 2m (6 × 6ft) and have attractive autumn leaf tints – they're good all-rounders. I have far too many of them, they are so irresistible.

Winter scent

For winter fragrance, my top two are wintersweet and the winter-flowering shrubby honeysuckles. Wintersweet (Chimonanthus praecox), *is a big open shrub, 3 × 3m (10 × 10ft) with translucent, yellow, bell-shaped flowers hanging all over the skeleton of bare stems in winter; they show up best against a background of evergreens. The winter shrubby honeysuckles are bushy shrubs, not climbers.* Lonicera × purpusii *has cream flowers on bare stems, and* L. fragrantissima *has white flowers and keeps its leaves in a mild spot – both grow about 2 × 2m (6 × 6ft) and are very strongly scented. Not to be missed.*

4

5

6

Filling in the fine detail

Trees, evergreens and flowering shrubs provide the background to the garden and some seasonal highlights, but what makes the ever-changing tapestry of colours are the flowers – roses, herbaceous perennials, bulbs, annuals, alpines and exotics.

Making plant associations

The smaller flowers are the next plants to add as your planting develops, but it's no good just picking your favourites and hoping they'll look good together, because they probably won't. You need to create plant associations – attractive groups – so that each plant shows its own best points, but also brings out the best in its neighbours. The one thing I'd always do if you are buying plants for a particular bed is to stand them in a group at the garden centre to see how they look together. At home, stand them in position on the actual spot and rearrange them as necessary until you hit the winning combination. Making good plant combinations is an art that grows on you with practice, but a few tips come in very handy for starters. It takes me ages to get it right, sometimes – but I still get a lot of pleasure out of doing it.

Contrast, contrast, contrast

Designers don't see things the same way as gardeners. Where we see a good plant, what they see is texture, height, shape, size and colour. When you make plant associations, try to think more like a designer, and leave your horticultural appreciation for later.

Tall, spire-forming perennials like delphiniums change the scale and form of the border as they grow – contrasting well with lower, fluffy plants.

The aim is to put plants together that contrast well. Go for contrasts of shape and texture first. A tall, upright, bony-looking plant, such as bamboo, looks good with a large, prickly, horizontal leaf, such as those of gunnera. Strappy-leaved phormium looks

great with a low, creeping carpet at its feet. Contrast shiny evergreens with rough-textured trunks or prickly stems. Big, round flower shapes, like those of the ornamental alliums, stand out well against a background of small, frothy, filler-flowers and upright spikes.

Think triangles

Keep thinking about making triangles. Choose one star plant, and a couple of less exciting but useful extras – even the most hard-bitten plantsperson won't believe how good it makes your best plants look. Try one spire-shaped plant with one bushy and one low, spreading type if you want a 'recipe'.

When you are grouping plants, odd numbers always look better than even ones – go for groups of three or five. The effect is bolder and less spotty than a mass of singletons. Arrange your threes and fives in triangle shapes and, if you find it too daunting to plan a whole bed, you can compromise. Make lots of three-and-five plant triangles, and link them with a carpet of something neutral, such as *Alchemilla mollis,* that runs through the entire bed.

Colours and colour schemes

It isn't luck that makes certain colours work well together. Make your mind up whether you want a hot scheme based on red, orange and yellow, or a pastel scheme that majors in pink, mauve, blue and purple – it's a heck of a lot easier not to mix the two together.

If you want a border of opposite colours then purple and yellow, red and green, or blue and orange contrast well. Don't overdo it: you'll soon get fed up with the visual argument. Try graduating colours in a border rather like a rainbow – from reds and oranges, through yellows and greens, to blues and violets.

If you want a border of many colours, try planning plant triangles each based on one set of complementary colours and then plant plenty of neutral-coloured foliage between them to give a sense of unity.

Contrasting strappy fountains of phormium (New Zealand flax) are offset well against the fluffy flowers and foliage of blue brachyscome and felicia and yellow bidens.

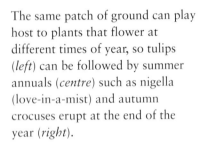

The same patch of ground can play host to plants that flower at different times of year, so tulips (*left*) can be followed by summer annuals (*centre*) such as nigella (love-in-a-mist) and autumn crocuses erupt at the end of the year (*right*).

Pinch ideas

Some of the best ideas you'll ever find are other people's, which is why keen gardeners spend so long taking photos and making notes when they visit flower shows and gardens. As soon as you need a bright idea for plants that go brilliantly together, there you are – a folder full of them.

Less is more

A traditional plant arrangement relies heavily on sheer numbers for impact, but if you are making a contemporary look then you want only a tenth of the number of plants, so each one needs to have ten times the charisma.

Three-dimensional chess

Yes, I know what you're thinking. It's all very well, but you'll end up with plants that all look their best at the same time. Well, you have to build in the seasonal factor. It's easy to add spring and summer bulbs, or annuals into the gaps between shrubs. If you can't wing it, make several tracing paper overlays of the same bed and mark in what's up and what's underground, what's in flower and what's evergreen. That way you'll cover the whole year and can see where the gaps are and think of ways to fill them.

Last word

If you get it wrong, *don't worry*! Beds and borders are not cast in concrete – plants can always be moved – and I have yet to visit a garden where every bed and border works. They are always being developed and changed. The important thing to do is to enjoy the journey – not turn it into a voyage to hell!

Roses

Unless you have a formal garden, you probably won't want traditional rose beds, but roses still have a place even in today's 'outdoor living rooms'. Bush roses cohabit well in mixed borders with shrubs and perennials, ground-cover roses are good for covering banks, and patio roses pack as much flower-power into containers as bedding plants, but are much less bother.

Consider scent as well as colour (which varies in its power) and also disease resistance, which will save you spraying regularly.

Here I've just chosen a few of my favourite roses – and even that's a hard call. My favourites won't necessarily be yours, so get yourself out there with a notebook and investigate some more – there are literally hundreds to choose from!

Learning the lingo – rose terminology

Hybrid teas (HTs)	Floribundas	Shrub roses	Ground-cover roses	Patio roses
HTs have 1–3 large flowers at the end of each stem, and they are repeat-flowering (remontant) roses. Nowadays we're supposed to call them large-flowered bush roses, which is how you'll often see them described in catalogues. The Botanical Police will probably turn a blind eye if you call them hybrid teas in the privacy of your own rose bed.	These are also repeat-flowering roses, with a large cluster of many flowers at the tips of their stems; they are now correctly called cluster-flowered bush roses.	This is a loose umbrella term for a group that includes old-fashioned roses, cultivated cousins of the rose species, and sometimes the more garden-worthy wild species themselves. Unlike modern bush roses, some shrub roses don't flower continuously all summer. For the ones that don't repeat, the main flush is in June–July.	These are a modern invention; some cultivars trail out over the ground and others are bushy and dense, and grow wider than they are tall. Many of them flower all summer.	These are small bush roses (dwarf cluster-flowered bush is the modern way of putting it) that look and behave just like floribundas but on a smaller scale, usually 30–45cm (12–18in) high. They aren't the same as miniature roses, which are smaller still and, frankly, aren't a patch on the patio roses.

Bush roses

For me, a rose without scent is only half a rose. It's good to see old-fashioned fragrance being bred back into many of the new cultivars that come out each year. Some of them are very good indeed, but a lot of the older cultivars are still tried-and-tested winners. Go for the more disease-resistant kinds if you don't want to do a lot of spraying.

Whisky Mac (**1**) appeals to some people because of the name, but it's really quite descriptive because the flower is a warm, bright, amber shade of single malt that's seldom found in roses. It's a hybrid tea, which on paper doesn't sound too clever as the disease resistance isn't all that special, but if you can live with that, it's well worth growing for the scent – which is rosy rather than whisky. It grows to a bushy 75cm (30in).

Margaret Merril (**2**) would be my bush rose of choice if I could have only one. A pure white floribunda with a perfume that knocks your socks off, she's vigorous, stands a shade over 90cm (3ft) high and has reasonable disease resistance.

1 *Rosa* Whisky Mac.
2 *R.* Margaret Merril.
3 *R.* 'Deep Secret'.
4 *R.* Fragrant Cloud.
5 *R.* 'Just Joey'.
6 *R.* 'Fragrant Delight'.

'**Deep Secret**' (3) is a hybrid tea for closet romantics who want a dark, black-red rose with a really rich scent. Unlike most roses of this much-sought-after colour, this one is quite a good do-er, strong and disease resistant, and about 90cm (3ft) tall.

Fragrant Cloud (4) is an old favourite hybrid tea, rather a loud coral red, and one of the strongest scents going. It's what they always used to call a bedding rose, which means it grows neat and compact – suitable for growing in blocks in formal rose beds. It grows to about 75cm (30in) tall, and, like most bush roses, is good for cutting. Not in the first rank for disease resistance, but not so weak that it becomes a martyr. If you want the classic, highly scented, fat-flowered hybrid tea, this is it!

'**Just Joey**' (5) is another distinctive hybrid tea, with scented, coppery-orange flowers that are slightly wavy round the edges. It looks good grown with coppery pink shades as well as more amber or yellow colours. It's a good bedding rose at 75cm (30in) tall and has stood the test of time.

'**Fragrant Delight**' (6) is a highly scented floribunda with large, coppery-pink flowers flushed yellow towards the centre. It has good disease resistance and makes a slightly more upright shape than some. It grows to about 75cm (30in).

Roses need not be confined to rose gardens; nowadays they are often used in mixed border settings. Here *Rosa* 'Geoff Hamilton', a shrub rose, is planted with a variety of colourful shrubs and climbers.

1 *Rosa* 'Geranium'.

Shrub roses

Shrub roses are ace for growing in mixed borders, and some make good rose hedges. I've included a couple of species roses here, too.

***Rosa moyesii* 'Geranium'** (**1**) is a selection of the species, with small, single, sealing-wax red 'wild rose' flowers. It is also grown for its large, scarlet, bottle-shaped hips. Excellent for the back of a big border or wild garden as it grows to 2.4 × 2m (8 × 6ft) and is very disease resistant. Honey bees love it.

Gertrude Jekyll (**2**) is an English rose bred to combine the long flowering season of modern bush roses with the scent and quaint flower shape of old-fashioned roses. It's rich pink, slightly ruffled and well scented, growing roughly 1.5 × 1m (5 × 3ft). Like most of the modern English roses raised by David Austin, *Rosa* Gertrude Jekyll is especially good if planted 60cm (2ft) apart in groups of three so that the branches intertwine, making a dense thicket of flowers.

Graham Thomas (**3**) is another real winner among the English roses, The flowers are the colour of a free-range egg yolk, with a tea rose scent, and a shape that is close to a peony. Irresistible. About 1.2m (4ft) tall, and disease resistant.

'Nevada' (**4**) is a real classic and, in June, has enormous single, cream-coloured flowers with golden stamens clustered in the centre. It's elegant, but does need a lot of room – it grows to 2 × 2m (6 × 6ft). It can succumb to black spot – but I love it!

'Roseraie de l'Hay' (**5**) has bright green, crêpe-paper leaves that never fall victim to mildew or black spot, and the fragrant, double magenta flowers appear right through the summer. It's a waist-high bush if you prune it back in spring, otherwise it will get to 2m (6ft) or more.

2 *R.* Getrude Jekyll.
3 *R.* Graham Thomas.
4 *R.* 'Nevada'.
5 *R.* 'de l'Hay'.

1

2

3

4

Patio and ground-cover roses

These are the roses to plant in 30–38cm (12–15in) pots of John Innes No. 3 compost on your patio, though they'll be just as happy at the front of a mixed border. There are lots of different cultivars and new ones come out every year; this is a very small selection of my favourites. They are hot on colour, less impressive on the nose.

Pruning patio and ground-cover roses

• Ground-cover roses don't need any pruning at all; just take out any dead or broken stems whenever you see them. You can also prune out any badly mildewed shoot tips as an alternative to spraying.

• Prune patio roses the same way as full-sized bush roses, but on a smaller scale. Don't cut them back lower than 15cm (6in) from the ground.

Magic Carpet (5) is a prostrate ground-cover rose that's also good for hanging baskets; the flowers are semi-double and lavender-pink with a faint scent. In the open ground, it'll cover a circle with a 1.2m (4ft) radius and about 30cm (1ft) deep.

Gingernut (6) is good for pots – a neat, bushy patio rose with lots of gingery-orange flowers produced all summer. It grows to about 45 × 38cm (18 × 15in), is very disease resistant but has little scent.

Sweet Dream (7) is very similar but with pale peach flowers; again good for disease resistance, but not much scent.

'Bright Smile' (8) is a small bush rose that grows to a width and height of about 45cm (18 in). Throughout the summer and autumn it bears clusters of lightly scented double yellow flowers.

5 *R.* Magic Carpet.
6 *R.* Gingernut.
7 *R.* Sweet Dream.
8 *R.* 'Bright Smile'.

5

6

7

8

Perennials

Whether grown for foliage or flowers, perennials are the flesh on the bones of any garden.

Unless you go the whole hog and plan a herbaceous border consisting of nothing but perennial flowers, the usual way of growing them is in gaps between shrubs in a mixed border to provide seasonal highlights. Perennials are, of course, plants that die down to an overwintering rootstock each autumn and grow up again the following spring.

Perennials perform best if you keep them happy by dividing them. Do this in spring if you garden on wet or heavy clay soil, and for all delicate perennials, or those with thick or fleshy roots. Autumn is okay for the more indestructible plants with fibrous roots as long as you have light, free-draining soil – otherwise the damaged roots can't heal and the plants rot.

But don't divide the plants until you need to; wait until they are obviously dying out in the centre, or they have spread too far. The most vigorous perennials may need dividing every 2–3 years; slow spreaders may not need doing more than every 6–7 years, if then.

Most of the perennials I've described are happy in any ordinary garden soil with reasonable drainage and some organic matter. They like non-scorching sun, or the kind of light shade cast by surrounding plants in an uncrowded border. If they like something different, I've said so. Otherwise, take it as read that they like standard conditions. Here's the cast in order of appearance.

Perennials for spring

Spring-flowering perennials are among the most welcome of all – partly because they show that the garden is coming to life again, and partly because they can be easily seen at a time when a lot of plants are not yet ready to emerge from dormancy. Many of them are good for shady borders – because they flower before the leaf canopy on the trees is fully developed.

Dicentra spectabilis (**1**) is called bleeding heart because of the locket-shaped, red-and-white flowers that hang down in rows from its arching, ferny-looking stems. It flowers in May and June, forming clumps about 45 × 45cm (18 × 18in). It dies down quite early, so you'll need plants nearby to fill the gap later in the summer.

Omphalodes cappadocica (**2**) flowers in May and looks just like a posy of long-stemmed forget-me-nots growing from the centre of a bouquet of nearly heart-shaped leaves. It grows to about 30 × 30cm (1 × 1ft). 'Starry Eyes' has flowers edged with paler blue.

Helleborus x hybridus (3) is the Lenten rose – quite a connoisseur's plant these days. To get your favourite colours, buy them in pots when they're in flower – late February to April. The spotted ones and the greeny or deep mauve-purple cultivars are especially sought after. They'll make evergreen clumps, 45 × 60cm (18 × 24in). Once established, hellebores hate being moved, but do self-seed – move the offspring while they are small.

Polygonatum multiflorum (4), Solomon's seal, sends fat buds poking up through the ground in April. These quickly grow into 60cm (2ft) tall arching stems with small bunches of white bell flowers dangling down between the pairs of leaves in May. Plants spread slowly for 60cm–90cm (2–3ft), but it's easy enough to dig up any that come up where you don't want them.

Pulmonaria 'Lewis Palmer' (5) is a clump-forming lungwort with oval leaves that are spotted with greenish white. Its flowers open pink and then turn blue, which is why, when we were kids, we knew it as 'soldiers and sailors'. 30 × 45cm (12 × 18in).

1 *Dicentra spectabilis.*
2 *Omphalodes cappadocica* 'Starry Eyes'.
3 *Helleborus × hybridus.*
4 *Polygonatum multiflorum.*
5 *Pulmonaria* 'Lewis Palmer'.

Tall, summer-flowering perennials

These are the big boys of the summer border, but don't assume they always need to be in the back row. They make great high points in your triangular set pieces too, and some of them make really fabulous specimen plants.

In summer, the herbaceous border comes into its own – a patchwork quilt of flowers that looks cheery even on dreary days.

Acanthus spinosus (**1**) is positively architectural; big and striking with great, thistly-looking leaves and 1.5m (5ft) stems topped with tall spikes of dusky mauve and pink, white-lipped flowers. These appear in June and July, but dry out on the plants and look good for most of the summer. Acanthus is happy in very well-drained and dry gardens in plenty of sun but doesn't like being disturbed once it's established, and it takes a few years to settle in. Grow it as a big specimen on its own, or team it with other drought-tolerant plants.

Salvia uliginosa (**2**) is nothing like the red bedding salvia. This has sky-blue flowers in loose spikes at the top of rather wiry stems in late summer and early autumn. It makes a slightly untidy, bushy shape, maybe 1.5m × 75cm (5 × 2½ft). It isn't the hardiest of plants, but cuttings root easily. Take a few when you take pelargonium cuttings and overwinter young plants under glass.

Phlox paniculata (**3**) is a traditional herbaceous border favourite that can be relied upon to put on a good show whatever the weather. Phlox have huge, domed heads of scented flowers from July to September at the tops of stems, 75cm–1.1m (2½–3½ft) tall, depending on the cultivar, and they come in clear, strong colours – violet, pink, orange, red, white and purple. Clumps slowly spread to 1m (3ft) before they die out in the middle and need dividing.

Achillea filipendulina **'Gold Plate'** (4) is also a sun-lover, but it's fine for a bright spot in a well-drained border with a little temporary shade. It's more spectacular than the average achillea – everything is about twice the usual size. The flat, bright yellow flower-heads are 15cm (6in) across, on 1.2m (4ft), ferny-leaved stems from July to September. The clumps spread slowly to maybe 1m (3ft) across.

Euphorbia characias **subsp.** *wulfenii* (5) takes as much sun as you can give it and needs well-drained soil, so it's good for a dry garden. The large, rounded heads of bright lime green flowers appear in April and May. It's evergreen and very architectural, forming a dome $1.2 \times 1.2\text{m}$ ($4 \times 4\text{ft}$). As with all euphorbias, the sap is irritant, so take care when you cut out the old, flowered stems out. You will need to cut them close to the base when the flowers are past it in midsummer to make room for the new stems and next year's flowers.

Geraniums (6) include so many brilliant hardy cranesbills. 'Mrs Kendall Clark' has pale blue flowers with dark blue veins, and at 1m (3ft) tall, likes a bit of support. 'Wargrave Pink' is low and restrained with lots of pink flowers, and the magenta-flowered *G. psilostemon* makes 1.2m (4ft) high mounds. All bloom from June to September.

1 *Acanthus spinosus.*
2 *Salvia uliginosa.*
3 *Phlox paniculata.*
4 *Achillea filipendulina* 'Gold Plate'.
5 *Euphorbia characias* subsp. *wulfenii.*
6 *Geranium psilostemon.*

Not-so-tall, summer-flowering perennials

Most of these are front-of-house plants and, one way or another, they put on a great show for most of the summer.

Dianthus (**1**), pinks, especially the modern ones such as 'Doris', flower from June to September – many have clove-scented flowers. They are mat-forming evergreens, 15×60cm (6×24in), for dry, sunny spots. They're short lived, so take cuttings to replace the old clumps after 2–3 years.

Hemerocallis (**2**), day lilies, make clumps of strap-shaped leaves, which are evergreen or nearly so, with straight stems topped by large, lily-like flowers in pink, red, yellow, white, orange or amber. Each flower only lasts a day, but the clumps keep flowering throughout July and August. Hemerocallis grow to 45–90cm (18–36in) tall, by as much across, depending on the cultivar. Shorter kinds are good at the front of the border – tall kinds are great fillers further back. One of my 'must-have' border perennnials.

Agapanthus (**3**) have strap-shaped leaves and long-stemmed spheres of blue or white flowers from July to September. Most reach 75cm (30in), but dwarf ones, half as tall, include the stunning 'Midnight Blue'. Great in a sunny, well-drained border, or in large pots in cold areas, which can be moved under glass in winter. Most aren't that hardy, but the 'Headbourne Hybrids' are pretty tough and will usually come through the winter in well-drained soil if given a protective mulch.

1 *Dianthus* 'Gran's Favourite'.
2 *Hemerocallis*.
3 *Agapanthus* 'Underway'.
4 Heuchera.

Heucheras (**4**) have good foliage – coloured, marbled or metallic – and they flower well too, in summer, with sprays of tiny pink, green or white bells. They like sun or shade and reach 30×30cm (1×1ft).

Perennials for late summer and autumn flowers

I hate coming home from my summer holiday to find the garden going over, so I make sure there are plenty of late starters ready to pick up the baton.

Sedum spectabile (5) is what we used to call the ice plant; it's second only to buddleia for attracting butterflies. It makes a 45 × 45cm (18 × 18in) cluster of waxy, blue-green leaves with flat-topped, pink or white flowers perched on short fat stems. Being semi-succulent, a well-drained, sunny spot is essential, otherwise it just rots off in winter.

Anemone × ***hybrida*** (6), Japanese anemone, flowers from August to October. The clumps do spread after a few years, so you might have to dig them up and divide them regularly to keep them in check. They grow to 1 × 1m (3 × 3ft), and the upright stems are topped by pink or white, single or semi-double flowers. They take a while to settle in – be patient.

Schizostylis (7) is such a reliable late-bloomer, I'm amazed everyone doesn't know it. *S. coccinea* 'Major' has strappy leaves and loose spikes of rosy-red freesia flowers. It starts in September and goes on till October or even November in mild autumns. There are pink ones – 'Mrs Hegarty' and 'Sunrise' – and *S. coccinea* f. *alba* has white flowers. Give them moist, rich soil in sun or light shade.

Aster novae-angliae (8), the New England aster, is the relatively mildew-free alternative to Michaelmas daisies. They look the same – big sprays of pink or mauve daisies – and late butterflies love them. For shorter ones, 75cm (30in) tall, a few twigs pushed into the clumps in late spring give enough support; the tall ones, at 1.2m (4ft), need a grow-through support from spring onwards.

5 *Sedum spectabile* 'Brilliant'.
6 *Anemone* × *hybrida* 'Honorine Jobert'.
7 *Schizostylis coccinea* 'Sunrise'.
8 *Aster novae-angliae* 'Herbstschnee'.

5

6

7

8

Grasses

Grasses and grass look-alikes, such as sedges, make good partners for perennials, as their linear forms and elegant seed-heads contrast well with all sorts of leaves and flowers. On a breezy day, grasses ripple – just like a field of barley – and it looks as though waves are running through the border.

Grasses are treated like most other perennials; clumps slowly increase in diameter and can be dug up and divided in spring when they outgrow their space or start balding in the middle. Cut herbaceous grasses down close to the ground in spring, so the dead rubbish is out of the way before new growth comes through, otherwise, they just look a mess.

In winter, grass seed-heads, evergreen leaves and dead stems of herbaceous plants look brilliant outlined in frost, so don't be in too much of a hurry to tidy them up. Although evergreen grasses don't need cutting back, it's worth pulling out dead leaves in spring, and if they look scruffy. It won't harm to give them a complete haircut – fresh growth will soon have them looking as good as new again.

Grasses really earn their keep – they have wonderful foliage, spectacular seedheads, and many even look good when they have dried out in winter.

Grasses for foliage

Some of the most eye-catching grasses are those with brightly coloured leaves or bold variegations; these are good for containers as well as for special places in borders.

***Hakonechloa macra* 'Aureola'** (**1**) is a choice, deciduous grass for borders – good for pots too, if it's kept well watered. The leaves are lemon with lime-green stripes. It likes sun and fertile soil that drains well but never dries completely. The clumps, 20cm (8in) tall, form elegant, waving carpets, 30cm (12in) across. Good in drifts at the border front, and magic with creeping *Lysimachia nummularia* 'Aurea', with mats of round, golden leaves, 5cm (2in) high.

***Imperata cylindrica* 'Rubra'** (**2**), Japanese blood grass, has bright red, semi-translucent leaves; with the sun behind them they look as if they are on fire. It's deciduous, about 38cm (15in) high, and grows slowly to make clumps 30cm (12in) across. It's fussier than some and likes a sunny site with fertile, moist but well-drained soil, which means plenty of organic matter and watering in hot weather.

Helictotrichon sempervirens (**3**) is a steel-blue, evergreen grass that forms architectural tussocks and, when it's grown alone, looks like a big pincushion, 45 × 60cm (18 × 24in), punctuated by 1m (3ft) long seed-heads. It needs good drainage and lots of sun, and is fairly drought tolerant, making it a good plant for a gravel garden.

1 *Hakonechloa macra* 'Aureola'.
2 *Imperata cylindrica* 'Rubra'.
3 *Helictotrichon sempervirens*.

Grasses for glamorous seed-heads

Whatever you do, don't let the flower arranger in your family pinch all the best seed-heads. They look good in the garden, even after they become a bit battered.

Stipa tenuissima (**1**) grows into thick clumps of fine, green, thread-like leaves and feathery seed-heads. Clumps grow to roughly 60 × 60cm (2 × 2ft). A very good grass for dotting between perennial flowers towards the front of a border and it's especially beautiful when animated by the breeze.

Miscanthus sinensis **cultivars** (**2**) include some very elegant tall, fountain-shaped plants with big, buff-coloured, feathery seed-heads and coloured or variegated leaves. They are brilliant in the middle of borders in between perennials, as they make good contrasts without taking up too much room. *M. sinensis* 'Morning Light' is one of the best of the variegated forms, with very narrow, grey-green and white-striped leaves, 1.2m (4ft) tall (if you include the seed-heads) and 60cm (2ft) across across. *M. sinensis* 'China' has a slightly reddish tinge to the leaves and red flowers that turn pinkish buff as the seeds form.

Pennisetum villosum (**3**), feathertop, is aptly named. It has the most spectacular seed-heads of all – big, fat and fluffy, outstanding for the front of a border – clumps grow 45 × 60cm (18 × 24in). It needs good, fertile, well-drained soil that isn't wet in winter. *P. alopecuroides*, fountain grass, is about the same size and even more sensational-looking, with great bristly, silvery-green bottlebrush flowers that turn to feathery, purple-flushed buff seed-heads when they mature. They are a tad tender, so they don't always survive a cold, wet winter unless you move them into a frost-free greenhouse.

1 *Stipa tenuissima*.
2 *Miscanthus sinensis* 'Undine'.
3 *Pennisetum alopecuroides* 'Woodside'.

Evergreen grasses

Evergreen grasses and sedges are good for year-round gardens giving structure when other plants have died back, as well as looking beautiful when covered in frost. The smaller grasses are especially good in pots if you are worryied about them being lost in the garden.

Festucas (4) are the grasses to choose if you want a small, drought-tolerant tussock with true-blue foliage. Go for a good named cultivar, such as *Festuca valesiaca* 'Silbersee', *F. glauca* 'Blaufuchs' or *F. glauca* 'Elijah Blue' if you want the very best colour. They are all good for rock features, seaside gardens, gravel gardens and pots, and grow slowly to about 30 × 30cm (1 × 1ft). They have delicate, feathery seed-heads. Try a small plantation of them – half a dozen or more – mulched with pieces of slate. The colour combination is stunning.

Carex buchananii (5) is a rather upright, clump-forming, evergreen sedge with stiff, reddish brown, thread-like leaves, that have coppery highlights and unusually curly tips. Growing to 60 × 30cm (2 × 1ft), it is good for pots, or for the fronts of borders with good, well-drained soil containing plenty of organic matter. It does best in sun, although it doesn't want scorching conditions. Plant one specimen in a 'rusted' container or mix a few in a prairie-style border. They look especially good planted among orange flowers.

Carex oshimensis **'Evergold'** (6) makes a shaggy, green-and-gold-striped mound, 20 × 30cm (8 × 12in); again it's a good plant for pots or the front of a border. It likes a cool, not-too-dry spot in light shade – the colour fades a bit in strong sun. One plant makes a focal point, several together make brilliant ground cover under taller shrubs and perennials.

4 *Festuca glauca* 'Elijah Blue'.
5 *Carex buchananii*.
6 *Carex oshimensis* 'Evergold'.

Ground-cover plants

From a design point of view, ground-cover plants create carpets of flowers or foliage. Ground cover can be used beneath trees or shrubs, or to help to pull everything together in a border, and they make great backdrops for spring bulbs. There is a practical angle, too, as they help to suppress weeds, so they're useful on banks or other places that are hard to weed. Mulching between the plants in spring holds back weeds and gives them extra nutrition, but sprinkle some general-purpose organic fertilizer round them as well. They don't need a lot of attention, but do need to be tidied up once a year. Prune woody kinds lightly to keep them in shape, in spring if they flower after midsummer, and just after flowering if they flower in spring. Herbaceous kinds die down for the winter and the dead stems need clearing away in autumn or spring.

Woody ground cover

If you use low-growing evergreen shrubs as ground cover plants then you can be assured that they will do their job all the year round.

Heaths and heathers (1) make good evergreen ground cover for sunny sites with acid, well-drained soil containing plenty of organic matter. They include *Erica*, *Calluna* and *Daboecia* species and cultivars, growing, on average, 25 × 60cm (10 × 24in). If you choose all three, you'll have flowers almost year-round, in shades of pink, purple and white and some have gold, red or orange leaves for extra colour. Clip them lightly with shears when the flowers fade; this removes the dead heads and makes them bushy, instead of leggy.

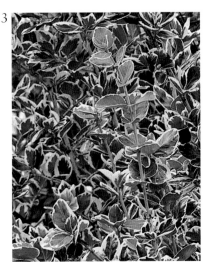

Cotoneaster dammeri (2) really hugs the ground as though it feels it might float away if it let go. Its leaves are dark green, oval and deeply veined, and in winter the bright red berries stand out well. In shady spots below trees and shrubs this is a really useful plant, and although it grows little more than 15cm (6in) high, it can spread sideways for a good couple of metres (6ft).

***Euonymus* 'Emerald Gaiety'** (3) is a more subtle alternative to the brighter 'Emerald 'n' Gold'. Where the latter's evergreen leaves are a confection of green and yellow, in 'Emerald Gaiety' they are green and creamy white, but none-the-less eye catching. Like 'Emerald 'n' Gold' it will also leg it up a wall if planted against vertical brickwork, and when planted as ground cover it may sometimes send a shoot or two up through a shrub, but this is nothing that cannot be kept in check with a light trim in spring.

Perennial ground-cover plants

You could argue that there is little point in ground-cover plants that are not in evidence all the year round. In that case, stick to the woody evergreens. But if you want a thick mat of growth that emerges afresh each spring and disappears in winter, then these are the plants for you. Over time the clumps will expand to fill all the avilable ground so that as well as the leaves smothering out weeds, the thick crowns will do the same.

Ajuga reptans (4), bugle, remains evergreen if conditions are kind, otherwise it ducks down for the winter and reappears in spring. In May and June, spikes of blue flowers appear, but the leaves can be green and white ('Variegata'), purplish-red ('Atropurpurea') or cream, green, and bronze ('Burgundy Glow'). Happy in sun or shade, it's not fussy about soil and grows to 8 × 60cm (3 × 24in), with 15cm (6in) flower spikes.

Tiarella cordifolia (5) is a useful little plant which is aptly named the foam flower. I say aptly because the domes of downy, maple-shaped leaves are covered with 30-cm (1-ft) high spires of tiny white flowers in summer, and they really do look frothy. Great in shade in any half-decent soil, and spreading into 30–60-cm (1–2-ft) clumps.

Brunnera macrophylla (6) is like a large-flowered forget-me-not. It's a perennial that gives a welcome splash of colour in early spring, making dense clumps, 30 × 60cm (1 × 2ft), of kidney-shaped leaves with sprays of delicate blue flowers floating above them. Over time it grows to carpet the ground with its attractive combination of long-stalked leaves and deep mats of flowers.

Planting ground cover

When using plants that don't naturally grow horizontally over the ground, plant clumps 25 per cent closer together than their anticipated spread after five years. Instead of making individual mounds, they'll blend together to form a complete carpet. The gaps between them will usually close up within 18 months of planting.

1 *Erica carnea* 'Springwood Pink' and *Erica* × *darleyensis* 'Arthur Johnson'.
2 *Cotoneaster dammeri.*
3 *Euonymus fortunei* 'Emerald Gaiety'.
4 *Ajuga reptans* 'Catlin's Giant'.
5 *Tiarella cordifolia.*
6 *Brunnera macrophylla.*

4

5

6

Bulbs

Bulbs emphasize the changing seasons, and they are a good way of packing even more plants into a limited space. Use them as carpets or clumps. Most bulbs need deep, well-drained soil. Spring bulbs are good 'naturalized' in grass (allowed to remain undisturbed), or under shrubs where they won't be watered in summer – enjoying the dry conditions they need when they are dormant. In wet conditions, they can rot. Summer-flowering bulbs are dormant in winter. Corms and tubers also tend to be loosely referred to as bulbs, although they are really condensed stems and roots, rather than buds.

Plant hardy kinds, such as lilies, in spring or autumn; they need good drainage and rich, fertile soil. Plant frost-tender, summer bulbs, such as gladioli, in late April or early May, so the frosts are over before the shoots appear above ground. They need digging up in autumn, drying off and storing under cover in much the same way as dahlias. Plant spring-flowering bulbs in autumn. As a rule of thumb, plant them three times as deep as the height of the bulb.

Dividing snowdrops

Snowdrops have a very short dormant season, and they transplant best if they are moved while they still have their leaves – a condition known as 'in-the-green'. Dig up the complete clump of snowdrops. Tease them apart with your fingers, don't use a knife or spade as you'll damage the bulbs and, if cut, they rot. Each new clump can have three to ten bulbs. Prepare the soil in the same way as for planting perennials, then plant clumps of snowdrops, about 15–20cm (6–8in) apart, to the same depth that they were planted previously. Firm them in lightly and water well.

Winter- and spring-flowering bulbs

These are bravest of all our garden plants, and therefore the most welcome. The real heralds of spring, everyone should grow them.

Snowdrops (1) are usually the first flowers to put in an appearance. There are many varieties with single or double flowerheads and they are best naturalized under shrubs or in grass so that they can come up year after year. The clumps increase in size, but can easily be divided.

Crocuses (2) are wonderful in shallow pots or seedpans which can add early spring colour. Species like C. *tommasinianus* can be naturalized in grass or in beds and borders and the amethyst spears of flower enjoyed in ever increasing numbers.

Anemone blanda (3) produces those short, white, pink or blue, star-shaped flowers you sometimes see carpeting the ground under shrub borders in spring, and that is probably the best way to use them. They grow about 15 × 10cm (6 × 4in) and, if left to naturalize, they slowly spread and produce a thicker carpet. Add clumps of taller or more sophisticated spring bulbs for contrast.

Narcissus (4) species and cultivars come in a huge range. The term 'daffodil' is saved for the tall, large-trumpet ones. All the rest we refer to as narcissi. Some of the most useful are the dwarf hybrids, such as 'Tête-à-Tête', 'February Gold' and 'Jetfire' which grow about 20–30cm (8–12in) tall. They flower earlier than large hybrid daffs, but the flowers are small and tough enough not to get battered by spring weather, and the foliage is compact so it doesn't create the usual eyesore – it is short enough to get swallowed up by all the summer perennials growing up round it. I reckon they are the best for garden planting, but they are also good for spring containers.

Tulips (5) are much more formal-looking flowers that were always used for spring bedding, for containers and other smart settings, but small groups of large, fringed parrot tulips, or elegant lily-flowered tulips – the ones with the wasp waists – look good tucked into a carpet of *Anemone blanda,* or when filling niches between shrubs. All tulips need a sunny spot with well-drained soil, but most of the species (the so-called botanical tulips) are choice kinds that need particularly free drainage and lots of sun. Tulip bulbs are prone to soil pests that bore holes in them, allowing rot to set in, so they are best dug up when the foliage dies down and stored in a cool, airy place for the summer. Plant bulbs in October or November; they don't root till then, and may rot if planted earlier in cold, wet soil.

5 *Tulipa* 'Ballerina' planted among forget-me-nots.

1 *Galanthus* 'Ketton'.
2 *Crocus tommasinianus.*
3 *Anemone blanda.*
4 *Narcissus* 'Tête-à-tête'.

Summer- and autumn-flowering bulbs

Gardeners who think that flowering bulbs are simply for spring, miss half the fun. Summer-flowering bulbs are even more spectacular and just as indispensable.

Lilium (1), the lilies, are treated more like clump-forming perennials that happen to have bulbs instead of fibrous roots. Plant three to five of the same cultivar in a group at three times their own depth, then leave them alone till the clump needs dividing – do this in early spring. Most like well-drained, rich, fertile, neutral to acid soil and a spot where their flowers are in sun but the bulbs are shaded. If you want strong scent, the best to go for are the Oriental hybrids, such as 'Star Gazer', which has deep red flowers edged in white and grows about 1.2m (4ft) high; 'Casa Blanca' is pure white. The tiger lily (*L. lancifolium*) is the old favourite with black-spotted, orange flowers whose petals curl out from the centre – it has no scent, but it doesn't mind light dappled shade or neutral soil. Tall and robust, it grows to 1.2–1.5m (4–5ft) high. I prefer to grow lilies in pots and stand them in beds and borders when they come into bud – that way I can protect them from slugs and snails, and from my misplaced hoe! They'll be happy in the same pots for three years if well fed.

1 *Lilium* 'Star Gazer'.
2 *Dahlia* 'Kenora Sunset'.
3 *Nerine bowdenii*.
4 *Allium hollandicum* 'Purple Sensation'.
5 *Gladiolus byzantinus*.

Dahlias (2) can be loud and vulgar, but I have a soft spot for them because they are so obliging. At last, they are coming back into fashion. They are not hardy, so unless you live in a mild area and are prepared to risk leaving the tubers in the ground (which needs to be well drained and thickly mulched with manure or compost), dig them up and store them in a frost-free shed in winter.

Storing dahlias

Leave dahlia plants in the ground until the leaves start turning black, showing they've been exposed to a frost – don't worry, it won't have been enough to harm the tubers underground.

Cut the plants down to about 15cm (6in) above the ground, then dig up the tubers and wash the soil off. Leave them out in the sun to dry. Store them in nets, or in stacking trays no more than one layer deep, in a frost-free shed where there is plenty of air circulation. Don't store them in a cupboard indoors unless it is an unheated room, or you'll prompt them to make early growth long before it's safe to replant them.

Nerine bowdenii (3) needs a hot, dry, sunny spot at the base of a south-facing wall. The pink, spidery, lily flowers appear in late summer or autumn, but the leaves don't appear until later, and they stand through spring. The bulbs are summer dormant, when they want a baking to prepare them for flowering. Plant them 30cm (1ft) apart and leave them alone: they don't like being disturbed.

Alliums (4) are wonderful bulbs to pepper through a border where their drumstick flowers will explode like fireworks. I particularly love 'Purple Sensation' which produces lilac-purple orbs on 1-m (3-ft) high stems in summer. Plant the bulbs in spring, in curving little plantations that will link other groups of flowers together. The bulbs will happily push up among them.

Gladioli (5) are the one flower that I do have a bit of a problem with. Well, they are so stiff and starchy. Grow them on the vegetable patch if you like them for cutting, or grow the much more graceful *Gladiolus byzantinus* in your beds and borders. This is the deep magenta gladiolus that grows wild in Cornwall and the one gladiolus I would plant in my garden! The large-flowered types (go on, grow them if you want to – don't listen to me!) need to be planted 10cm (4in) deep and 30cm (1ft) apart in spring, staked when they flower and dug up and overwintered in a garage. *G. byzantinus* can be naturalized 5cm (2in) deep and 15cm (6in) apart in sunny, well-drained soil.

1 *Musa basjoo.*

Exotics

Exotic plants give you a great excuse to exercise your design skills to create a tropical look for the summer, but whether you grow them in pots on the patio or plant them out, the tender kinds are only temporary residents – from mid-September to late May they need the protection of a frost-free greenhouse or conservatory.

Musa (1) is the botanical name for bananas. In the wild, bananas grow into short, squat trees with huge leaves. In the Caribbean, the leaves are tattered by the wind, but over here we normally see them with their leaves whole. *Musa basjoo*, Japanese banana, is the hardiest one, which means that it is hardy in sheltered spots in milder parts of the country, though it dies back to ground level each winter, so you seldom see a specimen much more than 1.2m (4ft) tall. If you can't find *M. basjoo*, then just put any banana plant you can find in the garden for the summer and move it indoors in winter. It will come as no surprise that you won't be picking huge crops of bananas, but enjoy those squeaky leaves.

Cannas (2) were once used as 'dot plants' for adding height to carpet-bedding displays, but they've made a comeback lately thanks to the exotics craze. They grow 2–2.4m (6–8ft) tall, and have big, loud, orchid-like flowers on straight leafy stems. Cannas come in a range of red-hot reds, oranges and yellows, and there are some that also have coloured leaves, such as 'Assaut' with dusky brown-purple leaves, and 'Roi Humbert' with royal purple ones. In winter they die down to big rhizomes that don't stand any frost, so they need lifting and storing under cover. Unlike dahlia tubers, they must not dry out completely, so it's best to pot them and leave them covered with potting compost that stays barely moist. Alternatively, you can grow them in big pots on the patio, when they won't grow quite so big.

Hedychium (3), the ginger lily, comes into the same bracket as cannas – spectacular – but not so well known or widely available. It makes large, 1.5–2m (5–6ft) clumps of straight stems with banana-like leaves and spectacular flowers with long wispy stamens sticking out all round. Then it dies back to a rhizome that needs treating the same as an overwintering canna. *H. coccineum* 'Tara' has orange flowers with red stamens and *H. gardnerianum* is lemon yellow, again with red stamens. In a mild area, leave ginger lilies in well-drained ground, but mulch them thickly to insulate the roots.

Plectranthus argentatus (4) is a loose, mound-shaped shrub, 30 × 90cm (1 × 3ft) with large, oval, silver, felty-textured leaves that have scalloped edges. It does flower – in summer, with clusters of pale blue to off-white flowers – but it's the leaves that I grow it for.

Dicksonia antarctica (5), Tasmanian tree fern, is just about hardy outside all year round in mild, sheltered gardens; I have a small grove of them at home that have survived for several years, but instead of being evergreen, as they are back home in New Zealand, the leaves turn brown with severe cold, and the head of the plant needs lagging in winter. We put inverted, lamp-shade-shaped cones of wire netting around the crowns in October and stuff them with straw. These are nailed on with metal staples and stay in place until the middle of April. Tree ferns aren't cheap plants, so if you don't want the risk, grow them in pots and put them in the greenhouse for the winter.

2

3

4

5

2 *Canna indica* 'Purpurea'.
3 *Hedychium coccineum* 'Tara'.
4 *Plectranthus argentatus*.
5 *Dicksonia antarctica*.

Eschscholzia californica, the Californian poppy, is a cheerful annual that will romp through your garden and provide a fabulous carpet of bright, sunny colours.

Annuals and biennials

Forget about the small bedding plants that are used in containers or formal bedding schemes (see page 130): the ones I'm thinking about are the taller, more unusual annuals and biennials for filling gaps around the garden while you are waiting for slower shrubs to grow, and for providing splashes of seasonal colour in mixed borders.

Remember that annuals are the plants that will grow from seed, flower and die within twelve months, whereas biennials grow from seed in their first year and flower and die in their second.

Hardy annuals

Handy gap-fillers for a mixed border, these have summer-long flowers. Sow them outdoors in early spring where you want them to flower, if you have light, weed-free ground, or better still sow them in pots or trays of 'cells' in an unheated greenhouse or cold frame and plant them out when they are big enough.

Cerinthe major **'Purpurascens'** (1) is a relative newcomer, with striking silvery blue, often silver-spotted leaves and tubular, purple-blue flowers. It makes an open spreading clump about 30 × 30cm (1 × 1ft), so plant 3–5 in a group so they beef each other up. Once established they self-seed, so transplant or thin them out to leave just those you want.

Eschscholzia californica (2), Californian poppy, is irrepressibly cheerful; it grows quickly and easily from seed and makes a 30cm (1ft) high carpet of large, silky flowers in warm, bright colours from early summer to early autumn. It self-seeds readily (rather too readily at times), but the seedlings are easily pulled out – don't bother trying to transplant them because, typically, like most poppies, they don't like disturbance. If it's not practical to sow the seeds where you want the plants to flower, sow small pinches in fibre pots and plant out pot-and-all as a ready-made clump before the roots grow out through the sides.

Helianthus annuus (3), sunflowers, come in several sorts. There are giants with single stems up to 4.5m (15ft) – good for competitions, or grown up against the wall of the house. There are also modern ones that are shorter and bushier, around 90 × 90cm (3 × 3ft), with multiple stems and lots of flowers. There are also sunflowers in velvety reds, mahogany and orange shades, as well as traditional yellow, and there are some with double flowers. They are all good for cutting and last an amazingly long time in water.

Half-hardy annuals

The taller half-hardy annuals are a bit neglected, but include some real show-stoppers. Sow seeds in a propagator in early spring and raise young plants in a heated greenhouse. They can't be planted out until after the last frost. Give them a warm, sunny site with well-drained soil, and water them until established.

Cleome spinosa (4) has heads of elegant, spidery flowers with narrow, curving petals in white or pale maroon-pink. It grows in upright clumps, 1.2m (4ft) tall. For great teamwork, grow it with cosmos.

Cosmos (5) has light, ferny foliage topped by enormous, fragile, slightly wavy flowers with a bunch of stubby stamens in the centre. The tallest are 'Purity' (white) and 'Sensation Mixed' (various colours) at 1.2m (4ft), but there are shorter kinds at 75cm (30in), if that's more in proportion to the gap you have in mind.

Tithonia rotundifolia (6) has chunky, orange or yellow 'daisies' on strong, upright stems. 'Torch' reaches 1.2m (4ft), but isn't as widely available as shorter ones, such as 'Goldfinger', at 75cm (30in).

1 *Cerinthe major* 'Purpurascens'.
2 *Eschscholzia californica*.
3 *Helianthus annuus*.
4 *Cleome spinosa*.
5 *Cosmos bipinnatus* 'Purity'.
6 *Tithonia rotundifolia*.

Biennials

Biennials are old-fashioned, but some kinds are creeping back into vogue. Many will self-seed, so once you've grown one batch, it's just a case of transplanting self-sown seedlings from then on. Start the ball rolling by sowing seeds in late spring or early summer, then transplant young plants to the flowering positions in early autumn.

Campanula medium (1) is the Canterbury bell, which – yes – is an old-fashioned flower, but it flowers in that awkward gap between spring and summer when you are glad of something to fill the gap between the spring bulbs and the summer bedding. The double ones, at 90×60cm (3×2ft), are particularly unusual-looking, though there are smaller cultivars and the more usual ones with single flowers in white, or shades of blue and pink.

Dianthus barbatus (2), sweet Williams, certainly have old-fashioned charm, but if you can't find room for them in the garden – and my favourite spot is under roses – then they are something to grow in a row on your vegetable patch and use for cutting. That's what my grandad did. The clove scent reminds you of supercharged carnations. They grow to 30×30cm (1×1ft) or thereabouts.

Verbena bonariensis (3) is a definite must for mixed borders. You don't really see the candelabra of the stems, because they're so upright and wiry with narrow leaves. All you notice are the tufts of airy, purple, gypsophila-like flowers that look as if they are suspended in space among shrubs and tall perennials. They go with anything and look good wafting through a whole border. Plants sometimes come up for a couple of years, and they self-seed but lightly. Transplant small plants in late summer to wherever you want them to flower the following year. Large plants can be potted up in autumn, overwintered in a greenhouse and used for cuttings.

1 *Campanula medium.*
2 *Dianthus barbatus* 'Oeschberg'.
3 *Verbena bonariensis.*

Rock plants

Rock plants are little gems; tiny mat- or mound-shaped plants to enjoy in close-up. Raised beds and rock features, or containers, are the best places to enjoy them. When planting, water new plants in well; rock plants in containers and raised beds need watering in hot, dry weather, even after they are established. Once planted, they can stay put for years, but do protect them from slugs and snails and weed rock features regularly, as small plants are soon swamped. Clear fallen leaves from rock features in autumn, and regularly pick plants over to remove dead flowers, dead leaves and old stems of those that die down for winter.

Spring-flowering alpines

Rock features usually look their best in the springtime as this is when all the dwarf bulbs and the majority of popular rock plants are in flower.

Phlox subulata (4) grows into small spreading mats, 10×38cm (4×15in), and is smothered in late spring with red, pink or blue flowers, similar to, but much smaller than those of the border phlox.

Mossy saxifrages (5) are the group of saxifrages that look exactly like patches of moss, 2.5×15cm (1×6in), and are covered in April and May with small pink or red flowers like upturned bells. *Saxifraga* 'Cloth of Gold' is especially pretty, as the foliage is bright yellow and lacy textured; it produces clouds of tiny white flowers.

Pulsatilla vulgaris (6), Pasque flower, makes small, upright clumps of silky foliage with large, single violet flowers in April. It needs alkaline soil. Allow 10×20cm (4×8in).

4 *Phlox subulata* 'Alexander's Surprise'.
5 *Saxifraga exarata*.
6 *Pulsatilla vulgaris*.

Alpines for summer colour

Summer is the time a lot of rock features start loosing their oomph unless you make a point of finding plants that are at their best then.

The traditional rock garden still has a lot going for it – provided you can fit it into your own style of gardening.

Campanula cochleariifolia **'Elizabeth Oliver'** (**1**) makes ground-hugging mats of foliage, 5 × 30cm (2 × 12in) that can spread quite a distance and pop up to start a new colony, but it's not invasive. The carpets of double, pale-blue bell flowers are very welcome.

Helianthemum (**2**), the rock rose, is a ground-coverer with masses of papery flowers that may be white, yellow, orange, pink or red, with a central boss of golden stamens. It grows no more than 30cm (1ft) high but a good 1–2m (3–6ft) across.

Lithodora (**3**), previously called Lithospermum, are old rock garden classics, with deep blue flowers on spreading, mat-shaped plants, 10 × 45cm (4 × 18in). *Lithodora diffusa* 'Grace Ward' and 'Heavenly Blue' are the well-known ones; both have star-shaped flowers from early summer to early autumn. They prefer acid, humus-rich soil.

1 *Campanula cochleariifolia*
  'Elizabeth Oliver'.
2 *Helianthemum* 'Rhodanthe
  Carreum'.
3·*Lithodora.*

Evergreen alpines

Any rock feature needs its share of evergreens for year-round interest.

Sisyrinchiums (4) look like mini-iris plants with stiff, upright, evergreen leaves and star-shaped flowers all summer; most of them grow to about 20 × 20cm (8 × 8in) and have purple-blue flowers. The *Sisyrinchium californicum* Brachypus Group, which has dark-veined yellow flowers, only grows to 10cm (4in). All of the sisyrinchiums are fairly drought tolerant.

Saxifrages (5) that are referred to as 'encrusted' saxifrages are a group of species with rosettes of evergreen leaves covered in a chalky white exudation. They produce airy sprays of delicate white flowers in spring. The most spectacular is *Saxifraga* 'Tumbling Waters', which makes a single, large, silvery rosette, 20cm (8in) across, but the plant takes several years to produce the trademark waterfall of white flowers, and then it dies.

Kabschia saxifrages make neat, tightly packed leafy mounds and flower prolifically each spring; *S.* 'Jenkinsiae' is a reliable favourite with large, round, pale pink flowers in March. Individual plants are about 2.5cm (1in) across, but they multiply slowly to make small mounds.

Sempervivums (6), alias houseleeks, were once grown on the roof for luck. They can survive heat, drought, and need next to no soil but, when properly planted in a container or bed, they'll certainly grow into much better-looking specimens. Plants are round and spiky, and pile up into knobbly, succulent clumps, 15 × 20cm (6 × 8in) or more across. Fat, hefty spikes of flowers emerge in June. Lots of different cultivars are available, with green or red leaves, plain or shiny. There is also *S. arachnoideum*, the one to grow for the cobweb-effect – the rosettes are decorated with spun silk.

4 *Sisyrinchium* 'Californian Skies'.
5 *Saxifraga* 'Tumbling Waters'.
6 *Sempervivum* 'Raspberry Ripple'.

5 WATER FEATURES

Design considerations

When you are planning a water feature, you need to bear in mind most of the things you'd take into account if you were making a new flower bed. Think about the shape and style that is going to suit you and your type of garden – will it be formal, informal, natural or contemporary?

A natural pond made alongside a contemporary deck to provide the best of both worlds.

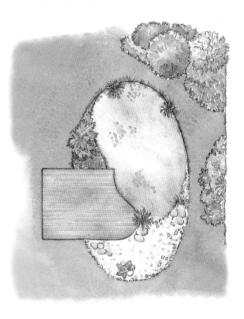

Ask yourself whether you want the main emphasis to be the water plants, fish, wildlife, or moving water itself. How much maintenance are you prepared for? If child safety is an issue, you probably won't want anything with open, standing water, even if it's only a few inches deep. Once you have organized your thoughts, choose the place that is both right for you, and for whatever is likely to live in the water.

Siting ponds

A pond is incredibly hypnotic, so you'll want to put it somewhere you can sit and 'switch off'. The patio is a good place, or you might want to put it in a quiet spot further down the garden where there's room for a garden bench opposite. It'll soon become your favourite outdoor retreat, where you can listen to the sound of running water and watch dragonflies, fish and wildlife. It makes you feel drowsy just thinking about it.

A sunny spot may be pleasant for anyone water-watching, but it's absolutely essential for the well-being of the pond's complex

Water world

Water plants need sunlight to photosynthesize, which is how they oxygenate the water. You can often see tiny bubbles coming up from them on a sunny day – and that's what enables fish and other water wildlife to survive. Oxygen is also crucial for all sorts of minute pond-life that clean the pond, right down to the friendly bacteria that clear up after everybody else.

Don't panic if your pond looks murky (*top*), and don't add tap water in the hope of clearing it, you will only make matters worse. The pond water will clear itself once it corrects its natural balance (*below*). Remove any leaves that might fall on the surface of the pond, but otherwise leave the pond undisturbed for a few weeks and you will start to see a difference.

ecosystem. Keep your pond well away from big trees and shrubs, even though they may seem to be an obvious background. Given half a chance, the roots can grow through the lining of a pond and make it leak, and repairing a pond liner is no joke. The leaves will also fill it up in autumn and foul the water.

Allow yourself enough space for a pond. You'll always need more room than you think. A very small, shallow pond isn't suitable for fish; the water will heat up too much in summer and can freeze solid in winter, which wrecks your water plants too. As a rule of thumb, don't make a pond any smaller than 60cm (2ft) deep, and at least 1 × 1.5m (3 × 5ft) across – preferably 60cm (2ft) or so bigger. Don't imagine you can cram it into a corner of the garden either. You need to leave enough room all round it for reaching in to do essential maintenance. End of lecture.

Small water features

If you choose a wall fountain or a pebble pool with nothing living in the water, then you can construct them in sun or shade. These features are a good way to add a sparkling focal point to a shady part of the garden – but you'll still find them easier to keep clean and the pumps will run more smoothly if they don't get clogged up with fallen leaves.

If you are worried about small children using the garden, these are safe water features since they don't contain standing water, but you'll need to put them close to an electricity supply to power the pump. Otherwise, go for a very basic type of water feature; a wide plant container without any drainage holes in the bottom, and a floating solar fountain, or a few temporary floating plants, such as water hyacinth (*Eichhornia crassipes*), on the top, which you just stand outside for the summer.

Both the movement and sound of water can be enjoyed in this simple feature. Water is pumped up through a central aperture in the stone column, and then falls into a hidden tank from which it is recirculated.

Ponds

There are all sorts of ponds to choose from to suit any garden style. Formal ponds have a geometrical shape, usually a circle or a rectangle, and normally have vertical sides. They are mostly used for waterlilies and goldfish, with a few oxygenating plants under the water surface to keep things healthy. Informal ponds have an

Where there's a bit of space to spare, a large sheet of water, a plank bridge and swathes of planting are nothing short of spectacular.

irregular, more natural-looking shape that suits the average family garden much better. This type will have planting shelves around several sides on which to stand baskets of marginal plants. They should have a sloping pebble 'beach' so that birds can get in to bathe safely, and baby frogs and hedgehogs (who will drop by for a drink) can climb out.

Wildlife ponds are more natural still; here, *all* the sides are gently sloping. You don't tend to find the same formally ornamental marginal plants growing round the sides, but bog plants will be at home in the soggy margins and a few deep-water or floating aquatics are happy in the middle. Instead of putting in fish, which will feed on naturally occurring water creatures, most wildlife gardeners prefer to wait for tadpoles and newts to turn up.

Pond care calendar

Don't just dig it, fill it and leave it. With a little regular maintenance your pond will be good to look at all the year round.

Spring

Anticipate that the pond water will turn green in spring; it should clear itself naturally after a few months, though a brand-new pond may stay green for the whole of its first year. Be patient.

Pull out blanketweed – those clumps of stringy green slime suspended in the water – with a wire-toothed rake, taking care not to puncture the liner. Always leave it on the pool side overnight, so that any pond creatures within it can escape back into the water, then consign it to the compost heap. Fish out duckweed with a fine-mesh net. Try to avoid using chemical 'cures' for algae or blanketweed and instead use one of the biological treatments that won't harm wildlife or pond plants. They work by increasing the numbers of naturally occurring, beneficial, water-cleaning bacteria.

Summer

Feed fish between May and September. Once the pond is established, the fish will also eat snails' eggs, mosquito larvae and other wild food for themselves. If you want a natural wildlife pool, fish are best left out altogether. Pull out handfuls of oxygenators regularly if the pond looks too full of them.

Autumn

When the pond has been there several years, you'll need to remove the excess deposits of silt that form naturally on the bottom. Don't empty the pond of water, just bale out as much as you can with a small plastic bowl, taking care not to perforate the liner. Don't be too thorough – leave a good 2.5cm (1in) layer of muck in the bottom for water plants to root into.

With the exception of the evergreen oxygenator, *Lagarosiphon*, most aquatics are perennials that die down in winter. To prevent debris building up, remove free-floating plants once they are killed by cold, cut down marginals flush with the surface of the water, and pull out decaying lily leaves. Keep autumn leaves off the pond with a net.

Winter

When you've done the autumn jobs, little or no pond maintenance is needed during the winter. If you have fish in the pond, however, place a plastic ball on the surface of the pond. If the water should freeze over, hot water can be poured over the ball so that you can remove it to leave an air-hole behind that allows fish to breathe.

Dealing with excavated soil

Use the soil removed when excavating a pond to make a raised bed, bank or rock garden somewhere else in the garden – not right behind the pool; it will always look like a spoil heap. Alternatively, if the topsoil is good, use it to top up beds and borders around the garden. Heavy clay is best disposed of in the footings for a path or paving, or just put it in the skip.

How to... **build a pond**

You'll see ready-made plastic or fibreglass ponds on sale in garden centres, but it's a lot cheaper and easier to do it yourself by digging a hole the shape and size that you want, and then lining it with flexible, butyl rubber or plastic sheeting to make it hold water.

Design your pond first, choosing a shape that fits easily into a rectangle based on the size of the lining material available, so you don't have to order special sizes, which are more expensive. Avoid having tight, fussy curves or acute angles; they are difficult to fit the liner round, and can create weak banks that easily cave in.

Calculating how much liner you need

Measure the pond length, multiply the depth at the deepest point by two, and add the two together. Add 50cm (20in) for overlap at the edges. Then do the same thing with the width. Those two figures tell you what size sheet you need, with enough spare to tuck in round the sides.

What you need

- *spade*
- *spirit level*
- *bottle of dry sand for marking out*
- *plank long enough to reach right over the pond*
- *soft building sand to cushion the liner from sharp stones*
- *sheet of butyl pond liner*
- *pool liner underlay, wooden pegs and craft knife*
- *paving or turf for edging*
- *hosepipe*

1 Clear the site to leave the soil bare and reasonably flat. Mark out the shape of the pond by trickling dry sand from a lemonade bottle.

2 Dig it out. Make the bottom of the pond firm, flat and stone free. Dig at least a third of the area 60cm (2ft) deep for fish and deep-water plants. The rest can be 45cm (18in) deep for most other aquatics. If you want marginal plants, make flat 'shelves' at the sides, 15cm (6in) wide and 20cm (8in) below the surface. Make very gently sloping edges where you want 'beaches'.

3 Lay the plank over the hole and rest a spirit level on top. The top of the pond sides must be level, otherwise the water will look as if it's all run down to one end. If they're not level, shift some soil to even it out – it has to be right. Check the levels from front to back and from side to side.

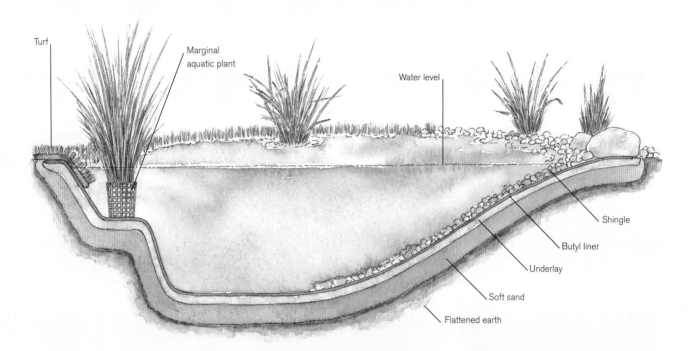

Turf
Marginal aquatic plant
Water level
Shingle
Butyl liner
Underlay
Soft sand
Flattened earth

4 Spread a 2.5cm (1in) layer of soft sand over the base, shelves and slopes. Then cover the whole area in pond underlay. Peg this into place. With one person at each end, lift the folded liner over the pond, position it centrally and carefully unfold it. Don't drag the liner about too much or walk on it. Put a few bricks on the edge of the liner to stop it blowing about.

5 Start filling the pond with water by leaving a hose running. As the increasing volume of water weighs the liner down into the hole, tug the folds of the liner so that they cling around the curves in small, neat folds. When the pond is full, trim the liner to a 30cm (1ft) overlap.

6 Laying paving stones at the rim of the pool will hide the liner – which can rot when exposed to the sun. Alternatively, for a natural-looking wildlife pond, lay turf so that it overlaps the rim and runs down into the water. It will be quite happy and makes a wild and woolly edging. Lower the plants into place, and allow oxygenating plants six weeks to establish before introducing fish.

Water features

You can create all sorts of water features by starting with a basic pebble-pool kit, which you can buy at most garden centres, and a pump that you have to buy separately. The kit consists of a reservoir container that you sink into the ground (with the pump inside), and a lid that covers it. The water outlet spout on top of the pump pokes out through the middle of the lid. When it's been installed, you lay a carpet of pebbles over the top, and the water appears to just run away – it's actually going back into the hidden reservoir container and being endlessly recycled.

Decorative detail

There's a lot you can do with a basic pebble pool, depending on how you finish it off. Like an iceberg, nine-tenths of it is underground, so all you see is the decorative bit on top. You can pile a heap of pebbles around the water outlet from the top of the pump, so that the water runs over the stones and looks like a small natural spring. If you want something more elaborate, either fit a nozzle on the top so the water sprays out as a fountain, or fit an ornament or a millstone over the top of the spout for the water to run over. All sorts of ornaments are sold especially for use with water features – such as terracotta jugs, seashells or what have you – and they've had a hole drilled through them for the water to run into or out of. Some are naff, some are classy. It's up to you.

If you fit anything over the top of the water outlet, make sure there's a good seal between the outlet and your ornament, otherwise the water will leak out there instead of being forced to come out where you want it. Fix everything together and make sure it is working properly before you cover the lid of the fountain with pebbles.

Care of water features

Top up the water once a week in spring and summer as there are bound to be some losses by evaporation.

The only way to prevent algae forming on the pebbles and anything else that stays wet all the time the pump is running is to add a chemical algicide to the water.

In a very cold area, where there may be a risk of the water in the reservoir or pipework freezing in winter, dismantle the water feature and clean and store the pump indoors to avoid damage. Generally speaking, though, the pump is best kept running for as much of the year as possible.

Pumping power

A pebble pool needs a power supply to run the pump, so it must be located close enough to a socket for the cable to reach. It can be plugged in indoors, if you drill through the wall close to a power point and allow room for the transformer. If you have power laid on to the shed or conservatory, you could also plug in there. You must always connect the pump to a circuit breaker (RCD, or residual current device) for safety. Employ a qualified electrician if electrics are a mystery to you.

How to... **build a water feature**

It's the perfect job for the weekend – not too strenuous, and capable of being constructed in the smallest corner of the garden. But if you plan on using heavy lumps of rock, enlist the help of a friend, and if you are hazy when it comes to the use of electricity, then get a competent electrician to lay the cabling for you. If you are not sure about what sort of pump you need, or indeed what size, explain to someone at your local garden centre what you are planning to build and they will be able to advise you what equipment will best suit your needs.

What you need

- *plastic reservoir*
- *submersible pump*
- *drilled rock or monolith*
- *wire grid and netting*
- *Jubilee clip, length of hose and silicone sealant*
- *screw driver and craft knife*
- *pebbles or shale*
- *electricity supply*
- *spade and spirit level*

1 Dig a hole large enough to take the reservoir. Remember that the larger the reservoir, the less frequently you will have to top it up. Sink the reservoir into the ground and check that it is level. Pack it with soil or sand so that it is stable. The pump needs to be attached to the electric cable by an electrician, and then placed in the bottom of the reservoir. Fasten a length of hosepipe to the pump outlet so that it can be fed through the stone. Add the water and check that the pump is functioning.

2 In order to stabilize the monolith, the wire grid, with finer netting over the top is now put in place, the hose threaded through it, and the mesh then covered with shale. The hose is then fed up through the monolith which is manoeuvred into the upright position and checked for stability. The flat cut top of the monolith needs to be checked to make sure that it is level, so that the water will flow evenly down all faces of the rock.

3 It is important that the hosepipe is sealed into position at the top using silicone. This ensures that the water runs down the face of the rock rather than down the inside of the aperture. The protruding piece of hose is cut off with a craft knife and the silicone allowed to dry for a couple of hours before the fountain is switched on.

Water plants

Plants are essential in ponds. They offer bed and breakfast facilities and act as crèches for the pond's various inhabitants, and provide vital services like air conditioning and waste disposal. All very necessary because, each year, a substantial layer of fish manure, and compost from decomposing water-weed, is deposited at the bottom of a pond.

Once a pond has grown into the landscape it will look as though it has always been there.

Plants also look good, providing foliage and flowers all summer. There are four types of water plants – deep-water aquatics, marginals, submerged oxygenators and free-floaters. For a pond to function properly, you need to include a few plants from each of the first three groups. Free-floaters are an optional extra.

Marginals, as the name suggests, are happiest at the margins of a pool, whereas the others prefer their roots to be in the water. Water plants tend to be grown in large, net-sided pots or plastic planting baskets, which stand on the planting shelves or floor of the pond. They stop plants spreading too fast and make them easier to lift out when dividing them. Plants are sold in small pots, and should be potted on into baskets about 25cm (10in) or more for the pond.

Water plants have evolved to live in low-nutrient environments, so use special aquatic compost for potting them. Don't use garden soil; it may pollute the water if it contains traces of garden products. And don't use ordinary potting compost; it contains nutrients that encourage algae to grow in the water and turn it green. If fertilizer gets into the pond – for instance, if it's washed out of surrounding beds by heavy rain – it will encourage a green algal bloom. Even the nitrates present in tap water can be enough to cause an algal or blanketweed problem; use rainwater to top up ponds if you can. Each time you remove excess water-weed, blanketweed or overgrown plants from the pond, you're removing a source of nutrients from the water.

Pond-life is sensitive to chemicals of any kind, so take great care not to use pesticides or weedkillers anywhere near a pond. If you use chemical water treatments for pond problems, always check that they're safe for wildlife, fish and the plants in your pond. Many products are only suitable for water features where nothing lives. I'd rather spend my time getting the balance right.

Dividing water plants

Like dry-land perennials, marginals and other water plants need dividing when the clumps get too big. Divide them in April, but don't do it unless you really need to; they're ready to split if they stop flowering or the leaves start growing vertically instead of horizontally. Fast-growing native plants, such as flowering rush (*Butomus umbellatus*), may need splitting every two years; water irises and dwarf reedmace (*Typha minima*) within 3–4 years, and waterlilies only after seven years.

Lift the basket out of the pond, taking care not to tear the liner, and swill it round to let tadpoles and other creatures back into the water. Tip the plant out or, if the roots have grown through the sides of the basket, cut the container to release it. Split the clump with a sharp spade, as you would with a border perennial. Choose a strong piece with healthy young shoots to replant and dump the rest on the compost heap. Replant into a basket of aquatic compost. Top with gravel to hold the compost in place and stop fish from disturbing it. When repotting waterlilies, only bury the roots – the rhizomes should sit on the compost surface. Sink the baskets slowly back into the pond. Don't worry if the water goes cloudy – it'll soon clear.

Planting depth

The one thing you must do when you buy a new plant is to give it the right depth of water to grow in – and when plant labels and reference books talk about depth, they mean the depth of water over the top of the roots, not the depth of water you ought to stand the pot in. Yes, it can be confusing till you get the hang of it.

Sometimes it's possible to prise out part of an overcrowded aquatic plant with an old knife, removing a good portion of the roots as well as some shoots. The parent plant can be topdressed and put back in the water, while the youngster is potted up in its own basket of aquatic compost, top-dressed with gravel and returned to the pond to grow away on its own.

Marginal plants

These are plants that grow in shallow water round the edge of the pond, and besides looking good, they do all sorts of good work for the pond community. Their vertical stems provide footholds for dragonfly nymphs to climb out of the water when it's time for them to turn into adult dragonflies, and their roots use up a lot of minerals in the water that would otherwise feed algae so, like other water plants, they behave rather like vegetable water-filters.

Renovating an overgrown pond

If a pond gets completely overcrowded and messy, it's time for a complete renovation job. Spring is the time to do it. You'll be up to your armpits in mucky water for hours, but it'll look a lot better when you've finished.

Take out all the plants, including the submerged aquatics, clear out as much silt as you can, all bar about 2.5cm (1in) of it anyway, leaving the original 'dirty' water behind. It's much better than new tap water, with its load of chlorine and nitrates. And this way, you can leave fish and frogs alone and don't need to worry about tadpoles.

Sort out your plants. Some will be worth dividing and replanting, but those that aren't up to much are best ditched on the compost heap so you can start again with new ones.

The water should settle within a few days. Take the time to tidy up round the edges, freshen up the surrounding planting, whip out any weeds and top-dress the ground with more pebbles or gravel.

Butomus umbellatus (1), flowering rush, has no leaves, just green, reed-like stems, 75cm (30in) tall, which, in late summer, are topped by 90cm (3ft) stems of pink, almost allium-like flowers. It grows in mud or in up to 13cm (5in) of water. Best in a medium to large pond.

Sagittaria sagittifolia (2), arrowhead, is a potentially invasive British native, but if you weed out the self-sown seedlings from the sludge in the bottom of the pond each spring, it's controllable. It grows 45cm (18in) high, with arrowhead-shaped leaves and three-cornered white flowers arranged in loose tiers up each spike in August. If you like this, but want more cultivated looks and less of a spreader, go for 'Flore Pleno' – double flowers, so no seedlings. It grows a bit taller but more slowly. For 8–15cm (3–6in) of water.

Typha minima (3) is the one to go for if you have a soft spot for bulrushes. The dwarf reedmace is only 38cm (15in) tall, with nearly round, brown 'fishing floats' impaled near the tops of some of the stems. It's well behaved and good for a small natural pond, as well as the garden kind, growing in 2.5–10cm (1–4in) of water.

Cotula coronopifolia (4), brass buttons, is good in small pools. It's a self-seeding annual, so once you have it, new plants reappear in the same spot each year. A neat clump, 15cm (6in) high, with flowers like daisies without petals – just the yellow boss in the middle.

Iris laevigata (5), Japanese water iris, flowers throughout June with large, single or semi-double, blue or white 'flags'. The rest of the time, clumps of upright, 45cm (18in) long, sword-shaped leaves make a background for the later flowers of other plants. Grow them in mud, or in up to 8cm (3in) of water.

Lobelia cardinalis (6), the cardinal flower, is a wet-loving version of the well-known bedding plant; but it's nothing like it. This grows to 90 × 60cm (3 × 2ft), with spikes of cardinal-red flowers in August and September; the cultivar 'Queen Victoria' is similar, but 60cm (2ft) taller and proportionately wider, with dark red flowers and beetroot red leaves – there aren't many pond plants this colourful. Grow them in mud, or in up to 8cm (3in) of water, but be prepared to lose them in winter in a cold area; neither is totally hardy.

1 *Butomus umbellatus.*
2 *Sagittaria sagittifolia.*
3 *Typha minima.*
4 *Cotula coronopifolia.*
5 *Iris laevigata.*
6 *Lobelia* 'Queen Victoria'.

Deep-water aquatics

These are plants that grow in much deeper water, so stand their baskets on the bottom of the pond a little way out from the banks. Some deep-water plants grow up out of the water, but others have leaves that float on the surface.

Aponogeton distachyos (1), water hawthorn, has long, oval leaves, like stretched waterlily pads, that float on the water, and odd-shaped clusters of white flowers that stick up just above the surface and look like mouthfuls of pearly-white sharks' teeth – a sort of friendly 'Jaws'. Water hawthorn is a brilliant all-round water plant; it's the first to start flowering each year and the last to stop. It's in business from April to October and it's also perfumed – the flowers have a strong scent of May blossom that, on still summer evenings, is strong enough to carry past the edge of the pond and fill the air with fragrance. At about 60cm (2ft) across, water hawthorn is small enough for even the tiniest ponds, as long as there's at least 30cm (1ft) of water. Don't submerge it more than 60cm (2ft) deep.

Orontium aquaticum (2), golden club, looks like a plant that can't quite make up its mind whether to lie flat on the water or stick out, so some leaves do one thing and the rest do the other. The flowers look like gold-tipped, white birthday-cake candles poking up out of the water in April and May. The leaves grow in a circle about 45cm (18in) in diameter. Give it 30cm (1ft) of water to grow in.

***Zantedeschia aethiopica* 'Crowborough'** (3) is the best of the arum lilies for growing outdoors; it's hardier than most. When it's grown in a pond, it can be left outside all year, since 15cm (6in) of water over the crown is enough to insulate it from frost. It has large, arrowhead-shaped leaves and big white spathes that appear on and off throughout the summer. It grows about 60 × 45cm (24 × 18in).

1 *Aponogeton distachyos.*
2 *Orontium aquaticum.*
3 *Zantedeschia aethiopica*
'Crowborough'.

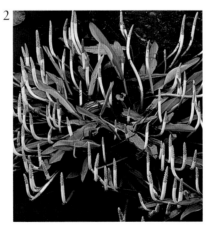

Waterlilies

Waterlilies are just another type of deep-water aquatic, with floating leaves and roots growing in a planting basket on the bottom of the pond, but because they are so popular there is a huge choice. If you've ever read *The Tales of Beatrix Potter*, you'll have a soft spot for waterlilies. I still can't look at a lily pad without thinking of Mr Jeremy Fisher.

The things to check before buying a waterlily are the spread and the planting depth, or you can come a cropper. Many waterlilies were bred about a century ago, when people had large lakes to accommodate them – cramped into a modern garden pond, they'd be crawling up the walls after a couple of years. If yours is a small pond, 1.2 × 2m (4 × 6ft) or less, with 60cm (2ft) of water to stand a waterlily in, these would be my top three. Don't get carried away because, in a pond that size, one waterlily is all you'll have room for. If you want a white one – and I would – that's a problem. Most grow too big for a small pond, and the dwarf white *N. pygmaea* 'Helvola' is probably too small. About 45cm (18in) across, it's very free flowering and has attractively marbled leaves. If you have a spot where it won't be swamped by more vigorous plants and where there'll be 15–25cm (6–10in) of water over the crown, try it.

Nymphaea **'James Brydon'** (4) has purple-splashed leaves and double, bright orange-red flowers, and it's one of the most prolific you can find for a small pond, making a circle of leaves 90cm (3ft) across.

Nymphaea **'Froebelii'** (5) has darker red flowers that are more bowl-shaped and it also grows to 90cm (3ft) across.

Nymphaea **'Laydekeri Liliacea'** (6) has pale pink flowers and bronze-marbled leaves; it'll spread about 60cm (2ft) across and has slightly smaller flowers than the other two.

> ### The right spot for waterlilies
>
> *Waterlilies are quite fussy plants. They won't grow under the spray from a fountain, or in moving water, so forget about combining them with fountains and waterfalls – it just won't wash. And if you try to grow them somewhere they aren't in full sun all day, they won't flower – but get it right, and you are on to a winner because a decent waterlily will flower all summer once it's had a year or two to become properly established.*

4 *Nymphaea* 'James Brydon'.
5 *N.* 'Froebelii'.
6 *N.* 'Laydekeri Liliacea'.

If you have a large expanse of water, you can really pack in the plants and still see the water beneath.

Oxygenators

Oxygenators are plants that live under the water, and their job is to provide the oxygen that is needed by fish and other pond-life, who also use the ferny stems of 'water-weeds', as they are often called, to hide and breed in.

Some oxygenators are far too vigorous for a small pond, and fill it with slippery stems that you then have to weed out regularly in summer. Really and truly, the most common one, *Lagarosiphon major*, comes into this category, but it's the one that is sold everywhere. It's evergreen, so instead of dying down in winter, like most of the others, it stays put and provides valuable hiding places for fish. It's also one of the first to get its feet under the table when you set up a new pond, so I'd bear with it. Just drop two or three of the weighted bundles they sell at pond centres into the water and they'll root just as they are. It's also called *Elodea crispa*, but for heaven's sake, don't be palmed off with the Canadian pond weed, *E. canadensis* – it really is a monster.

Eleocharis acicularis (**1**), hair grass, is exceptionally well-behaved. Grow it in small pots or in the silt on the bottom of a pond. It looks just like tufts of green hair, 15cm (6in) high and spreads slowly, to maybe 30cm (1ft) across, so you can leave it ticking away without having to worry about underwater weeding. In water 15–30cm (6–12in) deep; it's just about evergreen in winter.

Ranunculus aquatilis (**2**), water crowfoot, is a much better-looking oxygenator, because its 'working' parts, which look like swirling green threads, are under the water. On the surface, it grows as a buttercup-like plant with branching stems, floating leaves and single, white, yellow-centred flowers in May and June. It's not a big plant, maybe 60–90cm (2–3ft) across, so you shouldn't have problems with it in your average small pond.

1 *Eleocharis acicularis.*
2 *Ranunculus aquatilis.*
3 *Eichhornia crassipes.*
4 *Hydrocharis morsus-ranae.*
5 *Stratiotes aloides.*

1

2

Floating plants

Free-floating plants are a good way of providing instant shade for the surface of a new pond, before newly planted waterlilies and water hawthorn have had time to fill out and cover their rightful area. Some floating plants are not hardy and die off completely in winter, but some are natives that duck down in winter, then reappear each spring. They all look fascinating, but don't be surprised if they all end up at the far end of the pond when it's windy, as they don't have any anchors.

Eichhornia crassipes (3), water hyacinth, is a tropical plant that is killed by frost, so it's no good putting it out until June or so, as cold weather tends to blacken the edges. In a warm summer, its leaf rosettes make small knobbly clumps rather like leafy rafts, but don't expect to see any flowers; our climate isn't warm enough. Should that put you off growing it? No; because it is a fun plant, and children will love dissecting its foam-packed floatation chambers.

Hydrocharis morsus-ranae (4), frogbit, is a British native water plant that looks just like a minute waterlily, with leaves 2.5cm (1in) across and white, three-petalled flowers which are about the same size as the leaves. By midsummer, the original plants have produced 'pups', which grow strung together by fine strands. They spend winter as resting buds in the silt on the floor of the pond, and reappear late next spring.

Stratiotes aloides (5), water soldier, is another native Briton, this time making big spiky tufts, which are its chief attraction. Again a novelty that sinks to the bottom of the pond in winter, and gradually rises to the surface once more as the water warms up in spring.

How many plants?

Plants with floating leaves help to keep the water cool and provide some cover for pond-life, which is vital for keeping the ecology of the whole pond in balance.

You need to plant enough of these so that by the time they have had a couple of years to establish themselves, they cover between a third and a half of the pond's surface with foliage by midsummer. Use the sizes given here to help calculate how many you need for a pond of any size.

3

4

5

Bog gardens

Out in the countryside, natural ponds are often surrounded by boggy areas, where drifts of water-loving wild flowers form a natural backdrop to the water. At home, it instinctively feels right to make a bog garden next to a pond. A bog garden is also the answer to landscaping trouble-spots, such as natural hollows where water gathers, and other places where the soil always stays wet.

A bog garden has a lushness about it which few other parts of the garden can match.

Making a bog garden on wet ground

When you have a patch of ground that never really dries out, the very easiest way to tackle it is to turn it into a bog garden. All you do is dig in lots of well-rotted garden compost, manure, or some bags of composted bark, to improve the soil and make it richer and more fertile. Then, you put in plants that are natural moisture-lovers. Maintenance is simple. Mulch heavily each spring with more compost or bark. This tops up nutrients and helps prevent the ground drying out in summer, when the water table will be at its lowest. Sprinkle a spot of organic general feed around at the same time. That's all there is to it.

Since most bog plants are perennials, it's not difficult to have a bog garden that looks wonderful in spring, summer and early autumn, but there won't be much to see in winter unless you add a bit of window dressing. Chunky tree stumps, white birch logs and other boggy paraphenalia all help. If space permits, I'd strongly suggest putting in a framework of wet-loving shrubs that will look their best in winter, such as red-stemmed dogwood (*Cornus alba* 'Sibirica') and scarlet willow (*Salix alba* subsp. vitellina 'Britzensis).

Round the edge of a sunken bog garden, it's worth planting resilient shrubs, such as birches, cultivated elders, (try *Sambucus nigra* f. *laciniata*, with cut leaves and great autumn colour), or shallow-rooted evergreens. They'll make a bit more of a background and emphasize the amphitheatre feel.

Where the ground is slightly higher, it'll also be better drained and a tad drier, so you don't have to worry about sticking to real bog plants round the rim – just don't go for plants that actually need sharp drainage.

Making a bog garden where it's not boggy

When you want to make a bog garden where the ground is not naturally wet, it takes a lot more effort.

For a start, you need to treat the project a bit like making a pond, except you don't need to be quite as fussy. Dig a hole 60cm (2ft) deep and 1–1.2m (3–4ft) across, with sloping sides. Then line it. There's no need to buy proper pond liner – any old polythene will do. It doesn't even matter if there are the few odd holes in it – if you use a good sheet of new plastic, you need to stab a few drainage holes in it with a knife anyway. It's easiest to do when the liner is in place; just stand inside and make a dozen holes in a band all round and just above the bottom, so that water sits in the bottom of the hole, but can leak out if it gets too deep.

On normal soil, you don't even need enough plastic to reach right up the sides of the hole, but if you have very free-draining, light, sandy soil, it's worth doing to reduce sideways movement of water, which will soon drain your 'bog' in dry weather.

When you've dug your hole, refill it after mixing lots of organic matter with the soil you originally took out. Then plant with moisture-lovers and mulch as before.

Making a bog garden next to a pond

If you are making a bog garden right next to a pond, there's one thing you *must* do and that is keep the two features separate. There's one big difference between bog garden and pond conditions – bog plants need fertile soil, while the very last thing a pond wants is nutrients in the water.

Construct your bog garden 30cm (1ft) or more away from the pond. Make sure that the edge of the bog garden is a little bit lower than the rim of the pond – that way, in case of heavy rain, the pond overflows into the bog and not vice versa.

If you have enough room and it suits the layout of that part of the garden, then separate the two with a path. You'll find it very handy for getting at both bog and pond when you're working on them, without stepping in either.

Bog plants

'Bog plants' is simply a term for herbaceous perennials that are happy growing in permanently wet or damp soil.

You can often get away with growing the sort of marginal pond plants that will put up with growing in mud – which is what the plant labels mean when they say 0cm/0in of water – as long as you reserve the very wettest spots for them. But most damp-loving perennials can be grown in both a proper bog garden and a damp border, just as long as the ground doesn't dry out badly in summer.

Always check plant sizes before you buy, as a lot of bog plants grow enormous and, even if you are making a big bog garden, do include some smaller plants towards the front, otherwise all you'll see is a sea of stalks.

Small bog plants

These are the ones to go for in small bog gardens and at the edges of larger ones, especially if they're close to a pond; you don't want lots of leaves and dead flowers falling in to pollute the pond water.

Mimulus cardinalis (**1**) has orange-red, mask-shaped flowers that cover upright, 45cm (18in) tall clumps, from midsummer to autumn. It is borderline hardy so think of it as moisture-loving bedding – if it survives winter, it's a bonus. The original plants creep slightly, but it'll also self-seed gently, so you don't usually lose it entirely.

Lysimachia nummularia '**Aurea**' (**2**), golden creeping Jenny, looks like rows of gold coins strung together and laid on the ground. It has golden-yellow flowers all summer. It'll cover an area roughly 60cm (2ft) across in summer, and it's only 5cm (2in) high. The foliage colour is brightest in sun; in light shade, it's lime green.

1 *Mimulus cardinalis*.
2 *Lysimachia nummularia* 'Aurea'.
3 *Hosta* 'Gold Standard'.
4 *Houttuynia cordata* 'Chameleon'.
5 *Primula rosea*.

Hostas (3) are grown mainly for their large, blue-green, golden green, or variegated leaves. There are dozens that grow to around the 30–45cm (12–18in) mark. The shorter kinds can be dotted evenly around as ground cover, while clumps of larger types are good for between patches of summer-flowering perennials. The flowers of most hostas are subtle – spikes of off-white or bluish-mauve bells in early summer, though in some they are quite handsome. They are brilliant plants for growing in light dappled shade, but as long as the ground stays damp, they'll also tolerate a fair bit of sun.

Hostas are slow to spread, so you don't usually need to divide them for 5–6 years. It often takes them a year or two to settle down afterwards, so don't do it until you really need to. The things you must worry about when you grow hostas are slugs and snails; given half a chance, they reduce the plants to lace doilies overnight.

***Houttuynia cordata* 'Chameleon'** (4) is a 15cm (6in) high scrambler with ivy-shaped leaves, variegated in cream, red and green. It doesn't appear above ground until early summer, but soon spreads to make a ground-covering mat, 90cm (3ft) or more across. The flowers, in midsummer, are single and white with a yellow cone in the middle, but there aren't many of them and they're not the main attraction. It creeps by underground stems, so it's an easy plant to divide.

Primula rosea (5) is one of the very early-flowering bog plants, with shocking pink flowers, but in March, you are grateful for anything with that much punch. It's a tiny plant about 15cm (6in) high, so plant it in groups for impact. The leaves are soon swallowed up by neighbouring plants and it disappears in summer; mark the spot so you don't hoe it out.

3

4

5

Medium-sized bog plants

Plants in the 60–90cm (2–3ft) range aren't usually too big or spreading to rule them out for smaller bog gardens, where one of each is going to be enough. In a big bog garden, grow them in groups so that they'll make a bigger splash.

Astilbes (**1**) enjoy the same conditions as hostas and the two contrast well with each other. Astilbes make rather upright clumps with ferny foliage and plumes of fluffy flowers in mauve, purple, red, pink or white. Again sizes vary according to cultivar, but one that's always popular is 'Fanal', which grows to about 60 × 45cm (24 × 18in), with deep red flowers.

***Lythrum salicaria* 'Blush'** (**2**) is an improved form of the wild purple loosestrife – non-invasive, and with delicate, soft pink spikes on 1–1.2m (3–4ft) tall, bushy plants. If you don't have room for anything as big as 'Blush', then go for *Lythrum virgatum* 'The Rocket', which is a really neat upright clump, 60 × 60cm (2 × 2ft), with bolt upright, pink flowers like candles. Both of them flower from early to late summer.

1 *Astilbe × arendsii*.
2 *Lythrum salicaria* 'Blush'.
3 *Primula florindae*.
4 *Iris sibirica* 'Butter and Sugar'.
5 *Lysimachia clethroides*.

Primulas (3) are plants I'd never want to be without in a bog garden, but you have to choose the right ones. *P. florindae* is the giant cowslip, growing to 60 × 60cm (2 × 2ft), which has big, primrose-like leaves and stems topped by a shaggy head of nodding, yellow 'cowslip' flowers in July. The candelabra primulas are positively architectural, with their tiers of flowers; *P. pulverulenta* has 60–90cm (2–3ft) spikes of deep red flowers in June. *P. japonica* is similar, but about half the height and with crimson-red or white flowers in May. If you want a mixed bunch, the 'Harlow Carr Hybrids' take some beating – everything from glowing orange to shocking pink and rich crimson.

Iris sibirica (4) is the one to choose for bog gardens, which aren't quite wet enough for true water Irises like *Iris laevigata*. It's perfectly happy where the soil is just moist. It has upright stems and narrow leaves that look like stiff grass, and flowers between late spring and early summer. I fancy 'Butter and Sugar', which has yellow and white flowers that remind me of raw cake mixture.

Lysimachia clethroides (5) is an unusual loosestrife, growing in 90 × 75cm (3 × 2½ft) clumps, with arching, buddleia-like cones of white flowers at the top of rather upright stems, from late summer to autumn. It's quite a class act in comparison with the rampant yellow loosestrife (*L. punctata*).

Candelabra primulas of the 'Harlow Carr Hybrids' strain growing by the pond at Barleywood.

6 EDIBLE GARDENS

Growing your own

It's a real treat to wander out into the garden with a trug on Sunday morning to pick a few fresh vegetables for lunch, or to pop out after work to collect some salad for supper. It's also very convenient when you live miles from the shops, as we do.

'Growing your own' gives you a tremendous feeling of achievement and, even if you are short of space, it's still worthwhile cultivating your favourites because they taste so much better when you eat them within minutes of being picked.

Home-grown vegetables need not be grown in traditional allotment rows – they can be arranged in formal patterns.

For the flavour and feel-good factor, I can't recommend organic vegetable gardening strongly enough, even if you aren't so particular elsewhere. Yes, it means getting the hang of a few new techniques, but it's not difficult – and for anyone who likes to know what's happened to their food before they eat it, it's essential.

What's worth growing yourself and what's not

Don't even think about trying to grow everything. Unless you are a total enthusiast with time on your hands and plenty of room, life's too short to be truly self-sufficient and you'd just fill the garden with everyday stuff that, frankly, you might just as well buy at the shops.

No, what's really worth growing at home are unusual crops, and those that taste best picked and eaten straight from the garden. If you are short of time, don't take on more than you can manage – concentrate on a few quick, compact crops that you have time to grow well. That's much better than being forced to watch beds full of veg being ruined by neglect.

Won't it look awful?

Contrary to what a lot of people still think, growing things to eat doesn't have to mean turning the garden into a tip. Nowadays, it is fashionable to grow edible crops in ways that look good.

Even in a tiny space, you can grow worthwhile crops in tubs, growing bags or a small raised bed, or go for serious productivity in intensive deep beds. Where there's more room, a conventional vegetable patch can be as much of a feature as a flower bed – just add ornamental edging or a hint of architecture, and go for vegetables that are naturally more decorative. Most garden centres and mail-order seed catalogues stock golden courgettes (such as 'Gold Rush), purple French beans (try 'Purple Teepee', 'Royalty' or 'Purple Queen'), red lettuces with fringed or oak-shaped leaves, yellow tomatoes ('Sungold' or 'Golden Sunrise'), red-leaved beetroot ('Detroit Crimson Globe'), and blue pumpkins (Crown Prince), all of which taste as good, if not better, than the normal kinds.

Practical points

To grow veg, fruit or salads, you need deep, rich, well-drained soil and a sunny situation. The trouble is, when you are trying to fit a veg plot into an existing garden, you usually have to make the most of the space available.

If the soil isn't too special, there's quite a bit you can do to improve it. On poor, light soil, dig in lots of well-rotted organic matter – a barrowful per square metre/yard isn't too much. With clay soil, add organic matter *and* work in gritty horticultural sand at about a bucketful per square metre/yard. If the ground has a few inches of fairly good soil over impenetrable clay, stones or chalk, digging is not the answer – it just brings more rubbish to the surface. Instead, pile organic matter thickly on top.

Shade isn't easy to alleviate. You can thin out surrounding trees or shrubs to let more light in, but if the only available space is shady, don't waste your time trying to produce roots or fruiting crops – they'll never do well there. Stick to leafy kinds; brassicas, lettuce, sorrel and rocket, which will cope. Most herbs will grow in light shade, though connoisseurs say they don't develop their full flavour without sun – I don't agree. But see if there isn't somewhere sunny that you could grow a few crops, even in tubs or beds.

Start thinking of vegetables as ornamental plants and suddenly they can take on a dual role.

Little and often

The secret of good veg growing is to put in time little and often, so you keep on top of weeds and any problem pests and diseases. You can't 'catch up' all in one frantic weekend, just before you expect to be picking, because the odds are that your veg will have vanished by then. And anyway, a little light pottering is the best kind of gardening.

Deep beds enable plenty of vegetables to be packed into a small space.

Deep beds

Deep beds, popularised by my old friend, Geoff Hamilton, are a very intensive way of growing a lot of veg in a small space by growing them much closer together than usual in deeply worked, compost-rich soil, where the roots can penetrate a long way.

Making deep beds is hard work initially, as you have to dig out one trench at a time to about two spades' depth and back-fill it with a mixture of compost and topsoil, then move on till you've covered the bed – but you only do it once, and the results really pay off. You don't do much hoeing because crops are close-planted to smother out weeds. At the end of the season, there's no winter digging to do – just rake off rubbish and roughly fork the surface over after spreading more organic matter over it, the same as you do when you are replanting vacant rows during the growing season.

The reason deep beds work so well is because the soil never gets compressed – you work from paths either side. The soil stays fluffy and roots can burrow through it easily. Most people make deep beds 1.2m (4ft) wide, so you can work without stepping on the soil, and 3m (10ft) long, so you don't take short cuts across the middle.

Traditional plots

The usual way to grow vegetables is in rows, at the spacing recommended on the back of the seed packets and in reference books. With this method, you leave wide soil paths between rows of crops because you need to walk through your crops to work. There's more hoeing to do, as weeds come up on the paths, and the soil needs digging over properly at the end of the season, not just to work in more organic matter, but also to fluff up the soil, as the paths get seriously squashed down.

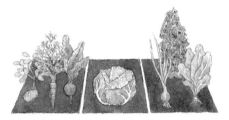

Root vegetables Brassicas   Salads, peas,
                                beans, onions

What about crop rotation?

If you grow vegetables the traditional way, you should practise crop rotation. The idea is to divide your patch into three and grow each of the three main groups – root veg, brassicas (the cabbage family), and salad crops, plus peas, beans and onions – in its own area. Each year, you move everything on to the next space so that the same crop never grows in the same ground more than one year in three. This way, each type of crop receives exactly the right soil preparation, each benefits from whatever the last crop has left in the ground, and there is less risk of plants picking up root diseases from a previous crop.

Salads, peas,   Root vegetables Brassicas
beans, onions

Crop rotation is certainly a good thing to do if you have an allotment or other large-scale veg patch but, it has to be said, that with today's small modern gardens it isn't always that practical. If you don't have a plot that can conveniently be divided into three, or you don't want to grow veg from all three groups, then my advice would be to forget it. Just avoid growing the same type of plant in the same bit of ground two years running, and don't try to grow root crops on ground that has had a good dose of manure in the last six months, which just makes them fork. You'll be very unlucky to run into problems, and if you do, just grow something else.

Brassicas   Salads, peas,   Root vegetables
                  beans, onions

Getting organized

Even if you don't go in for crop rotation, it's a good idea to plan what you'll be putting in where. It helps make the best use of the space – you won't have ground that doesn't produce anything for ages, then have three rows of lettuce that all need eating at once.

Divide a piece of paper into columns, one for each container, bed, or block of space, and list in each one what you want to grow there. Start at the beginning of the veg growing calendar, and show what will occupy each bit of ground through the season. Bear in mind that some crops, such as Brussels sprouts, take a whole growing season to mature, while others, such as lettuce, take only 3–4 months. You don't have to follow it slavishly, but it's a start.

Routine jobs

The veg growing year has quite a soothing routine to it. Autumn, winter or early spring is when you prepare the ground. Spring is the main sowing and planting time. Then, in summer, as you finish up fast-growing early crops, you clear away the remains and put something else into the gap as soon as you can. The last seeds or plants will be going in around July or early August, although if you have gaps between your winter brassicas and leeks in the autumn, you can plant overwintering onion sets to keep the ground fully employed – they'll be ready to eat by the following June.

The basic jobs of sowing, thinning and transplanting are the same regardless of which veg you are growing.

Sow veg seeds thinly in shallow drills made with the tip of a cane, or the corner of a Dutch hoe, held against a taut garden line.

The soil must be really well prepared and well nourished. Cover small seeds to a depth of no more than 6mm (¼in), and large ones, such as beans, to their own depth. On grotty clay soil, it's best to cover seeds with a sprinkling of horticultural vermiculite or seed compost, instead of soil. They'll come up better and faster. Remember not to sow root crops in ground that has been manured within the last six months.

Thin out seedlings to 2.5–5cm (1–2in) apart when they first come up, while they are easy to handle, then thin them again to their final spacing a few weeks later. You can transplant seedlings that are to be moved elsewhere when they are big enough to handle. Don't transplant root crops – it makes the roots split or the plants run to seed prematurely, and with carrots, the aroma you release will attract carrot fly.

Hoe between rows of veg regularly to stop weeds swamping your crops. It's easiest to do when you can barely see the weeds germinating; if you wait till they have a good hold, you need to hand weed with a trowel, which takes a lot longer.

Water veg regularly in dry spells, and feed long-stay crops, such as courgettes, brassicas, leeks and tomatoes, several times during the growing season. You can either sprinkle general-purpose organic fertilizer between the rows and water it in, or you can use diluted liquid feed that you put on with your watering can, aiming the stream at the roots. Don't get feed onto leaves, as it can scorch them. If you do, wash it off with plain water.

To draw a seed drill, position a taut garden line on the soil, stand on it and draw the corner of a Dutch hoe along it in short bursts to make a furrow of the required depth.

Gather crops frequently and while they are young and tender – there is no pleasure in eating big toughies.

Control pests and diseases organically. Pick off blackfly, greenfly and caterpillars by hand any time you see them. Cover brassica and carrot plants with very fine woven mesh to screen out cabbage root fly, cabbage white butterflies, and carrot fly. Grow disease-resistant varieties whenever you can. 'Fly Away' or 'Sytan' are carrot varieties resitant to carrot fly, 'Trixie' for clubroot-free calabrese, avoid rust in leeks with 'Toledo' or 'Porvite' and keep viruses in courgettes at bay with 'Tarmino' or 'Defender'. Encourage beneficial insects, which prey on insect pests, by planting nectar-rich flowers, such as French marigold (*Tagetes patula*), poached egg flower (*Limnanthes douglasii*), and *Phacelia tanacetifolia*.

Gather crops little and often without waiting for a whole row to be ready, or you won't be able to use them all in time and some will go to waste. I find keeping hens a good solution to sudden gluts – they appreciate the varied diet, and it does wonders for the eggs.

Protect very early or late crops with a row of cloches, or use the economical modern equivalent – cover them over with sheets of horticultural fleece.

Traditional vegetables

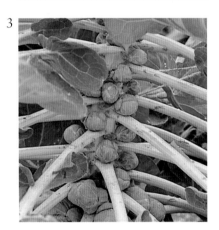

1 Onions.
2 Leeks.
3 Brussels sprout 'Maximus'.
4 Beetroot.
5 Carrots 'Early Nantes'.
6 Potatoes 'Pink Fir Apple'.

There are lots of essential vegetables you might want to grow that aren't decorative enough to show off in a trendy potager or in pots on the patio; they are the ones to pack into your intensive deep bed if you want maximum output for minimum input – or just grow in a traditional veg plot down the garden or on the allotment.

Onions and spring onions (1) are easiest grown from sets, which are like tiny dry baby onions that you push down into well-prepared soil in rows, about 15cm (6in) apart, in March. There's no thinning out: all you do is keep them hoed. Most people who sow them from seed, do so in the greenhouse and prick out the seedlings into pots to plant out in spring when they are big enough to see properly; the tiny seedlings look like grass and are easily lost in the garden. If you must, sow seed in shallow drills and thin the seedlings to 15cm (6in). Spring onions are sown outside in the same way, but for regular pullings sow every three weeks from March to July. Or be crafty and sow for dual-purpose – use the thinnings as spring onions and leave the rest 15cm (6in) or so apart to grow into autumn bulb onions.

Leeks (2) are a lot easier than onions to grow well – you are less likely to clobber them with the hoe, and they produce more food from the same area. They are good all-purpose veg for the kitchen. Real leek-lovers need to grow two varieties, one for use before Christmas and another for afterwards, as the early kinds don't stand for long without rotting, and the lates don't bulk up early. Sow in shallow rows in March or April, and transplant when big enough to handle. Foodies might like fashionable baby leeks, so sow a row of 'King Richard' and don't transplant but thin them out to 2.5cm (1in) apart – they are ready once they reach pencil thickness, from July onwards.

Brussels sprouts (3) are the vegetables kids love to hate, but now there are sweeter varieties without the bitter taste. As with a lot of winter veg, you need to grow two varieties – an early and a late – if you want to pick from autumn to spring. Sow sprouts in a seed-bed in March or April, thin the seedlings out to 5cm (2in) apart, then, in May or June, transplant them to their final positions spacing them about 5cm (2in) apart. Sprouts need a rich, fertile soil that's been well manured, but the secret of growing hard, round, tight sprouts is to plant into very firm soil – tread it down well. Don't plant sprouts in a newly-prepared deep bed as the soil is too fluffy at first – wait till it's several years old so the ground settles. As the plants grow up, tie them to a stake, so they don't blow over in winter.

Beetroot (4) is making a come-back. Avoid sowing it too early or it may bolt; early varieties are designed to solve this problem, so sow them first, in late April; others in May and June. Sow thinly as traditional varieties have several seeds in each cluster, then thin to 10cm (4in) apart – don't try and transplant root crops or they will 'fork'. Choose from neat round varieties or tubular 'tankard' beet.

Carrots (5) need a deep, fine, well-drained soil; they dislike stodgy clay or stony ground. Stick to tried-and-tested varieties for reliable bulk. If you like designer veg look out for trendy white or yellow carrots, but if carrot fly are a problem grow a resitant variety, otherwise you'll need to cover the plants with fine insect-proof mesh to eliminate egg-laying adult flies. Avoid planting in recently manured ground or they will 'fork'. Sow the seed thinly along a shallow drill – early varieties in March, April and July, August for pulling as new baby carrots about 10-12 weeks later, and main seasons in March or April for pulling in late summer and autumn. They keep best in the ground, but if you can't use them all before the ground turns claggy, they can be dug up and stored under cover.

Potatoes (6) for planting need to be proper seed potatoes bought from seed firms or the local garden centre – don't plant potatoes from the greengrocer as they can carry viruses. These days, old heritage spuds and show-winning varieties are widely available; look out for modern pest- and disease- resistant varieties if you've had problems before and prefer to grow veg organically. Plant potatoes in deep fertile soil, but not where you've recently dug in organic matter or you're asking for problems with keeled slugs (the underground sort). Plant them in April, 13cm (5in) deep with 38cm (15in) between them in rows spaced 75cm (30in) apart. Plant second earlies in the first half of the month, and maincrops in the second half. It's not essential to let maincrop seed potatoes sprout before planting them in April, it's only the earlies you need to bother with.

Recommended varieties

Onions – 'Ailsa Craig' a large reliable favourite; 'Red Baron' red-purple skin.

Spring onions – 'White Lisbon' a reliable favourite; 'Redmate' red-purple variety to grow as spring onions or as bulbs.

Leeks – 'King Richard' early; 'Toledo' late rust-resistant; 'Musselburgh' a winter favourite.

Beetroot – 'Boltardy' round, bolt-resistant; 'Cylindra' large tubular shaped beetroot.

Carrots – 'Autumn King' reliable variety; 'Early Nantes' early; 'Yellowstone' yellow roots; 'Kuttiger' white roots.

Brussels sprouts – 'Peer Gynt' use till Christmas; 'Trafalgar' ready from Christmas; 'Icarus' child-friendly bitter-free variety.

Potatoes – 'Edzell Blue' blue-skinned heritage variety for roasting or mashing; 'Kerr's Pink' heavy cropper for baking or roasting; 'Sante' good pest and disease resistance ideal for organic growing; 'Pink Fir Apple' late gourmet salad variety.

4

5

6

Ornamental vegetables

1 Runner bean 'Painted Lady'.
2 Sweetcorn 'Sweet Nugget'.
3 Courgette 'Ambassador'.
4 Mangetout Sugar Snap.
5 Pumpkin Rouge vif d'etamps.
6 Black Tuscany kale.

If you don't have a traditional veg patch, you can still grow useful amounts of mainstream crops in the garden. Try growing groups of tall veg in borders with flowers around them, or train climbing crops up obelisks, on trellis or over arches. Or how about an ornamental potager, based on a circle or octagon and divided into segments with a different crop in each. Put an obelisk in the middle for climbing beans, and surround with a dwarf edging of herbs. Following William Morris's dictum, it's both useful *and* beautiful.

Climbing French and runner beans (**1**) do well on trellis and arches, and can also be grown in a trough against the patio wall, given some netting or trellis to climb up. The flowers are similar to sweet peas, though in fewer colours – just red, pink or white. Runners are the beans to grow for quantity – they're very productive and you can keep picking from the same plants all summer. Go for a stringless cultivar, or pick them when still tender, at 10–15cm (4–6in) long; don't let them grow huge. Climbing French beans are usually thought to have the finer flavour, but they run out of steam at half time so, for beans all summer, make a second sowing to follow on. Neither is frost-hardy – don't put plants out until late May.

Sweetcorn (**2**) is another good-looking edible crop that is fun to grow, but it's no good for containers, and not worth dotting around in a border. Because sweetcorn is pollinated by the wind, the only way to be certain of corn cobs setting properly is to grow a decent-sized block of it. Still, you can grow them either in a decorative vegetable patch or potager, where it makes a good centrepiece to a geometric design, or you can grow it in a conventional veg patch. Raise plants in the same way as pumpkins and courgettes, though you can sometimes buy them in May – don't put them out until any risk of frost has passed.

Courgettes (**3**) are very easy to grow – sun, fertile soil, a bit of fertilizer and plenty of water. These days, most are bush cultivars that make a mound of leaves with the fruit tucked away in the middle. Sow seeds in a frost-free greenhouse in mid-April and plant out after the last frost. Bush kinds can be grown in 38cm (15in) tubs, or in growing bags on the patio. Those with golden fruit are more ornamental than the green ones, which are better in a veg patch. They are terrifically productive, if you keep cutting the courgettes regularly – turn your back for a day or two, and suddenly you have giant marrows. Don't despair – stuff 'em with savoury mince.

Mangetout and sugar snaps (4) are peas you eat complete with their pods; 6–12 plants give a worthwhile crop from a small space. Grow them up twiggy sticks in the veg patch, or in troughs on the patio against a not-too-hot wall with netting or trellis for support. For an early crop, sow seed in pots in a greenhouse in March and plant them out during a mild spell in April. Or sow where you want the plants to crop in late April – you'll need to make several sowings between then and early July to keep yourself in mangetouts all summer.

Pumpkins and squashes (5) look spectacular and, if you stick to those with smaller fruit, there is no problem with letting them scramble up trellis and obelisks, though they need tying up. Large-fruited sorts are too heavy to grow this way – they need to run along the ground, but they look good growing over a bank. Squash and pumpkin plants are fast-growing vines with spiny stems and big, prickly-backed leaves; they need regular watering and heavy feeding, but they are fun to grow and children love them. Sow them like courgettes. Summer squashes are ready to eat, like courgettes, when they are big enough, but winter cultivars need to ripen on the plants and are ready to pick in late September.

Brassicas (6) look wonderful in a potager with nasturtiums or annuals to attract beneficial insects, especially if you go for the pretty ones, such as red cabbage, purple kale, red-leaved Brussels sprouts, or the Black Tuscany kale with frilly leaves of darkest green. These taste as good as they look. Don't confuse them with ornamental cabbages and kales sold for winter bedding; they aren't worth eating. To grow your own brassicas, sow seeds in drills in well-prepared ground in April or May and transplant seedlings to their final positions when they're a good size, 6–8 weeks later.

Recommended varieties

Climbing French beans – '*Hunter' flat beans; 'Cobra' pencil beans; **runner beans** – 'Desiree' white flowers, stringless; 'Sunset' pink flowers, early.*

Sweetcorn – 'Honey Bantam Bicolor' supersweet yellow and white kernels; 'Sundance' good for poor summers.

Courgettes – green 'All Green Bush'; golden – 'Gold Rush'.

*Mangetout – 'Oregon Sugar Pod'; **sugarsnaps** – 'Sugar Snap'.*

*Pumpkins – 'Atlantic Giant' for size; **summer squashes** – 'Patty Pan' greenish-white; 'Sunburst' yellow; **winter squashes** – 'Butternut' beige tubular squash.*

*Red cabbage – 'Red Drumhead'; 'Red Jewel'; 'Red Winner'; **purple kale** – 'Redbor' crinkly; **red sprouts** – 'Falstaff'; 'Red Delicious'.*

4

5

6

Salads

If you never grow any other edibles, a salad bed is one thing you shouldn't be without. From an area no more than 2m × 60cm (6 × 2ft), you can pick enough salads to keep a small family well stocked for most of the season. If you don't have a veg patch, make a small raised bed, or use a packing crate as a large container.

Salad leaves

Fertile ground and constant moisture are essential for salads to grow quickly and stay succulent and tasty. If they run short of water, or suffer a check, they'll bolt or fail to heart-up properly, and be tough and bitter to eat. Sow salad leaves in short rows and thin seedlings, first to 2.5cm (1in) apart, and later to the final spacing. Use the small plants you pull out as salad leaves. Clear the ground when you've cut the whole row, remove debris and work in a little organic feed. Then sow or plant the next batch straight away to keep the ground fully occupied. To extend the growing season, cover early spring and late autumn crops with horticultural fleece, or a row of cloches, to protect them from the weather.

Lamb's lettuce (1), or corn salad, are small plants, like compact 5cm (2in) lettuces. The flavour is like a very superior lettuce. Sow it in early spring, and again between August and September for late crops. It's small and fast growing, so it's ready in weeks – cut the whole rosette. The thinnings also make very good salad.

Chicory and endive (2) can be tricky to grow – they don't heart up as reliably as lettuce. Different types vary in sowing times, so check the back of the packet – most are sown in early summer for eating in autumn. Thin or transplant to leave the plants about 20cm (8in) apart. Non-forcing types of chicory should form a heart naturally towards the end of their growing season. Endive makes a loose, open head rather than a tight heart, and tastes bitter unless you blanch it. Cover each plant with an upturned bucket for a week or two before cutting. Watch out for snails; they enjoy blanched endive.

Salad rocket (3) has a hot, peppery taste. Sow a short row any time from April to July, thin to 8cm (3in) apart, and pick a few leaves when they're big enough, leaving the plant to grow on. You can pick from the same plants all summer but, after flowering begins, rocket won't grow new leaves; that's the time to sow again.

Recommended varieties

Red lettuce – 'Lollo Rosso' very frilly; 'Blush' small iceberg type tinged red-bronze; oakleaf – long, decorative indented leaves; 'Cerize' red; 'Cocarde' red/yellow tinged, loose leaf; 'Funly' green frilly, red and green; 'Salad Bowl'; pick a few leaves and leave the rest to grow.

Cos lettuce – 'Little Gem' and 'Sherwood', both exceptionally well-flavoured mini cos; no need to tie up as you do the large cos lettuces.

Chicory – 'Sugar Loaf' green-hearting non-forcing winter-hardy; 'Pallo Rosso' round red radicchio; 'Rosso di Treviso' pointed red radicchio.

Endive – 'Frisee' finely divided and curly.

Lettuce (4) is the staple salad leaf for many, and most types can be sown from March to early August. The different types include: red, oak-leaved, the conventional green, hearting kind, loose-leaf lettuce that doesn't form a heart – just pick a few leaves at a time and leave the rest of the plant to keep growing – and the upright cos lettuce. 'Little Gem' is easier to grow than full-sized cos, which need tying up with raffia to make them heart up properly. To keep a constant supply all season, sow part of a row each time you thin the last batch. It works better than sowing every 2–3 weeks; lettuces grow faster in warm weather, so regular sowings catch up with each other. Space 20–30cm (8–12in) apart, depending on cultivar.

Oriental leaves (5) are dual-purpose plants, used cooked in stir-fries, and raw as salad leaves. Sow them in July and August. Use the thinnings for stir-fries or salads; the rest mature 6–8 weeks later. Chinese cabbages need time to form a heart – space them 25–30cm (10–12in) apart. Space the quicker-growing pak choi 15cm (6in) apart. The large, loose-leaf oriental veg, such as mizuna and mibuna, need 30–38cm (12–15in) of space. Watch out for slugs, snails and flea beetle; they're all fond of oriental leaves.

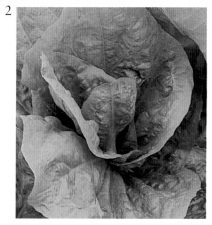

1 Lamb's lettuce.
2 Chicory.
3 Salad rocket.
4 Lettuce 'Little Gem'.
5 Oriental leaves.

Growing in containers

Growing veg in containers is just like growing bedding plants – treat them exactly the same way. Yes, really!

Choose good-looking and highly productive plants such as herbs, strawberries, climbing French or runner beans, tomatoes, courgettes or salad leaves. Hardy crops, such as strawberries and lettuces, can be planted in spring, but leave the tender kinds, such as tomatoes and French beans, until after the last frost, around the end of May.

Use any good brand of multi-purpose compost to fill the containers. After planting, water the veg to settle them in, and from then on, water often enough to keep the compost moist. This will probably mean every day when the weather is warm, but do the finger test if you want to be sure. A quick prod reveals all. Damp as a freshly wrung-out flannel? It's fine. A touch dusty? Water it. Four weeks after planting, the nutrients in the compost will have been used up, so start liquid feeding once a week at first, rising to twice weekly as the crops grow bigger and fill the pots. As salad leaves become big enough to eat, pick little and often so you don't denude the display overnight.

Provided the container is of adequate dimensions, most vegetables will be happy growing in a restricted space, just make sure they do not go short of food and water.

How to... **plant an edible hanging basket**

Hanging baskets make good use of space and they are a great way to stop slugs and snails swiping your crops. They'll look good and be productive too, which is very satisfying. Put them in an open spot with good light, but with some shelter from wind. You will have to feed and water a hanging basket regularly, as it contains only a limited amount of compost. And don't forget that hanging baskets dry out more quickly than ground-level pots because they're more exposed to the air and evaporation will be greater – water-retaining gel crystals help here. But because the basket is suspended, it will probably have better access to light all round than it would at ground level – and you don't even have to bend to pick. You could also try tumbling outdoor tomatoes in a hanging basket.

What you need

- *35cm (14in) diameter wire-framed hanging basket*
- *hanging basket liner*
- *medium-sized bag of multi-purpose compost*
- *water-retaining gel crystals, so it holds more water*
- *selection of small basil, parsley, coriander plants*
- *one trailing bush tomato or small-fruited outdoor cucumber plant*

1 Position the basket on an empty flowerpot so that it is stable. Put the liner in place and tuck its folds neatly together. All kinds of liner are available – from polythene to jute and organic matting materials. Avoid sphagnum moss which, like peat, needs to be conserved. The purpose of the liner is to prevent the compost falling through the mesh but also to help keep plant roots cool.

2 Add a little multipurpose compost mixed with water-retaining granules to the bottom of the basket. Water the plants well, then tap them out of their pots and position them so that their shoots emerge through the upper sides of the basket – you can push them through from the outside, squeezing the rootball, or the inside, carefully feeding the shoots through – whichever is easiest.

3 Add more compost and then plant the centre of the basket with more herbs and the trailing tomato plant or the cucumber. A small depression in the centre of the basket will allow for easier watering. Water the basket at least once a day and feed once a week with dilute liquid tomato feed during the summer.

Patio crops

Quite a few of the bushier vegetables make attractive patio plants; if you didn't know that they were edible crops, you'd think they were something exotic.

Colourful crops

Cucumbers, tomatoes and peppers occupy their pots all summer, but it's also worth considering shorter-term crops for the patio. Dwarf beans can be planted out from mid-May until late July – purple-podded ones are particularly attractive. They're about 30cm (1ft) high, and you'll fit a dozen in a 30cm (12in) pot, or fifteen in a 38cm (15in) tub. Feed and water them like bedding plants. When you've picked all the beans, pull out the old and put in some more.

New potatoes (**1**) are a good early crop in a 38cm (15in) tub. Plant tubers in February or March in a frost-free greenhouse, then put them out on the patio after the last frost. Or plant them outside in early April, 15cm (6in) deep. Kept fed and watered, they'll be ready to harvest in June – grow a pot of mint to go with them.

Recommended varieties

New potatoes – 'International Kidney' waxy textured early variety popularly known as 'Jersey Royal'; 'Red Duke of York' delicious heritage variety with yellow flesh; 'Swift' extra early 'early' good for starting in pots in the greenhouse.

Outdoor cucumbers – 'Crystal Apple' small round golden cucumbers; 'Burpless Tasty Green' digestible 12" mini-cues.

Sweet peppers – 'Bell Boy' traditional 'square' green variety ripening red; 'Redskin' dwarf variety good for pots.

Chillies – 'Habanero' short fat red and very fiery fruit; 'Cayenne' long thin red and mild.

Tomatoes – 'Tumbler' dwarf cascading plants for hanging baskets; 'Tornado' good doer in an iffy summer; 'Sungold' orange-gold cherry toms; 'Ildi' hundreds of tiny yellow cocktail sized toms; 'White Beauty' pale green toms that turn white then ripen to pale cream; 'Tangella' old bright orange variety; 'Tigerella' red and gold tiger-stripes.

Chilli peppers and other tender vegetables will enjoy the hot and sheltered conditions of a patio which will help them ripen their fruits.

Outdoor cucumbers (2) also enjoy patio conditions, and they are fast-growing and productive, so you should be picking a couple of cucumbers per plant from about June onwards. Don't worry about training and removing sideshoots, as you'd do if you grew them in a greenhouse. On the patio, cucumber plants look more decorative rambling over trellis, or tied up to an obelisk standing in the middle of their pot, sideshoots and all. That way they grow more, smaller, cucumbers, which are usually a lot more welcome than an occasional whopper. Feed and water cucumber plants the same as tomatoes and peppers.

Pepper and chilli (3) plants are very decorative, but all of them have green fruit at first – it's not till they ripen in late summer that they turn yellow, red or purple. Treat them exactly the same as bush tomatoes. They are slower growing and need more warmth, so you won't get a very big crop from plants grown outdoors – they are really only worth trying on the patio. You can grow aubergine plants the same way, if you have a really warm, sheltered, sunny spot outdoors, but they aren't worth bothering with otherwise.

Tomatoes (4) were originally brought to this country as decorative plants that nobody thought of eating. Now, you can get tomatoes with pink, gold or white fruits that are as tasty as the familiar red kinds, so they make a really colourful addition to the patio. They are easy to grow and, like other frost-tender crops, tomatoes benefit from the warmth and shelter of a sunny patio, which is the next best thing to being grown inside a greenhouse. Keep them well-watered and feed them once or twice a week with liquid tomato fertilizer. Don't overdo it on either score or you'll spoil the flavour and they'll make soft growth which is more susceptible to disease.

1 New potatoes.
2 Cucumber 'Burpless Tasty Green'.
3 Pepper.
4 Tomato 'Gardeners' Delight'.

How to... **grow outdoor tomatoes in pots**

Tomatoes are such a popular crop that you'll probably find lots of different cultivars on sale in the garden centre – and that's a lot easier than growing your own from seed. Look for outdoor cultivars – the indoor ones need a lot more warmth to ripen properly. They come in two kinds: upright or vine tomatoes for growing on a single stem, and bush tomatoes, which are – well – bushy. The bush ones are easier to grow outdoors and need no special training – the tomatoes appear at the end of every stem.

What you need

- *30–38cm (12–15in) pots*
- *broken crocks for drainage*
- *John Innes No. 2 potting compost*
- *1.2m (4ft) canes and soft twine*
- *tomato plants – any outdoor cultivar*
- *bottle of liquid tomato feed*

1 After the last frosts, around the end of May, stand the pots in a sunny, sheltered spot. Put in a layer of crocks, fill with compost and plant a tomato plant in the middle of each. Push a cane in behind the plant, 5cm (2in) away from the stem, and tie it loosely up to it with soft garden twine. Water the plant in, and keep the compost slightly on the dry side for the first two weeks or until the first truss of flowers opens – it helps to persuade plants to concentrate on flowering and fruiting instead of growing leafy.

2 Give a dilute liquid feed once or twice a week – as much diluted feed as it takes to wet the compost thoroughly. As the plants grow, keep tying the stem to the cane. Bush cultivars don't need trimming or training, but use several canes to support the stems, so they don't break under the weight of fruit. Train upright varieties as a single stem; nip out sideshoots as soon as you see them, but take care not to break off the flower trusses. Nip the growing tips out after 3–4 trusses of fruit have formed.

3 Because you reduce the fruit trusses on upright varieties, the fruit will swell and ripen fast, and you won't be left with a lot of half-grown green fruit at the end of the season. Expect outdoor tomatoes to start ripening in early August; they'll continue until cold autumn weather stops any further growth, then the plants will be killed by the first frost, so pick any remaining green fruits to ripen indoors or just make chutney.

Fruit

Contrary to what a lot of people think, you don't have to have a huge garden with a fruit cage and orchards to grow fruit. Nowadays, there are all sorts of dwarf fruit trees, but even in a tiny garden you can grow apples in tubs, strawberries in pots and fruit bushes trained flat against a wall, all of which look good and produce worthwhile crops.

Practical stuff

To grow any kind of fruit, you need deep, fertile, well-drained soil and a sheltered site with plenty of sun. Avoid an east-facing spot like the plague, because most fruit flowers early, and if frozen flowers thaw out fast in the early morning sun, they'll be killed, which means no fruit for a year. If you don't have the right spot, frankly, you'd be better off growing something else and buying fruit from the shops. You'll get so little return that it just won't be worth the space.

Yes, you can improve less than ideal conditions, as long as they aren't too awful. For example, you could plant a shelter belt to protect an exposed site, improve shallow or poorly drained soil by adding lots of compost – and sharp grit in the case of clay – or prune overhanging trees to let in more light. But it's often easier just to grow a small amount of fruit on sunny walls or in containers on the patio.

The easiest fruits to fit into a small garden are strawberries – cultivated with the minimum of effort in a modest-sized bed.

You can even grow strawberries in a hanging basket outside the back door.

Planting and aftercare

Autumn or spring are the very best times to start growing fruit, though plants that are sold growing in pots can be put in at any time of year, as long as the soil is workable. Prepare the ground well, with lots of organic matter, and plant them just like normal trees or shrubs. Fruit trees need to be staked. Leave a 1m (3ft) circle of bare soil around them if you are planting them in grass so that there's less competition for food and water.

Each spring, mulch all fruit generously with well-rotted manure and feed with a general-purpose organic fertilizer. If the weather turns dry when the fruit is swelling, keep the plants watered – otherwise you'll have small fruit at best, and at worst, it'll all fall off prematurely. It's a good idea to get into the habit of sprinkling a handful of organic rose fertilizer to each square metre/yard of soil around the plants in August, and watering it in – it helps encourage the current year's growth to mature and promotes good flowering next year, which bodes well for the next fruit-picking season.

Choosing fruit

There are lots of different cultivars of most popular fruits available in garden centres, and even more if you look to see what specialist nurseries have to offer in their catalogues. So how do you decide which to choose? Taste is the first thing to go for. Go to an apple tasting event (advertised in the gardening press and local newspapers in late summer), or try fruit from a friend's garden, and ask the name of those you enjoyed eating. But important though it is, taste is not the only thing you need to take into account.

Most fruit trees need a pollinator – another cultivar of the same type of plant – to produce fruit, so you actually need two plants. Clearly any old two won't do – they both need to flower at the same time and must be sexually compatible. I'm not joking – some fruit tree pollen just does not mix happily, so check before buying.

If space is tight, stick to self-fertile cultivars. They produce fruits when fertilized with their own pollen. Alternatively, buy a family apple tree – they have several compatible individuals grafted onto one trunk. You can have a couple of different eating apples and a cooker all growing on the same tree. You don't have this problem with fruit bushes and canes; all the popular types are self-fertile.

Then there's the question of flowering time. In a cold area or exposed situation, choose a late-flowering cultivar to avoid frost damage to the flowers, which wrecks your chances of a crop of fruit. If you are growing several different cultivars of the same type of fruit, it's worth choosing a mixture of early, intermediate and late-ripening kinds to stretch your harvest.

How to... plant a strawberry pot

A strawberry pot is the ultimate solution for gardeners who think their patch is too small for fruit. Alright, you won't become self-sufficient, but the pleasure of picking a fresh strawberry or two for your morning cornflakes is well worth the space taken up by a single flowerpot. You'll be surprised just how much fruit a single pot can produce – and some strawberry pots are very large. That said, avoid the massive ones as they contain a huge amount of compost that can become cold, soggy and inhospitable to plants. A pot up to 30cm (12in) in diameter and 45cm (18in) deep is plenty large enough, and shallower half pots or pans are also suitable.

After fruiting, cut the plants back to within 5cm (2in) and feed once a week with dilute liquid tomato feed until September. Reduce watering in winter and stand the pots by the house for shelter. Start feeding again in April and the plants will produce a second crop, after which you can pension them off.

What you need

- *suitable pot with wide rim or planting pockets up the sides*
- *John Innes No. 2 potting compost*
- *crocks or other drainage material*
- *liquid tomato feed*
- *strawberry plants*
- *horticultural fleece*

1 Spring is the time to plant your strawberries. Put the drainage material over the holes in the bottom of the pot and then add sufficient compost to bring the level up to the first planting hole. (You can also plant strawberries in a hanging basket if you have a sheltered spot in which to hang it.)

2 Water the young plants well, then squeeze the rootballs and ease them through the planting holes and into the compost. Lightly firm the compost around them. A strawberry pot has the advantage of keeping developing fruits clear of the ground so that there is no need to protect them with mats or straw. Slugs and snails are also likely to be less of a problem (though they will not be absent altogether).

3 Plant up the top of the pot, water the container well and stand it in a sunny, sheltered spot. If frost threatens when the plants are in flower, wrap the pot with horticultural fleece and remove it when the danger passes. Frosted flowers turn black in the centre and no fruits are produced. Use netting to protect the ripening fruits from birds if necessary.

Soft fruit

Soft fruits are the ones that grow on canes, on bushes, or, in the case of strawberries, on herbaceous perennial plants.

Gooseberries and redcurrants (**1**) are usually grown as bushes on a 'leg' – a short trunk – that makes it easier to get a hoe or a mower beneath the branches. Both can be trained as cordons (grown on a single stem) to grow flat against a wall, which saves space, and gooseberries also make very good standard plants, trained in the same way as standard fuchsias. Whichever method you prefer, plants need pruning regularly – tackle them both in the same way. In early July, just after the fruit has been picked, shorten all the sideshoots that have grown in the current season back to about five leaves from their base. In winter, when the leaves have fallen, shorten the leaders (main shoots) by about half their length. Not that difficult to master, really.

Blackcurrants (**2**) are big bushes whose shoots all grow out from below ground level, and they don't take to being pruned into fancy shapes. If you don't have room for one, and they usually make 1.5×1.5m (5×5ft), you are best doing without. They are one of the few fruits that doesn't mind wet or heavy soil, but they are also very greedy plants that need a good mulch of manure each spring. With these, you prune in winter – thin the bush out by cutting out a few of the oldest and woodiest stems close to the ground, and trim back fruited stems to just above a strong sideshoot. Alternatively, if you find it easier, instead of picking the fruit as usual, cut the whole stem to take indoors and pick in comfort, and that acts as combined picking and pruning for the year.

Raspberries (**3**) are most people's favourite soft fruit, but unless you have lots of room, I'd give the summer-fruiting kind a miss. Go for autumn-fruiting cultivars instead. They are ready to pick from early August and go on until the first serious frost of autumn. The plants are about 1m (3ft) tall, you don't need to put up post and wire supports, or tie them up. And instead of worrying about which canes to cut off and which to keep, as you do with the summer sort, you just chop the lot down to about 5cm (2in) above the ground every February. You don't even have to grow them in rows – a raspberry thicket in a small bed will provide all you can eat without making very much work at all. The very best thing about autumn raspberries is that although they taste as good as the summer sort, birds don't seem interested. Yes, you'll lose a few, but unless you protect summer raspberries under nets or a fruit cage, you'll lose the lot.

Recommended varieties

Gooseberries – 'Whinham's Industry' large red fruit for eating fresh from the bush; 'Invicta' popular heavy-cropping pie variety.

Redcurrants – 'Jonkheer van Tets' large early currants.

Blackcurrants – 'Ben Sarek' small bush with frost resistant flowers and heavy crops of large fruit; 'Jostaberry' cross between blackcurrant and gooseberry with gooseberry sized 'blackcurrants'.

Autumn raspberries – 'Autumn Bliss' red raspberries; 'Allgold' yellow fruit.

Strawberries – 'Elvira' early variety, well flavoured heavy crops; 'Elsanta' midsummer variety well flavoured high yielding commercial variety; 'Cambridge Late Pine' old variety with lightish crops but one of the best ever strawberries for flavour; 'Mara des Bois' the flavour and fragrance of wild strawberries but full-sized fruit, in late summer.

Strawberries (4), being small plants, are often the most convenient fruit to grow in today's gardens. Buy young plants in pots in spring. Plant them in well-prepared soil in a sheltered sunny situation, spaced 45cm (18in) apart in rows 90cm (3ft) apart. At flowering time, spread straw all over the soil, tucking it well under the plants, or fit special strawberry mats round them, so that the fruits don't get splashed with mud each time it rains and go mouldy. As soon as small green fruits have 'set', cover the plants with anti-bird netting. After all the fruits have been picked, go over the plants with shears and cut them down close to the ground – you can afford to be quite rough with them – then rake up the rubbish and put it on the compost heap. Sprinkle organic rose fertilizer (which is high in potash) all over the strawberry bed at a couple of handfuls per square yard and water it well in; the old leaves are soon replaced by healthy strong young growth ready for next year. Replace old plants every 3–4 years, using runners produced from a few parent plants that aren't cut back after fruiting.

Individual information

All the information you need about pollination, flowering and ripening times should be found on the label, in the nursery catalogue, or in the adverts in gardening magazines at about the time you are making up your mind about which fruit to buy. New cultivars are constantly coming along and, with fruit, new ones often offer significant advantages over the old ones.

1

2

3

4

1 Gooseberry 'Whinham's Industry'.
2 Blackcurrant 'Boskoop Giant'.
3 Raspberry 'Leo'.
4 Strawberry 'Pandora'.

Apples – 'Ashmead's Kernel' vintage variety for a warm garden, superb aromatic flavour; 'Discovery' crisp early yellow and red apples; 'Egremont Russet' nutty-flavoured russet apple with brown 'suede-like skin'; 'James Grieve' reliable eater/cooker; 'Sunset' like Cox but more reliable and easy to grow.

Pears – 'Concorde' like a newer 'Conference', early and self fertile; 'Red Williams' sweet, juicy, fat red pear-shaped 'Williams'-type pear; 'Onward' quality aromatic early pear.

Cherries – 'Sunburst' dark red eating cherries, self-fertile.

Plums – 'Marjorie's Seedling' late September purple eater/cooker good in cold areas; 'Victoria' classic August cooker/eater but often 'misses' a year; 'Early Transparent Gage' superbly flavoured early red-flushed golden greengage.

Peach – 'Rochester' reliable outdoor variety, ripe early August; 'Bonanza' dwarf patio peach with large yellow fruit.

Nectarine – 'Lord Napier' old faithful for outdoors, ripens early August; 'Nectarella' dwarf patio nectarine.

Apricot – 'Moorpark' popular outdoor variety, ripe in August; 'Aprigold' dwarf patio apricot.

Tree fruit

If you like the easy life, the best way to grow fruit such as apples and pears is to grow standard trees. Buy one with a good branching shape in the first place and you won't need to do much pruning for years. You don't really have to prune them at all, but if you thin out the growth slightly, you'll have better quality fruit – bigger, and better coloured – though in smaller quantities.

Apples, pears, plums and cherries can all be grown as standard trees and, as long as you choose cultivars grown on dwarfing rootstocks, they'll stay fairly small and compact.

All apple cultivars are grafted on to rootstocks that control their vigour – dwarfing rootstocks have been developed to make the trees suitable for small gardens.

More vigorous rootstocks produce taller trees that are better suited to commercial orchards. You can grow dwarf fruit trees instead of ornamental trees in a small garden; the blossom is every bit as attractive as that of flowering cherries and crab apples and you have the bonus of a delicious crop of fruit.

Fruit and vegetables mix well in a cottage garden.

Apples (**1**) can be bought on very dwarfing rootstocks, which produce fruit within the first year or two after planting. These rootstock produce a tree that only grows to 2.4 × 2.4m (6 × 6ft). A few self-fertile apples are available, such as 'Greensleeves'.

Peaches, nectarines and apricots (**2**) would be my first choice for a warm sunny wall. They can be fan trained, and you only need one as they are self-fertile. You'll be able to pick an incredible amount of fruit and it's easily protected from birds by draping a net over it. Buy a fan-trained tree and tie the main branches to horizontal wires fixed at 45cm (18in) intervals up the wall. Each year, in late spring-early summer, cut out any shoots that grow out from the wall or in towards it, and tie in all the rest to increase the cropping area. There are naturally dwarf varieties of nectarine and peach, sold as 'patio peaches', that are small enough to grow in pots.

Cherries and plums (**3**) are worth growing if you have room; there is a dwarfing rootstock for cherries, which produces a slow-growing tree about 1.5 × 1.2m (5 × 4ft), but nothing for plums that gives a tree less than two-thirds normal size – too big for most small gardens. 'Morello' and 'Stella' cherries are self-fertile, as is the plum 'Victoria'. You can grow fan-trained forms against a wall, which makes it easier to protect ripening fruit from birds. All the pruning needs to be done in summer, to avoid silver leaf. The disease enters the tree through open wounds, but in summer, the flow of sap stops the silver-leaf organism getting in.

Pears (**4**) are best trained against a sunny wall as espaliers (with several horizontal tiers of branches). The fruit ripens far better in a warm spot, and it's a good way of controlling vigour; no very dwarfing rootstocks are available yet for pears. 'Conference' is self-fertile. 'Doyenne du Comice' is the fattest and juiciest.

1 Ballerina apple.
2 *Prunus persica* 'Flat China'.
3 Plum.
4 Pear 'Doyenne du Comice'.

Herbs

No cook wants to be without herbs for the pot, and no gardener wants to be without them for fragrance. They have the advantage that many of them are perennial, that they can be squeezed into pockets on the patio or corners of borders and that a little goes a long way. Any reasonable soil and a sunny spot is all they require.

Herb gardens

Formal herb gardens are traditionally round or square, often with a clipped, dwarf evergreen hedge round the outside as a year-round outline, something architectural, such as a sundial or container, in the middle, and a tapestry of herbs filling the remaining space. Alternatively, you can design something more complicated, based on a knot garden, with gravel paths in between the beds, and clipped rosemary or lavender making the scented outlines of the knot's pattern.

In an informal herb garden, you can make mixed borders using woody, perennial and annual herbs, just as with ornamental shrubs and flowers. Don't limit yourself to culinary herbs, which can look terribly green – add medieval medicinal plants, such as lavender, foxglove and the apothecary's rose (*Rosa gallica* var. *officinalis*) to give the garden a bit more colour. You could also bring in other useful plants – those that attract butterflies, bees or beneficial insects – without losing the thread of your herbal theme.

Herbs are also good for contemporary gardens; they look as much at home growing in containers made of stainless steel or other non-traditional materials, surrounded by pebbles or glass nuggets, as they do in traditional terracotta. The strong green shapes of herbs, combined with their scent and, in some cases, clippability, make them a good foil for way-out designs and unusual surroundings. So long as the growing conditions are right, they'll be quite happy.

The majority of herbs, and especially the culinary ones and the aromatic herbs, such as lavender and rosemary, are natives of the Mediterranean and grow best in warm, sunny conditions with very well-drained soil. It doesn't have to be particularly fertile, but I would recommend adding lots of grit to keep the drainage up to scratch. These herbs really don't like too much winter wet standing around their roots.

There are lots, though, that are bone hardy and that thrive in wetter soils and some that even tolerate some shade – most of the mints and sorrel come into this category.

A formal herb garden with sundial surrounded by camomile is only one way of growing herbs.

Herb care

Herbs are some of the very easiest edible crops to look after.
Mediterranean-style herbs such as bay, rosemary, thyme and sage
must have a warm, sunny spot with very well-drained soil, and
basil is very fussy about warmth and shelter but it doesn't like hot,
searing sun – it's best grown in pots of soilless potting compost in
semi-shade. Other herbs, such as tarragon, parsley, sorrel and mint
are happiest in normal garden conditions in sun or light shade with
soil that holds moisture but where they won't have wet feet.

Plant perennial herbs in spring and frost-tender herbs in
summer, shortly after the last frost, so you have the longest season
in which to use them.

Remove flowers from short-lived leafy herbs like basil and
chervil to keep them going longer, also from coriander and dill if
you want them for leaves rather than seeds. But there's no need to
bother taking flowers off perennials.

Enthusiasts claim herbs have more flavour if they are kept short
of water and not fed so they have to struggle, but most of us treat
them more kindly – water lightly when the soil dries out, and use a
general purpose liquid feed regularly every 2–3 weeks for herbs in
containers. Only big loutish perennial herbs like mint need lots of
water and heavy feeding; when you grow mint in pots you can
hardly be too generous.

Herbs also lend themselves to being
grown in a contemporary setting
and in sleek containers.

Cottage gardens are the natural home of herbs and here culinary and ornamental varieties are most easily combined.

Evergreen herbs

These are the Mediterranean herbs that put up with any amount of heat and drought, once they are established, which makes them particularly good for growing in containers, gravel gardens and in gaps between paving. They are also good for courtyard gardens and patios where there is a lot of reflected heat and light. Wherever you grow them, good drainage, not-too-rich soil and plenty of sun are the essentials.

Rosemary (*Rosmarinus officinalis*) (**1**) makes a spiky, balsam-scented bush about 90 × 90cm (3 × 3ft) with lots of tiny, pale blue 'lipped' flowers in spring. There are various named cultivars, such as 'Sissinghurst Blue'; tall and columnar with rich blue flowers, 'Majorca Pink', which is compact and has pink flowers, and 'Severn Sea', which is short and squat with flowers of bright blue.

French lavender (*Lavandula stoechas*) (**2**) is the one to grow for culinary use – the flowers are dried, rubbed from the stems and cooked with lamb, if you are feeling experimental, or mixed with other dried Mediterranean herbs. French lavender has a pair of long purple petals waving from the top of the flower-head, like streamers, and the foliage is narrower and more needle-like than other lavenders. It is not so hardy as the likes of 'Hidcote', though the similar *Lavandula* 'Helmsdale' is quite tough.

Bay (*Laurus nobilis*) (**3**) can eventually grow into a large evergreen bush or tree, up to 6 × 3m (20 × 10ft), but in a herb garden, it is usually kept pruned to size, or grown in a large pot or tub, which acts like a corset. It can be trained into a standard and grown in a pot, used as the centrepiece of a formal herb garden, or stood on a doorstep or on the patio. In a pot, it's not good at coping with a long, cold winter in the open, so move it under cover temporarily.

Culinary sage (*Salvia officinalis*) (**4**) has thick, wrinkled leaves and grows a bushy 75 × 60cm (30 × 24in) or thereabouts, with a strong chicken-stuffing scent and flavour, but its coloured forms – purple sage (*S. officinalis* 'Purpurascens'), golden sage (*S. officinalis* 'Icterina') and tricolor sage (*S. officinalis* 'Tricolor') – look a lot more decorative. They are slightly smaller, with more delicate leaves that 'mummify' on the plants in winter instead of remaining truly evergreen and, although they aren't so strongly scented, they are still good for cooking.

Thymes (**5**) come in two basic types. The creeping ones run to about 5 × 60cm (2 × 24in) and the upright thymes usually come in at about 30 × 30cm (12 × 12in). All of them have pink or mauve flowers around midsummer, and tiny, strongly scented leaves. Some, such as 'Doone Valley' (creeping) have gold-variegated foliage, and several, such as Thymus serphyllum 'Lemon Curd' (creeping) have citrus-scented foliage. 'Fragrantissimus' is orange scented. *T. herba-barona* has a caraway scent and was traditionally put under a joint of beef while it roasted. Try it!

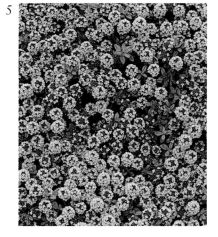

1 Rosemary (*Rosmarinus officinalis* 'Sissinghurst Blue').
2 Lavender (*Lavandula stoechas*).
3 Bay (*Laurus nobilis*).
4 Sage (*Salvia officinalis* 'Purpurascens').
5 Thyme (*Thymus pulegioides* 'Bertram Anderson').

Herbaceous herbs

Perennial herbs that die down each winter and come up again each spring are happiest in normal garden soil, and though they want sun, they don't like scorching hot conditions. Treat them just like herbaceous flowers, and cut the plants down close to the ground in autumn when they die down naturally.

1 Herbs like chives, with its lilac pom-poms, are spectacular when in flower.

Chives (*Allium schoenoprasum*) (**1**) grow in 25 × 15cm (10 × 6in) clumps like bunches of slim spring onions; the hollow leaves have a mild oniony flavour. If you are serious about your chives, cut the plants almost down to ground level periodically during the summer to get rid of old or yellowing leaves and 'force' a new crop of strong young leaves for cutting. If you don't bother, the clumps will have tufts of spiky mauve flowers that are as good as ornamental alliums any day, and bees love them.

Sorrel (*Rumex acetosa*) (**2**) looks like dock but on a smaller and more refined scale. It reaches 30 × 30cm (12 × 12in) with flower stems 90cm (3ft) high. Pick the small young leaves to use in salads or omelettes, or to cook like spinach. The larger leaves are handy to use as 'home-grown tin-foil' for wrapping meat you are baking or barbecuing. Sorrel will grow in light shade.

Mint (**3**) is a real thug if you let it spread, so most people grow it in a large plastic pot sunk to the rim in the ground. It likes plenty of moisture and it's a greedy plant, so when it's grown in a pot, give it liquid feed every few weeks. In the ground, mulch it heavily each spring with rich compost and dose it with general-purpose organic feed. Dig up a few roots to start a new mint patch every 2–3 years, as it soon exhausts the ground. If you want fresh mint in winter, pot up a few roots in autumn to keep on a windowsill indoors.

There are several kinds of mint to choose from: spearmint, *Mentha spicata*, is the best for mint sauce, but the furry, round-leaved 'Bowles mint' (*M. × villosa* var. *alopecuroides*) is the one to put in the pan with your home-grown new potatoes. For something prettier for containers, try gold-variegated ginger mint (*M. × gracilis* 'Variegata'), or white-edged pineapple mint, (*M. suaveolens* 'Variegata') in pots by the back door. Or try them mixed with bedding plants, such as mimulus, which enjoy similar conditions.

Fennel (*Foeniculum vulgare*) (**4**) has feathery, aniseed-flavoured leaves that are mostly used for cooking with fish – don't confuse the herb fennel with the fat, swollen Florence fennel that is used as a vegetable. Bronze fennel (*F. vulgare* 'Purpureum') looks prettier, if it's a more ornamental effect you want, and the foliage can be used for cooking in the same way as the plain green sort. The flat yellow flower-heads look pretty, but if you let fennel run to seed – which it does naturally after midsummer, making a plant 1.2m (4ft) tall and 60cm (2ft) across by then – you can anticipate a plague of self-sown seedlings next year.

2 Sorrel (*Rumex acetosa*)
3 Mint (*Mentha suaveolens* 'Variegata').
4 Fennel (*Foeniculum vulgare* 'Purpureum').

Annual herbs

Think of annual herbs as culinary bedding plants – they'll do best in richer soil, with a degree of shelter and plenty of food and water. If you want to produce industrial quantities for drying or freezing, then grow them in rows in the veg patch. If you only need a few, grow them in a multi-storey planter by the kitchen door, team them with annual flowers in tubs and hanging baskets, or plant them in a potager with other crops. For best results, sow annual herbs in pots in a greenhouse, or on a windowsill indoors, in spring and plant them out when the soil warms up a bit.

Parsley (1) comes in flat-leaved and curled-leaved cultivars; the flat-leaved sorts are considered to have the better flavour, the curled looks better as garnish. Seed germinates best at 21°C (70°F) and even though it will come up outside, it is very slow. Sow it thinly in small pots indoors and plant out the whole potful without disturbing the roots – seedlings don't like being pricked out. In any case, a potful grows quickly into a thick clump, 23 × 23cm (9 × 9in), that produces much more parsley than a single plant. Parsley is biennial, so although it comes up again in its second year, it only does so in order to flower. It then runs to seed straight away, so you need to sow a new batch each spring.

Basil (2) is indispensable, and specialist seed producers and herb farms offer a range of cultivars, from the large lettuce-leaved, to the highly perfumed Genovese basil, including types with fringed leaves or purple foliage. Basil is a real lover of warmth, whose seedlings do best at room temperature – don't plant them out for a couple of weeks after the last frost to be on the safe side. All basils grow about 30 × 15–30cm (12 × 6–12in); nip out the tips regularly to keep plants leafy instead of running to seed. Even so, you'll still need to sow 2–3 lots of basil over the growing season, because plants lose the urge to grow bushier once they reach flowering stage. Most people love them with tomatoes and mozzarella cheese, but try them on buttered carrots, too. Wow!

Coriander (3) has leaves that look very similar to flat-leaved parsley, but the flavour is slightly peppery – add a few to salads or to home-made curries just before you serve them. Like basil, it's popular as a leafy herb, but unless you sow a named cultivar that is bred specially for leaf production, it will try and run to seed. The seeds, if left on the plants to ripen, are the source of coriander spice that is used in curries. Grind your own in a peppermill – used straight away it has much more flavour than the ready-ground stuff you buy.

Chervil (4) has fine ferny leaves with a delicate, aniseed-like flavour, but it is quite a short-lived annual, 15 × 25cm (6 × 6in) which runs to seed within a few months. Pick all the leaves you can use before it flowers, then pull it out and sow some more.

Dill (5) is like fennel that's been on a diet; it has the same feathery leaves and similar upright, bushy shape, and if you let it run to seed you'll recognize the family resemblance in the flat heads of yellow flowers. If you are growing dill for the leaves, keep it closely cut to delay flowering, but if you want it for seed then avoid cutting the leaves – it'll reach 90 × 30cm (3 × 1ft). Let the seed ripen naturally on the plant, then complete the drying process by hanging the heads upside down in paper bags in a cool airy shed.

Borage (6) is pretty rather than terribly useful, but essential if you want a herb garden that attracts bees. The prickly oval leaves make a rosette at first, then throw up a thick succulent stem hanging with blue flowers, which are brilliant in Pimms. If you want to be very fancy, freeze the flowers in an ice tray and add them to other summer drinks too.

1 Flat-leaved parsley.
2 Sweet basil (*Ocimum basilicum*).
3 Coriander.
4 Chervil.
5 Dill.
6 Borage (*Borago officinalis*).

7 WILDLIFE GARDENS

Gardens and wildlife

The last fifty years have seen a gradual role reversal. Nowadays, it's often the countryside that is highly manicured, and it's gardens that wildlife rely on for a living.

The popularity of garden ponds has meant a huge increase in the numbers of newts and frogs; many butterflies that are now scarce in the country find everything they need in gardens, and several once-common countryside birds now rely on gardens for food supplies, especially in winter. At Barleywood, we have thriving colonies of long-tailed tits, wrens, tree creepers and woodpeckers, which, years ago, you'd never have seen.

Much of the difference is due to the far lower usage of pesticides in gardens than on farmland, even among people who don't go completely organic, but a lot of gardens are also being designed and managed with wildlife much more in mind. It's a good thing for all concerned, even if it does mean learning a slightly new way of gardening.

Once the garden has been designed and planted up, leave it alone as much as possible – the less disturbance it gets, the better your chances of attracting scarce creatures such as newts, slow worms and stag beetles. Don't tidy away old perennial flower stems until spring; spiders and other beneficial insects use the dead plants to hibernate in during the winter.

But don't give up gardening – even in a wild garden, you still need to clear out brambles, nuisance weeds and unwanted sycamore saplings before they become established. Mulch woodland corners in spring with leaf-mould, for preference, or bark chippings, and in autumn, allow fallen leaves to pile up naturally. Cut down pond-side plants and wild flowers in late autumn, after they've shed their seeds, or leave them till early next spring, just before the new growth starts.

What's in it for you?

A little wildlife adds a lot to the garden. There's always something to watch – a mother blackbird teaching her babies how to tug worms out of the lawn, or frogs gathering for their ritual get-together in the pond each spring. There's a background of natural sounds from the dawn chorus, croaking and buzzing, to territorial calls of birds and, if you're lucky, grunting hedgehogs on the lawn on summer nights. There are butterflies, birds and bees, and strange insects to identify, and with something to interest the whole family, the garden can become – dare I say it – educational.

Garden ponds have become a stronghold of the common frog (*top*) whose natural habitats are fast disappearing. Frogs are great slug eaters, too. Flowers with good nectaries, such as sedum, will attract butterflies like the small tortoiseshell (*bottom*).

From an ecological standpoint, all those different kinds of creatures interreact with each other in some way, and that can be a very good thing for the gardener because, in time, a natural balance establishes itself. The 'good' wildlife cancels out the 'bad' wildlife and will take care of garden pests automatically. Well, partially at least.

By doing something as simple as not spraying the greenfly on your roses, all sorts of creatures, such as lacewings, hoverflies and blue tits, will turn up to feed on them. Once insects take up residence in gardens, larger creatures such as birds, bats and hedgehogs drop in to feed on them, and they all do their bit to help.

Nature is an intricately balanced and interdependent network of organisms, from insects to birds and mammals, and any interference by the gardener is bound to upset things. The trick is to try and rub along with everything and just tweak here and there, rather than wade in with a sledgehammer.

In time, predators and pests achieve a natural balance, and although you never get rid of your pest problem entirely, there won't be enough pests to do much damage – if pest numbers rise, then predators will increase in proportion to mop them up before there's a problem. It's biological control at its best – effortless and free and, above all, natural.

How to start the ball rolling

The first step in natural gardening is to quit the chemical habit. If you've been a chemical user for a long time, you'll have eradicated most of the beneficial creatures from the garden and it will take them a while to find their way back. They won't put in an appearance until there's a supply of food to attract them, so you can anticipate a 'difficult' gardening season or two when you first stop using chemicals. The ubiquitous pests, such as greenfly and slugs, will inevitably build up before the good guys move in – but stick with it.

Anything you can do to make the garden more wildlife-friendly will help, even if you don't create a special wildlife garden – just incorporate a few of its features around your existing garden. Leave uncleared patches of old plant stems and long grass, at the back of borders or round the edges of the garden, where beneficial insects can overwinter; then they'll be ready to go back to work straight away in spring.

You don't fancy giving up on chemicals? Well, more and more garden chemicals are being withdrawn from the market every year on safety grounds. That gives you food for thought, doesn't it? You might just as well look to sensible alternatives before there are none left at all.

Caterpillar food plants

Attracting adult butterflies is one thing, but any responsible wildlife gardener gives them somewhere to lay their eggs and provides food for their caterpillars. Stinging nettles will feed caterpillars of the small tortoiseshell, peacock, red admiral and comma butterflies. Holly and ivy feed caterpillars of the holly blue; wild flowers in the crucifer family, such as lady's smock, attract orange-tips and green-veined whites, and privet is the food of privet hawk moths. Many moths will lay eggs on apple, willow, hawthorn or poplar trees.

Hang feeders for birds in autumn to sustain them through the winter.

Making a wildlife garden

It makes sense to design a garden so that the features you use most, like a patio and the lawn, are closest to the house, with your 'best' flower beds forming a view from the living-room windows, leaving the more natural-looking area further down the garden.

It's the most practical arrangement – this way, you avoid walking lots of muck indoors; it helps the garden to blend in to surrounding fields if you live out in the countryside, and wildlife won't be disturbed because you won't need to walk through 'their'

This wildlife area is positioned at the far end of a long, narrow garden. Although cultivated, it takes its inspiration from the lines of the natural landscape.

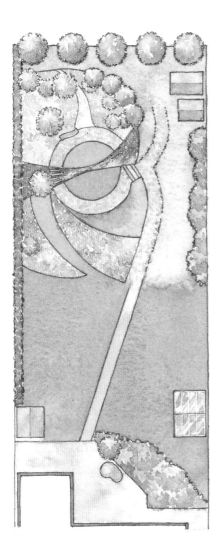

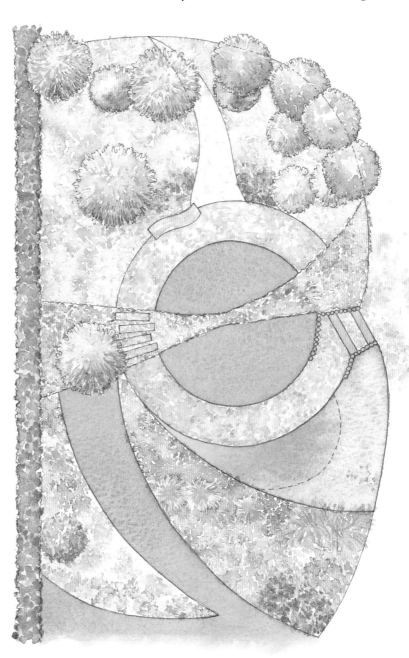

patch every time you put out some washing or go to the shed. Even quite shy creatures will be attracted, in time.

That's the way I've planned Barleywood – when you go out the back door, there's a paved courtyard garden, followed by several different flower gardens, but the higher up the hill you go, the more natural the garden becomes, until you reach the top, when it levels out into a wild-flower meadow surrounded by woods.

But don't go away with the idea that you have to live in the country to have a wildlife garden – far from it. In a small town garden, you can dedicate a special wild area, but if you have space to make a separate wildlife garden 'room', screened off behind fences, hedges or shrub borders, it's as good as having the countryside right on your doorstep.

Making it happen

To attract wildlife, the garden needs to provide certain basic facilities. A supply of food is essential – both naturally occurring food, such as insects and thistle-heads, and food you put out specially, such as bird seed. Water is vital for drinking, but birds also need to bathe, and amphibians need larger areas of water to breed in, so think about making a pond. All wildlife needs shelter and security, so they'll feel more at home given patches of long grass, dense shrubs, ivy on walls, trees for birds to perch, roost and nest in, stacks of logs, dead leaves, old plant stems and rotting vegetation.

The challenge of a wildlife garden is to put together all these ingredients, which are usually turfed out of 'polite' gardens, in a way that looks attractive to humans as well.

My ideal small wildlife patch would contain one good-sized tree, a few fruiting or berrying shrubs, some long grass with a short path mowed through it, and banks of wild flowers. A mixed hedge would provide food and shelter for birds, insects and mammals, and a pile of logs held together with soil would suit the creepy-crawlies. Remember that 40 per cent of woodland wildlife lives in rotting timber.

Give yourself a bench or a fallen log to sit on, and position it in front of a pond – the sort with shallow edges, so it makes a natural bathing beach. If you don't have room for them all, simply select your favourites, but the more features you can fit in, and the greater the diversity of plants you include, the more types of wildlife your garden will attract.

How to encourage birds

Birds will visit the garden out of curiosity, but the more they like it, the more you'll see of them. There are several things you can do to make your garden into a mini bird sanctuary.

Bats

Night-flowering plants, such as the 90cm (3ft) tall, white tobacco flower (Nicotiana sylvestris) *and wild thornapple* (Datura stramonium), *attract moths that also draw in bats, which feed on night-flying insects. Moths will also be attracted by a light left on in the garden at night. Now that modern houses don't have the easy access to roof spaces that old buildings once did, you might think about putting bat boxes up in tall trees – they look like nest boxes for birds, but with letter-box-like slots instead of the usual round entrance holes.*

Grow plants that provide them with natural food – seeds of ornamental and wild grasses, berries and fruits, sunflowers and thistle-like plants, such as teasels. Put out bird seed, suet, bits of cheese, and dried fruit – especially in winter, when there's not much natural food around, and in spring, when they have chicks to feed. Peanuts are fine in winter, but don't put them out in spring because baby birds can choke on them. Real enthusiasts have live mealworms delivered to put out for the robins in spring.

A shallow bowl of water is always popular for bathing in, if you don't have a pond with shelving edges for birds to use, but sparrows particularly enjoy dust baths, so a border with fine powdery soil that stays dry in summer becomes a popular stop-over. Otherwise, spread some fine sand in a small hollow in a garden bed, which birds will soon find.

Trees and large shrubs are essential for birds; they need cover to get away from predators. Birds always feel happier about feeding where there's a thicket nearby that they can escape to when they feel threatened. A tall tree with a pointed top, or a bare horizontal branch sticking out, always makes a popular place for cock birds to sing their territorial songs to warn off other males in the area. The more perching and roosting places the better, but you need quite dense foliage for birds to stop and nest.

Creating a wild flower lawn

A bird table and feeder (*above*) bring life to any garden, while plug plants (*below*) can be established in existing grassy areas more easily than wild flower seeds. Even cowslips (*right*) can be encouraged to grow in profusion within a couple of years.

If you have a wild flower meadow, cut it once in early spring then leave it long till August, mowing short grass paths through it to allow access. Use a scythe or strimmer to cut it, rake up the 'hay' and cart it away. If your grass is a more normal lawn that contains short-growing wild flowers, such as primroses, violets and bird's-foot trefoil (see page 274), cut it once a month or so with the blades set high so that they pass safely over the flowers.

Ten cultivated flowers for butterflies and bees

Sedum spectabile
ice plant, 60 × 45cm
(24 × 18in); chunky
succulent stems
topped by flat
clusters of pink
flowers, are very
sought after by
butterflies and bees
in late summer and
autumn.

Helenium
75 × 60cm
(30 × 24in);
marmalade orange
or yellow daisies in
late summer that are
very popular with
bees.

Lavender
60 × 90cm
(24 × 36in); mauve
or purple scented
flowers in summer,
much loved by bees.

Marjoram
30 × 45cm
(12 × 18in); sprays
of pink flowers on
aromatic plants in
summer attract a
good variety of
butterflies as well
as bees.

Mint
90 × 90cm
(36 × 36in); short
spikes of mauve
flowers in summer
attract butterflies
and bees. Buddleia
mint has the biggest
spikes of flowers
and attracts most
insects, including
beneficial kinds.

Achillea
milfoil, 75 × 45cm
(30 × 18in); flat-
topped summer
flowers in red, pink
or yellow that attract
butterflies, bees and
red soldier beetles.

Centranthus ruber
valerian, 90 × 60cm
(36 × 24in); clusters
of small red, pink or
white flowers at the
tips of the stems in
summer attract
butterflies and bees.

Solidago
golden rod, 90 ×
90cm (36 × 36in);
spires of yellow
flowers from mid- to
late summer attract
bees and butterflies

Scabiosa
scabious, 75 × 45cm
(30 × 18in); large
'anemone' centred
blue or white
flowers, brilliant
for butterflies.

Aster novae-angliae
Michaelmas daisy,
105 × 75cm
(42 × 30in); sprays
of small autumn
daisies in pink,
mauve, purple and
blue shades on tall
stems, good for
butterflies and bees.

1 *Crataegus persimilis* 'Prunifolia'.

Wildlife-friendly trees

Wildlife-friendly trees are the sort that provide fruit or berries for birds to eat and provide them with good cover from predators. They'll also be ideal places for birds to perch during the day, roost at night, or make nests. Nearly all trees house an insect population too, another food source for the birds.

Tree species that have attractive blossom are doubly valuable in the garden – all those I've listed here are suitable for a fairly small garden, and they look good enough to grow in a normal garden as well as in the wildlife kind.

Hawthorns (**1**) are all good wildlife trees, but *Crataegus persimilis* 'Prunifolia' is a form that has everything; white May-blossom in spring, large, red oval berries in late summer and autumn that persist well into winter, and probably the best autumn colour of all the thorns. The berries of this, and many other hawthorns, are a great favourite with blackbirds. It reaches 4.5 × 2.4m (15 × 8ft).

Elder trees (*Sambucus nigra*) (**2**) make bushy trees, around 3.6 × 2.4m (12 × 8ft) with corky bark and a naturally craggy shape. The bark is a great insect refuge and the flat-topped clusters of white flowers in midsummer are followed by purple-black berries that birds enjoy. Wild elders can be pruned to shape or cut back to a stump in early spring – you can cut them as hard as you like, they'll still grow back. Cultivated forms of *S. nigra* have finely cut, coloured or variegated leaves, some of them with great autumn colour. They also carry bird-friendly fruit, though not in such large quantities as the wild species.

Holly (*Ilex* species and varieties) (**3**) have berries which are often left untouched until quite late in the year. Male and female flowers are carried on different bushes and only the females which have been fertilized by male pollen will carry berries, so you may need one of each sex. However, *Ilex aquifolium* 'J.C. van Tol' is a female variety that does not require cross-fertilization to carry fruit.

Crab apples (**4**) are more decorative than culinary apples and equally appreciated by wildlife. They have attractive white or pale pink spring blossom and large crops of small, red, orange, purple or yellow, apple-shaped fruit. They are often little larger than big berries and usually vanish by Christmas. Some cultivars have fruits that hang for a long time on the trees, providing useful late winter food for birds, and if that's your main requirement go for *Malus* 'Red Jade' (small red fruit) and 'Golden Hornet' (lots of yellow fruit). Anticipate roughly 4.5 × 3m (15 × 10ft).

Cotoneaster (**5**) berries are great favourites with birds and are usually taken as soon as they ripen in late summer, but a big tree cotoneaster, such as *Cotoneaster frigidus* 'Cornubia', at 5.4 × 5.4m (18 × 18ft) makes a spectacular focal point in a garden. It provides so much bird food that the berries last quite a fair time before they're all gone.

Snowy mespilus (*Amelanchier lamarckii*) (**6**) has clusters of beautiful and delicate white spring blossom, which appears just about the same time as the young foliage is opening out to pale bronze. Small red berries ripen to black in late summer, when the branches are full of birds in search of a meal, well before most other berries are at the eatable stage. Most amelanchiers also colour well in the autumn – a bonus for the humans. Allow 4.5 × 4.5m (15 × 15ft).

Apple trees (**7**) provide valuable perching places for birds, and are also inclined to attract greenfly and other insects for them to feed on; in late summer and autumn, windfall apples are eaten by blackbirds and fieldfares. A standard apple tree on a semi-dwarfing rootstock will occupy a space of about 3–4.5m (12–15ft).

2 *Sambucus nigra* 'Guincho Purple'.
3 *Ilex* 'J.C. van Tol'.
4 *Malus* 'Golden Hornet'.
5 *Cotoneaster* 'Coral Beauty'.
6 *Amelanchier lamarckii*.
7 *Apple* 'Winston'.

Shrubs to attract wildlife

These are plants to grow in a mixed hedge or shelter-belt; you can also plant them in a border with decorative shrubs or grow them in groups in a wildlife garden.

Alder buckthorn (*Rhamnus frangula*) (**1**) is a deciduous shrub with bright red autumn leaves, and red berries that turn black when ripe in autumn. Allow about 2.4 × 2.4m (8 × 8ft). It will grow in grim conditions, including boggy, acid soil, but is also happy in normal garden soil. It is the larval food plant of the brimstone butterfly.

Guelder rose (*Viburnum opulus*) (**2**) bears clusters of white flowers, followed, in late summer, by bunches of red berries; it is a tall, upright, bushy shrub, about 2.4 × 1.2m (8 × 4ft). It's good for wet, heavy clay soil and very tolerant of poor conditions in general. You need two plants for a good crop of fruits, so put both into the same hole when you plant if you don't have much room.

Privet (*Ligustrum vulgare*) (**3**) might not appear a natural choice for wildlife, but a hedge of it is a housing estate for wrens, blackbirds and sparrows. If you don't want a hedge, grow one as a shrub. Unclipped privet has white flowers that attract insects and insect-eating birds, and the flowers are followed by black berries.

Firethorn (*Pyracantha*) (**4**) makes a good, predator-proof hedge, and if you don't have room for a large, free-standing shrub roughly 2.4 × 2.4m (8 × 8ft), it's also very attractive trained flat against a wall. Besides making a safe place for birds to perch and nest, the berries are in great demand in winter, and are usually left until after cotoneaster berries, which birds generally prefer.

Butterfly bush (*Buddleja davidii*) (**5**) is well known for attracting butterflies into gardens, but wild seedlings turn up all round railway lines, so it's quite acceptable in a wildlife garden. The cone-shaped purple, mauve, blue or white flowers appear from mid- to late summer and attract several species of butterflies with their nectar.

Berberis (**6**) of all sorts offer thorny shelter and berries, though for a wildlife garden, the large and prickliest evergreens with the biggest crops of berries are probably better than the smaller and more 'polite' garden kinds – they have orange or yellow flowers in early summer. The best include *B. darwinii* and *B. × stenophylla*, both about 3 × 3m (10 × 10ft), which have black berries.

1 *Rhamnus frangula.*
2 *Viburnum opulus.*

Roses (7) that produce hips are good specimen shrubs for a wildlife garden, but if you want a hedge for an open, windy spot, then the best are cultivars of *Rosa rugosa*, which have wrinkled leaves and big, squashy, tomato-shaped hips. They include 'Scabrosa', 2 × 1.2m (6 × 4ft), with mauve-pink flowers, and 'Fru Dagmar Hastrup', 1 × 1m (3 × 3ft), with pink flowers. They have the biggest hips, and birds go mad over them. *R. pimpinellifolia,* which has ferny leaves and small black hips, is as good, but choose cultivars with single flowers as double-flowered forms don't usually have hips. *R.* 'Geranium', 2.4 × 2m (8 × 6ft) has single, red flowers that bees love, followed by scarlet, bottle-shaped hips.

Rubus species (8) include several that are prickly, edible-fruited scramblers for wildlife gardens; Japanese wineberry (*R. phoenicolasius*), with handsome, red-bristly stems, is good for training along a fence, say 1.2–2.4m (4–8ft). Use the strawberry-raspberry (*R. illecebrosus*) for covering a bank – it'll reach about 30cm–2m (1–6ft), but it's not self-fertile, so you need two plants. But if you have room, then cultivated blackberries and loganberries always find a firm following with birds, and even foxes will take blackberries.

3 *Ligustrum vulgare.*
4 Pyracantha.
5 *Buddleja* 'Lochinch'.
6 *Berberis* 'Goldilocks'.
7 *Rosa rugosa.*
8 *Rubus* 'Loch Ness'.

There is something particularly pleasing about a patch of native wild flowers – even if we do get the feeling that nature can manage perfectly well without us.

1 *Cardamine pratensis.*
2 *Caltha palustris* var. *palustris.*
3 *Menyanthes trifoliata.*

Wild flowers

Wild flowers are more than just decoration for a wildlife garden, they are wildlife in the vegetable sense of the word. A good range of wild flowers is vital to attract insects and feed the caterpillars of butterflies and moths. To grow your own, sow seeds in pots or cell-trays – annuals in spring, perennials in autumn – then plant them out into soil that has been forked over – but *not* fertilized.

Mix grassland species with grass seed and sow them as you'd sow a new lawn – without the fertilizer. Better still, plant young plants into short grass; cut out a plug of turf and plant into the gap in autumn. Sprinkling wild flower seed into existing grass doesn't work.

Wild flowers for damp ground and around ponds

Some of our natives are happiest with their feet in water, or at least in mud. They make a perfect bridge between pond and garden.

Lady's smock (*Cardamine pratensis*) (**1**) is a slender, 60 × 15cm (24 × 6in) plant with watercress-like leaves, from which 15cm (6in) spikes of lilac-pink flowers emerge in April and May. Good for moist, sunny places, including short grass, or beside ponds.

Marsh marigold (*Caltha palustris*) (**2**) or kingcup, makes a rounded, 60 × 60cm (2 × 2ft) clump of heart-shaped leaves; it flowers from March to June with yellow flowers that look like large, single buttercups. It grows in boggy ground and in shallow water.

Bog bean (*Menyanthes trifoliata*) (**3**) is a native water plant that's ideal for boggy ground or at the edges of a wildlife pond. The leaves run out over the water, to about 1.2m (4ft), with delicate white flowers on 15cm (6in) spikes sticking up above them.

1

2

3

Wild flowers for long grass

There are two main groups of wild flowers that live in long grass: annuals and perennials – the latter being those that will persist by self-seeding without cultivating the soil in between times.

Ox-eye daisy (*Leucanthemum vulgare*) (**4**) is like a giant version of the lawn daisy, with yellow-centred, white-petalled daisies standing up on stems 45–60cm (18–24in) tall, in mid- to late summer. It's very impressive spaced out evenly in a stand of long grass, and it's a perennial so it comes up every year. Introduce it as plugs and you'll have it forever.

Field poppy (*Papaver rhoeas*) (**5**) is one of the first wild flowers to colonize newly cleared ground and, after years of absence, is now once again a familiar sight in cornfields. You can recreate the effect in the garden by sowing a mixture of annual cornfield flowers, such as field poppy, corn cockle (*Agrostemma githago*) and scentless mayweed (*Matricaria perforata*) along with hay seed. They all grow to about 30cm (12in) high with a 20cm (8in) spread. After the first year, self-sown seeds will be in the soil, so they'll come up again automatically – provided that it is raked over and disturbed. Allow it to remain untouched, and the grasses will take over and the cornfield weeds will disappear.

Yellow rattle (*Rhinanthus minor*) (**6**) looks like a feeble stinging nettle, grows to 60cm (2ft) tall, but often less, with small leaves and big, pale yellow flowers. It doesn't sting and it's actually a semi-parasite of grass, so it's handy for curbing the vigour of coarse grasses that often make a meadow look out of control. The hollow seed-heads rattle in the wind, or when the long grass is cut, hence the name. It's an annual or short-lived perennial that can take a while to get established, but then it persists by self-seeding.

4 *Leucanthemum vulgare.*
5 *Papaver rhoeas* Shirley series.
6 *Rhinanthus minor.*

Wild flowers for shade under trees

This is where you can create a little patch of woodland fringe – where many birds take shelter and some butterflies and moths rear their young.

Wood anemone (*Anemone nemorosa*) (**1**) is a perennial spring flower, 15–20 × 15cm (6–8 × 6in), that grows from a slow-spreading underground stem, and dies down shortly after flowering. The flowers look fragile – white, single and starry – growing just above delicate, buttercup-shaped foliage. It needs to be grown in carpets to make an effect, and it takes time to establish, but it's absolutely charming. It needs light shade, as in a woodland clearing – in too-dense shade, it can remain dormant for years until there's more light.

Celandine (*Ranunculus ficaria*) (**2**) is usually a nuisance in gardens, but in damp, shady ground under trees and shrubs in a wildlife garden, it makes cracking carpets of gold that really light the place up from March to May. By mid-June, the foliage has died down and the plants have disappeared until next year.

1 *Anemone nemorosa.*
2 *Ranunculus ficaria.*
3 *Geranium phaeum.*
4 *Digitalis purpurea.*
5 *Fragaria vesca.*

Dusky cranesbill (*Geranium phaeum*) (**3**), or mourning widow, is a British native that's been domesticated in gardens, but once you've bought a plant, it'll self-seed gently, coming up between shrubs and among other flowers, in well-drained to dry soil, including shady places. The flowers are deep maroon, almost black, but lilac and white forms often turn up as self-sown seedlings.

Foxglove (*Digitalis purpurea*) (**4**) is a short-lived perennial that self-seeds, so you'll find seedlings coming up here and there, and it'll grow in light shade under trees, as well as in clearings on any soil that's not too dry. Plants can reach 2m (6ft) where they are happy, but mostly they are about 1–1.2m (3–4ft), with a basal rosette of large leaves up to 60cm (2ft) across; plants look best in groups. The spotted, mauve-purple, thimble-shaped flowers, arranged in rows up the stems, are great favourites with bumble bees.

Wild strawberry (*Fragaria vesca*) (**5**) looks like a miniature version of the cultivated strawberry plant, with three-lobed leaves and white flowers in summer. They are followed by red, finger-tip-sized fruits, which are tasty to eat but very fiddly to pick, so they're best left to the birds. It spreads slowly by runners, making loose, open mats maybe 1 × 1.2m (3 × 4ft); good for fruiting ground cover in damp, shady places under trees.

Look upon a grove of foxgloves in late spring and admit to yourself that there's no sight more elegant or breathtaking.

Wild flowers for short grass

These are for those who can't get to grips with a full-blown meadow; just mow the turf with the blades set high enough to miss these little treasures.

Cowslips (*Primula veris*) (**1**) flower in April and May, with tubular golden flowers in clusters at the top of a 20cm (8in) stalk. They prefer drier ground and more open situations than their cousin, the primrose, so while you'll find primroses growing wild in ditches and hedges, cowslips will be the ones growing out in the meadow.

Bird's-foot trefoil (*Lotus corniculatus*) (**2**) likes dry, sunny spots and can be a lawn weed on sandy soils. The yellow pea-flowers are often streaked with red, hence the common name 'eggs and bacon'. They are visited by several butterflies in search of nectar and the leaves feed caterpillars of dingy skipper and green hairstreak butterflies.

Primrose (*Primula vulgaris*) (**3**) makes 10 × 15cm (4 × 6in) clumps of pale yellow flowers in March; it'll grow in bare soil in a bed in between shrubs, but it's happiest in short, damp, shady grass.

Violets (**4**) are plants of moist shade that make small clumps of heart-shaped leaves that are studded with typical violet flowers. Sweet violet (*Viola odorata*) has scented flowers from January to March or April and spreads by runners to make low ground cover up to 45cm (18in) wide. The dog violet (*V. riviniana*) flowers in May and June, but is unscented and remains as clumps. Heartsease (*V. tricolor*) is more like a miniature pansy than a violet; the plants are upright, with 20cm (8in) stems topped by minute pansy flowers in cream, yellow and purple. Heartsease grows in poor-quality, underfed lawns, but it's worth planting in a wild flower lawn, where it will self-seed, though never enough to be a nuisance.

1 *Primula veris.*
2 *Lotus corniculatus.*
3 *Primula vulgaris.*
4 *Viola tricolor.*

How to... **build a bird box**

Of course, you can cheat and buy a ready-made nest box, but if you have a few odd bits of timber kicking around, you don't need a degree in civil engineering to make your own des res for local birds. Put up the nest boxes in autumn and then you give the birds a chance to suss them out before they start prospecting for spring nesting sites. You will also be offering the likes of wrens a suitable roosting place for the winter months. Site nest boxes above head height, and where they will present a challenge to marauding cats. Avoid facing them into the prevailing wind.

What you need

- 1.5cm (⅝in) timber cut into six pieces – front 20.5 × 11.5cm (8 × 4½in); 2 sides 14 × 25cm (5½ × 10 in); back 25 × 11.5cm (9¾ × 4½in); bottom 11.5 × 10.5cm (4½ × 4¼in); roof 20 × 15.5cm (8 × 6in)
- nails and screws
- hammer and screwdriver
- roofing felt or reinforcing timber strips

1 Make the nest box from pieces of wood cut to the sizes specified in the list (top right). You can use weatherproof plywood or old floorboards (although the latter might have a more limited life). Cut one end of each side piece at an angle so that the shorter side measures 11.5cm (4½ in). Nail the bottom, back and side sections together.

2 The roof can be more elaborate, either with reinforcing ridges (made from semicircular 3.5cm (1¼in) battens), or with a piece of roofing felt to make it more weatherproof. The front of the box should have a hole 3 cm (1⅛in) in diameter, which will suit many species. Robins and flycatchers prefer a box where only the bottom half of the front section is solid, and the opening is like a deep letterbox.

3 Cut a channel through the lower edge of the front, then screw the section in place about 5cm (2in) from the top edge. Hammer a headless nail through the channel and bend it over to act as a fastening. At the end of the winter, swivel the headless nail and swing open the front so that you can remove old nests and clean out the inside. A clean box is more likely to attract new occupants.

8 COVERED GARDENS

Greenhouse gardening

In gardening terms, glass is what you might call a luxury. You can get by without it, but if you take the plunge and invest in a greenhouse or conservatory, you'll never regret it. Gardening under cover opens up so many new opportunities – new plants to grow, more propagation techniques to try – and, it has to be said, it's great fun. Under glass, you are in your own little world where you can get away from it all, forget everything else, and just potter about with plants – whatever the weather.

A greenhouse can be used for practical or decorative purposes – most folk use theirs for a bit of both. If you incline towards the decorative, you'll probably want to use it for plants that are too delicate to put out in the garden, or a collection of specialist plants for which you need complete control over the growing environment. If you fall into the practical camp, the odds are you'll be raising crops like tomatoes, peppers and melons, which produce far heavier yields in a greenhouse than in the open. You'll also be able to propagate plants on a much bigger scale than you could manage on the windowsills indoors.

Greenhouses are rather like boats – the smaller the size, the greater the pleasure.

If you're buying a new greenhouse, it's worth the extra expense of putting in some heating. You'll not only be able to add frost-tender plants to your collection and keep tender patio perennials through the winter, you'll also have a winter retreat where you can garden all the year round. But it's not worth heating a whole greenhouse just for a couple of geraniums – if you are going to heat it, use it to the full and fill it up with exciting plants that justify the expense.

Where do I put it?

When you start with an empty garden, it's no trouble to find a spot for a greenhouse. You can pick the perfect place and just work the rest of the garden around it. Does that sound a bit drastic? The trouble is, by the time most people get round to buying one, they already have a fairly well-filled garden, so it's a case of putting it wherever you can. You may be able to dig up a patch of lawn, or take a chunk out of the veg garden. It might mean taking down a tree to let more light in, or clearing part of a border to make room.

You see, a greenhouse needs plenty of light, and there must be easy access for glass-cleaning and general maintenance all round. It needs to be well away from trees that cut out sunlight and which might drop branches or leaves on top. You don't have to hide a greenhouse away down at the end of the garden; if you choose a good-looking one and fill it with displays of pot-plants, it can be quite a feature of the garden, just like any other garden building. The greenhouse at Barleywood is the star of its own Mediterranean garden. But if you're going for a more functional house, to grow tomatoes and raise cuttings, then it's most practical to put it close to the shed and the vegetable patch.

You also need to think about other facilities you'll need in the greenhouse. You'll need a water and electricity supply nearby, and a hard path leading up to it. These can be quite expensive to lay on, so it pays to choose a spot not too far from existing services.

Types of greenhouse

The cheapest greenhouse you can buy is a standard-sized, aluminium-framed one from the DIY stores, usually about 2.4 × 2m (8 × 6ft). But if price isn't your top priority, it's worth looking around at various greenhouse manufacturers' catalogues to see what else is available. There are various other styles and sizes that might suit you better – it just depends on how much you want to invest.

Timber greenhouses have a traditional look and feel, and any time you want to put shading or insulation materials up inside, you can just use drawing pins instead of having to buy special gadgets.

Plants round a greenhouse

Unlike a shed or gazebo, you can't really plant trees and shrubs to fuzz the shape of a greenhouse, because you don't want anything that'll plunge it into shade. But that doesn't mean it has to stand out like a sore thumb.

You can grow a carpet of low plants around it, or go traditional and plant narrow beds of flowers for cutting around the sides. Plants like nerines, Amaryllis belladonna and winter-flowering Iris unguicularis are traditional favourites; they enjoy the sun and warmth reflected by the glass, but don't cast any shade.

Otherwise, you can screen the greenhouse by planting a bed of shrubs, or some trellis with climbers, closer to the living room windows than the greenhouse, so that they mask it from view but don't block out any of the light.

Try to make sure that a greenhouse fits comfortably into a garden, rather than sticking out like a sore thumb.

The down side is that you need to treat the timber with preservative every year to stop it rotting and, as wooden greenhouses age, they start needing quite a bit of maintenance.

Metal greenhouses need little maintenance, and modern glazing means they are sealed against draughts, so there are no worries if you are heating them. If you fancy a change from the functional type, you could choose one of the mock-Victorian styles, or go for a coloured structure instead of bare metal – mine is this sort, in dark green. The plastic-coated alloy is virtually maintenance free.

Besides the conventional rectangular-shaped house, you can also find six-sided greenhouses, which are rather like glass gazebos – good for really tiny gardens where looks are important. You can pack them with plants, as they have staging on all sides except the one with the door. Both metal and timber models are available.

Lean-to greenhouses have rather gone out of fashion, since most people would rather have a conservatory these days. But if you have very little space, try a slim lean-to greenhouse, which is more like a glass cupboard with shelves. This can be a handy way of raising a few bedding plants, or making an under-cover plant display, and it's economical to heat in winter. Over-heating can be a problem in summer though, unless you watch the ventilation; the temperature shoots up when the sun is shining on it.

Polythene tunnels don't look great, but if you can tuck one out of the way, they're a cheap alternative to a greenhouse for growing tomatoes in summer. You can also use them as walk-in cold frames for out-of-season veg, bringing on young plants, or hardening off bedding. They don't need foundations like a proper greenhouse, but you do need to replace the plastic every 4–5 years; it goes brittle and tears after prolonged exposure to sun. Mine makes a valuable overflow from the greenhouse in winter, when it's bursting with plants that just need a little protection from frost.

Fitting out the greenhouse

There's no point in buying a lot of specialist greenhouse gear until you know how you'll actually use the house. If you'll be growing crops in beds in the ground, you don't need much, other than a row of paving slabs down the middle to divide the area into two soil borders, so that you can work without stepping on the soil.

If your main interest is in propagation or displaying a collection of pot plants, you'll need staging and possibly some shelves to make good use of the space, maybe a heater and propagating case too. People who want to grow a bit of everything compromise by paving half the floor area to stand staging on, leaving the other half as a soil border, which should be deeply dug, with lots of well rotted manure added.

Greenhouse jobs

There's no big mystery about gardening under glass: you simply do the same jobs you'd do outdoors – watering, feeding and weeding. But instead of just looking after plants, you have to control the climate as well, by heating and ventilating when necessary.

Feeding and watering

Most greenhouse plants are grown in containers of some kind, so feeding and watering will come as second nature to anyone who's ever grown houseplants, or looked after tubs on the patio. The big difference is that, under glass, plants dry out a lot faster in summer, because the greenhouse interior heats up so quickly when it's sunny.

The easiest way to keep greenhouse pot plants watered in summer is by standing them on capillary matting, which is like a thin, water-absorbing blanket covering the surface of the staging. If the pots are well-watered initially, they'll soak up all they need as long as you use plastic pots with plenty of holes in the base and keep the capillary matting damp. Just give it a good drenching with the hose each morning when it needs it. Large containers are best watered by hand, or fitted with a drip-irrigation system.

I have to say, I prefer to stand my plants on staging covered with pea shingle – it keeps them stable, improves atmospheric humidity, and leaves the pleasure of watering to me. I call it gardening. Regular feeding, every week or ten days, is essential throughout summer, when greenhouse plants are growing fast. Liquid or soluble feeds are the best to use for plants in containers. If regular feeding isn't practical, then mix slow-release fertilizer granules into the compost you use to pot up the plants in spring. It should last them for the rest of the season.

When the weather is colder, in autumn and spring, plants won't be growing very fast, so they need very much less feed and water than in summer, and in winter, they are barely ticking over. At this time, avoid watering any more than you have to, so that the humidity stays low. Cold, damp air encourages fungal diseases to attack resting plants.

Ventilation and shading

Keeping the greenhouse cool in summer helps to prevent plants drying out too fast, and prevents other problems, such as scorched leaves, shed fruitlets and aborted flower buds. The obvious way is to open the ventilators. Aim to do so as soon as the temperature rises above about 13°C (55°F). Fit automatic ventilator openers that can be preset to operate at a chosen temperature. That way

Remember that ventilation in summer is every bit as important as heating in winter.

Your greenhouse doesn't just have to be a functional addition to your garden (*opposite*), it can also be geared to ornamental plants and used as a conservatory.

you don't even have to think about it, and your plants won't burn up while you are away at work. It also helps to 'damp down' daily by splashing water onto the greenhouse floor, which cools and humidifies the air as it evaporates.

Cutting out some of the sun is another way of preventing a greenhouse overheating, so paint liquid shading on the outside of the glass each summer; it washes off again easily in autumn when you need the extra light. Alternatively, go for the luxury of blinds, which can be raised and lowered as necessary.

By ventilating, damping down and shading, you keep the atmosphere inside the greenhouse much more tolerable; plants carry on growing, instead of shutting all systems down. Wilting is the first symptom of stress, but with regular watering and proper greenhouse management, you should be able to avoid it easily.

Heating and insulating

In winter, greenhouses suffer from exactly the opposite conditions; cold and damp are the cause of a lot of problems. From September to May, the greenhouse needs heating, if you are going to use it for anything other than hardy plants.

The easiest way to do this is with an electric fan heater. Buy a greenhouse model, which has waterproof connections designed for use in a damp environment, although it won't stand being splashed with water. Position the heater roughly at the centre of the greenhouse – low down, but not directly on the floor since it will ingest a lot of dust and dirt, which wrecks the motor. Gas heaters that run off a cylinder are available for greenhouses that don't have a power supply, but they are expensive. If you try to maintain temperatures higher than about 7°C (45°F), they produce a lot of water vapour that can encourage fungal diseases. Paraffin creates the same problem, but it is less often used for greenhouse heating nowadays due to the high price of the fuel and the bother of carriage and storage.

Whichever type of heating you choose, aim to keep the temperature in the greenhouse just above freezing, around 3–5°C (38–40°F). To help reduce your heating bills, pin bubble-wrap insulation up in the roof or round the walls. Leave the ventilators free, so they can still operate normally. If it's totally sealed, the greenhouse environment will become very humid, and that really encourages fungal disease in cold, dull weather.

If you are heating the house, I'd strongly advise buying a maximum-minimum thermometer, so you can keep tabs on the overnight temperature and adjust the heater thermostat if need be. Thermostats aren't always accurate, so buying a thermometer could save you a fortune.

Greenhouse crops

There's a lot of satisfaction to be had from growing something to eat under glass. All those I've listed here are summer crops, but if you can turn on some heat in spring and autumn, they'll have a longer cropping season, which means bigger total yields.

Tomatoes (1) produce roughly 3kg (7lb) of fruit per plant under cold glass, and up to 7kg (15lb) if you plant early in a heated greenhouse. Both greenhouse and outdoor cultivars can be grown under glass, but greenhouse types really need warmth. Upright, cordon cultivars take up less room than the bush kinds. In an unheated house, it should be safe to plant in late April or early May; you'll be picking ripe fruit from early July onwards. If you turn the heat up to 10°C (50°F) at night, you can plant in late March and start picking around early June, but they'll be expensive tomatoes. It's more economical to plant in late April and turn on the heat to 5–7°C (40–45°F) as the nights turn cold in autumn – you'll have tomatoes almost till Christmas.

After planting, water plants lightly to start with. Tie each plant to a 2m (6ft) cane as it grows and remove sideshoots as they appear. After the first flower opens, water more and feed regularly with liquid tomato feed. Leave tomatoes on the plants until they turn red, so the full flavour develops. Don't remove the bottom leaves until they turn yellow – it doesn't make the fruit ripen any faster. Nip the plants' tops out eight weeks before you want to pull them out at the end of the season; it helps partly developed tomatoes swell and ripen, so you're not left with a lot of little green ones.

1 Greenhouse-grown tomatoes being tied up to stop them from falling over.

Figs (2) fruit best when their roots are confined in a 38–45cm (15–18in) pot; when they are given a free root-run, all they grow is masses of leaves. Plant a fig tree in spring or summer, using John Innes No. 2 potting compost. Train it into a fan shape, by nipping out misplaced shoots while they're tiny. Stand the tree flat against the greenhouse wall, where it won't take up much room. In summer, feed it regularly with liquid tomato feed and water heavily, especially when the fruits are swelling. Prune in mid-winter when it is dormant. Just reduce the size and improve the shape, so it doesn't get out of hand. No heat is needed if you grow 'Brown Turkey' or 'Brunswick'.

Aubergines, sweet peppers and chilli peppers (3) belong to the same family as tomatoes, and you can grow them in almost the same way (see page 283), but since the plants grow short and bushy, the only support they need is a short cane for the main stem. You won't get a huge crop of peppers, especially if you leave the fruit to turn red instead of picking them green, but one or two aubergine and chilli plants will produce enough for most households. They're a tad more tender than tomatoes, so plant 2–3 weeks later. The same goes for cucumbers and melons.

2 Fig (*Ficus carica* 'Brown Turkey').
3 Aubergine.
4 Cucumber 'Painted Serpent'.
5 Grapes.
6 Melon supported in a net.

Cucumbers (4) give incredibly high yields under glass, so a single plant is usually enough. You can expect to pick at least a couple of cucumbers each week, and 3–4 or more if you grow the short, mini-cucumbers. To save greenhouse space, grow one of the all-female F1 hybrid cultivars. In ordinary cultivars, if a female flower is pollinated by a male, the cucumbers become bitter. Always pinch off the chaps, the ones without a miniature cucumber behind them. Train the main stem up a tall cane, and remove all the tendrils and sideshoots. With the F1 type, the fruits grow from flowers that appear in the leaf axils, where a leaf joins the main stem.

Cucumbers can be touchy when first planted, so water them sparingly until they are 60cm (2ft) high. Then increase the supply, and feed them weekly with a general-purpose liquid feed – they like more nitrogen than you find in tomato feed. As a change from the usual kind, try lemon cucumbers, which have round, yellow, lemon-sized fruit. Grow them in exactly the same way, but *don't* remove the sideshoots, as that's where the lemon cucumbers grow from. Train them in the same way as cantaloupe melon plants.

Grape vines (5) take up a lot of room, and create quite heavy shade, so don't try growing sunlovers, such as tomatoes, underneath. No heat is needed unless you want to grow late-ripening, specialist cultivars. Plant the roots in rich soil in a well-prepared border and train one main stem up the back wall of the house and under the ridge. Thin out the sideshoots to 30cm (1ft) apart and train them down the glazing bars of the roof. These become your permanent framework of stems. Each year, sideshoots that grow from these will bear flowers, followed by grapes. After one or two bunches of grapes have 'set' on each sideshoot, nip back the growing tip to a few leaves beyond the bunches. If you want big fruits, thin out the bunches when the grapes are about pea-sized, using narrow-nosed grape scissors to remove every other grape.

Keep the vine well-fed and watered in summer. Prune in mid-winter when it is completely dormant, cutting all the sideshoots back to the main framework.

Cantaloupe melons (6) are grown just like F1 hybrid cucumber plants, apart from the training. Melons don't grow from the main stem, but from sideshoots, so leave them to grow until you spot a swelling fruit and then 'stop' that shoot; cut the tip off about two leaves beyond the baby melon. You should get 4–6 melons per plant over the summer, but to be sure of a crop, it's essential that the flowers are pollinated. If there aren't many bees about, hand pollinate the flowers with a small soft brush by dabbing it into all the fully open flowers, one after another, every couple of days.

Recommended varieties

Tomatoes – in unheated greenhouses grow any patio variety (see Chapter 6), plus beefsteak varieties such as 'Dombito' and 'Marmande'. Try medium-sized 'Marion', 'Sonato' and, 'Stupice', which is very early.

Sweet peppers – grow any listed in Chapter 6 for outdoors, plus large-fruited 'Jumbo Sweet' or 'Big Bertha'; exotic 'Carnival Mixture' grows green, red, yellow, violet and purple-black.

Chilli peppers – grow any listed in Chapter 6, but also very hot varieties such as 'Thai Dragon'.

Aubergines – 'Moneymaker' (reliable purple-black fruit); 'Red Egg' (orange egg-sized fruit ripening red); 'Chinese Ancestors' (mauve, white, striped, fat and thin fruits).

Cucumbers – 'Pepinex 69' (traditional long and green); 'Carmen' (virus and disease resistant); 'Athene' (good in unheated greenhouses).

Cantaloupe melons – 'Amber Nectar' (aka 'Castella'), salmon-pink flesh, superb flavour; 'Sweetheart' (scarlet flesh, good flavour, very reliable).

Grapes – 'Black Hamburgh' (sweet black grapes for an unheated house); 'Crimson Seedless' (superb red grapes).

Figs – 'White Marseilles' (ripen gold); 'Rouge de Bordeaux' (purple with deep red flesh).

Pick over ornamental plants such as pelargoniums every few days, removing faded leaves and flowers. It keeps them looking neat, and it removes a potential source of fungus disease.

Ornamental plants

Greenhouse pot plants provide seasonal colour for staging and shelves. If you don't have a heated greenhouse, stick to annual, summer varieties that are thrown away at the end of their flowering season, rather than tender greenhouse perennials that need to be kept frost-free in winter.

Coleus (*Solenostemon*) (**1**) are grown for their very colourful, nettle-shaped leaves; plants are easy to raise from seed sown in a heated propagator in early spring. If you have named cultivars, then take cuttings in spring or summer. Coleus plants look good between flowering plants in a greenhouse display, and they like fairly generous feeding and watering in summer. Nip out the flower buds as soon as you see them; the leaves fade if the plants are allowed to flower. Coleus need a temperature of 18°C (65°F) to get them through the winter, so keep cuttings in a heated propagator, take the parent plants indoors, or raise new ones from seed each spring.

Cyclamen (**2**) make a great show under glass, from autumn until late spring, given a minimum temperature of 5°C (40°F) and gentle watering and feeding. Cool, bright conditions are to their liking – too much heat and water and they will wilt, never to recover. Tug out dead flowers complete with their stems, and treat yellow leaves the same way. In early summer, the plants start yellowing, which indicates they are ready for their annual rest, so gradually reduce the watering until the tubers are dormant. Stand the pots outside in a cool, shady place for the summer. Repot in late July, and begin very gentle watering until the plants are growing strongly again, then move them back to a shady part of the greenhouse in September, before the first frost.

Freesias (**3**) are easy to grow under glass; plant the corms, six to a 12cm (5in) pot in late summer or early autumn and, during winter, keep them very lightly watered and free from frost. As the flower spikes start appearing in spring, tie them to split canes with raffia to keep them straight, and begin feeding with diluted liquid tomato feed. When the flowers are over, or you've cut them to take indoors, continue feeding until the leaves start to turn yellow, then reduce the watering and allow the bulbs to dry off gradually for their summer rest. The same bulbs should flower again for many years, but grow small offsets in a 'nursery' pot while they plump up, as they won't flower till they are big enough.

Fuchsias (4) are regular summer favourites. The best kinds to grow under glass all year round are those with particularly large or fragile flowers, such as the California Dreamer Series and the exotic-flowered species, which would soon be ruined by the weather if you risked them outside. They enjoy light shade.
Pot up rooted cuttings or repot young plants in spring, water freely all the time they are growing well and give half-strength tomato feed every week or ten days. Reduce the watering in autumn, then keep plants almost dry and at a minimum temperature of 5°C (40°F) in winter, when they are dormant.

Achimenes (5), or hot water plants, are sold as tiny 'tubercles' in spring. Plant three or five to a 10cm (4in) pot, covering them to their own depth with compost. Water sparingly, and stand them in a heated propagator, at 10–15°C (50–60°F), until the first shoots show, then move them to a shady part of the greenhouse. The plants grow to about 30cm (12in) high and flower their socks off through summer and early autumn. Feed and water regularly.
In late autumn, reduce watering to allow the tubercles to dry off gently, and store them in their pots in a frost-free place for the winter, ready to repot next spring.

1 Coleus.
2 *Cyclamen persicum*.
3 *Freesia* 'Ballerina'.
4 Fuchsia.
5 *Achimenes* 'Scarlatti'.

6 *Streptocarpus* 'Falling Stars'.
7 *Primula malacoides*.
8 *Clivia citrina*.
9 Cactus.
10 *Pelargonium* 'Fringed Aztec'.
11 Regal pelargonium.

Streptocarpus (6) is another very glamorous plant, flowering from midsummer to mid-autumn, and some of the new cultivars will bloom all the year round. Repot plants in spring – a 12cm (5in) pot is the biggest they'll ever need; they only have small root systems. Keep the compost moist and feed regularly in summer, when plants need to be grown in light shade as they scorch easily. In winter, they'll tick over at 5–7°C (40–45°F) if they're kept almost dry, but they'll be happier kept just moist and at room temperature, so move them to a windowsill indoors.

Primula malacoides (7) is a popular winter-and spring-flowering pot plant for a frost-free greenhouse that's kept at 5–7°C (40°–45°F). Grow your own from seeds sown in late spring. Keep the seedlings cool and shady in summer, and pot them into 8–12cm (3–5in) pots when they are big enough. They are usually thrown away after they finish flowering. *Primula obconica* is larger in all its parts, more robust and easier to grow, though its leaves can bring some people out in a rash. I love it and it has been a firm favourite since my Parks' Department days.

Clivia (8) is an exotic-looking, evergreen bulb with strap-shaped leaves and several stems topped with large, long-lasting, yellow-centred, orange trumpet flowers in late winter or early spring. Plants need good light, but the leaves scorch easily, so keep them in light shade during summer. Water clivias all year round, but only sparingly in winter, when they need a minimum temperature of 5°C (40°F). Begin feeding with half-strength liquid tomato feed as soon as you see the first flower buds, and continue till late summer. Repot after flowering if necessary. Raise new plants from seed removed from the ripe 'berries' that sometimes follow the flowers, or split big old plants when they have 'pups'.

Cacti and succulents (9) are very collectable – they look good all year round, they put up with any amount of sun and heat, and many of them flower each spring. Contrary to what a lot of people think, the plants need plenty of water and occasional weak liquid feeds in summer. In winter, they need to be kept almost dry, in a minimum temperature of 5°C (40°F). They are quite slow growing and only need repotting every 2–3 years, in spring, using a well-drained, gritty cactus compost, or John Innes No. 1 potting compost mixed with lime-free grit at the ratio of 4:1.

Zonal pelargoniums (10) are commonly known as 'geraniums' and they are, for me, a must in the greenhouse. All right, so they are common bedding plants, but you can grow all kinds of beauties in a frost-free greenhouse. Try 'Appleblossom Rosebud' with its fully double rose-shaped flowers of white tipped with rose pink, or miniature varieties like 'Red-black Vesuvius' whose leaves are deep purple-grey, setting off the scarlet flowers. The 'Angel' pelargoniums are miniature versions of regals (see below) and they have a charm all their own. All demand full light and hate soggy compost. Given these requirements they are happy as pie.

Regal pelargoniums (11) are the posh relatives of the bedding pelargoniums, with jagged-edged leaves and orchid-like flowers that are too fragile to last outside. They need to be grown on a sunny windowsill indoors or under glass, where they flower through summer and well into autumn. Pot rooted cuttings into 8cm (3in) pots, or repot young plants into 12cm (5in) pots in spring, using John Innes No. 2. Water lightly until they fill the pot with roots. In summer, water more generously, feed once a week with liquid tomato feed, and pick off yellow leaves and dead flower-heads regularly. In autumn, slowly cut back the watering and stop feeding. Plants need to be kept fairly dry in winter – keep them at 5°C (40°F). Propagate by stem tip cuttings taken during the summer.

The conservatory

A conservatory isn't just a greenhouse tacked on over the patio doors; it is part of the house – a room used by people in which plants are part of the furniture. A conservatory needs to look good, so there's no place for things like potting benches, propagators and sprayers, and there's no place for plants that don't look their best. It's a show house, not a work place.

A traditional conservatory is a matchless addition to any period house.

Choosing and siting a conservatory

This isn't a do-it-yourself project. You need professional help. Several firms specialize in conservatory design and construction and they'll be able to suggest a style and proportions that look right for your house, as well as undertaking the work.

Victorian-style conservatories are very popular, but in some situations, a fifties-style structure, with stained-glass window panels, a contemporary design, or a one-off that's been designed specially for you will look much better. When it comes to construction, hardwood looks smart and needs little maintenance but if, from the looks point of view, a white-painted job will suit the situation better, then frankly I'd go for PVC. Yes, I know it's not natural, but it'll save you no end of painting and routine maintenance. And if you live near the sea, or in an exposed situation, where painted timber deteriorates rapidly, it'll last an awful lot better.

The one thing I would insist on is washable flooring – ceramic tiles, quarry tiles, or a good quality vinyl, because there's bound to be a certain amount of water and plant mess. You'll want to be able to clean up easily and carpet will soon look a bit jaded.

When it comes to siting a conservatory, the only practical place on a lot of houses is outside the living room, with access through French windows or sliding patio doors – but be imaginative. You could use a conservatory to link the kitchen and living room so that it becomes a garden-dining-room. Maybe you can knock through a passageway wall and turn what was previously wasted space at the side of the house into a summer sitting room. That's where a good firm comes in; they can show you all the possibilities.

A sunny, south-facing spot isn't essential – far from it. A conservatory built in that situation will be like an oven in summer unless you put in lots of blinds and fans. A shadier aspect will stay far more comfortable, and it also means you'll be able to grow a wider range of plants.

Managing a conservatory

A conservatory is rather like a cross between a living room and a patio, so looking after conservatory plants is the same as for any other plants in containers. They may be part of the furniture, but they need more than an occasional dusting. They need regular watering; more in summer and less in winter. Feed them weekly from late spring to early autumn, using quarter-strength tomato feed for flowering plants and general-purpose liquid feed for foliage kinds. To stop plants making a mess, spend some time each week picking off dead leaves and flowers – it's surprisingly therapeutic, and they look so much better afterwards.

You probably won't want to use pesticide sprays in the conservatory even if you use them elsewhere. Look for organic alternatives, but if you don't overload the conservatory with plants, you won't have half the pest problems. If you stand affected plants on the patio for the summer, most pests clear off all on their own.

The only extras you need worry about are shading and ventilating in summer, and heating in winter. Various kinds of internal blinds are available to keep things cool in summer, and roof fans will circulate the air to supplement roof vents. If you use the conservatory all year round and want to keep it at room temperature, the best way is to have extra radiators added to the central heating system. Otherwise, use electric skirting heaters along the bottom of the walls. If it's only used occasionally and you don't grow plants that need much warmth, there's no point heating it more than enough to keep it frost free, and a normal greenhouse fan heater will do that nicely.

Against a modern house you can afford to be more outlandish – and sit among the plants whatever the weather.

Conservatory plants

Stagger home with a mature bougainvillea and the Mediterranean touch is yours.

This is where a conservatory has nothing in common with your living room because, with few exceptions, conventional houseplants aren't all that happy in the conservatory. That's because the sunlight is a lot stronger and temperatures may fluctuate quite dramatically. Proper conservatory plants are best suited to the conditions, and – as always – a few big specimens look much better than lots of little ones. But when you are choosing plants, besides looks, the thing to check is what temperature they need to be kept at in winter.

Bougainvillea (**1**) is a large, spiky climber that's covered in pink, apricot or purple bracts for most of the summer. It's good for training on a sunny wall. It puts up with quite high temperatures, and although it appreciates generous feeding and watering during the growing season, it's relatively drought-proof. Bougainvillea is a very good choice for a conservatory that's heated to between 5–13°C (40–55°F) in winter; it needs a cool, dryish spell then to initiate flower buds – if you keep it too hot when it wants to be resting, it won't flower. In early spring, prune the plant back to within a few buds of its main framework of stems to keep it tidy.

Brugmansia (**2**) is what we used to call datura, or angel's trumpet. It has large, oval leaves and huge, trumpet-shaped flowers in white, yellow or an unusual sort of burnt orange. It grows like crazy in summer, when it needs lots of food and water. It's also quite prone to greenfly and whitefly, so that wants keeping an eye on. Prune it quite hard in spring, just before it starts growing, to stop it growing too big and untidy. It's at its absolute best trained as a standard, when you only need to trim up the head the same as for a standard fuchsia. Keep it at 5°C (40°F) or above, in winter.

Geranium maderense (**3**) is a spectacular biennial for a 30cm (12in) pot, growing leaves one year and producing flowers the next. It makes a 1–1.2m (3–4ft) tall, geometrical arrangement of lacy leaves and the stems are topped by mauve-pink, cranesbill-like flowers. Grow plants from seed sown in spring, and keep them at a minimum of 5°C (40°F) in winter.

Plumbago capensis (**4**) is another south-of-France special, best trained as a wall shrub in a sunny spot, where the sky-blue flowers appear from midsummer well into the autumn. Give it the same treatment as bougainvillea and you won't go far wrong.

Stephanotis (5) is the climber to choose if yours is a slightly shady conservatory and you can keep a fairly steady, living-room temperature all year round. It's evergreen with large oval leaves and big clusters of scented white flowers in summer. Train it up ornamental trellis, or round a plant support frame stuck into its pot. It needs to be slightly pot-bound to flower well so only repot it in spring when it really needs it and then only give it a slightly bigger pot.

Oleanders (*Nerium oleander*) (6) are tender trees or large shrubs with a Mediterranean air, and clusters of waxy-looking pink or white flowers for most of the summer. Grow them in tubs in a hot, sunny conservatory and stand them out on the patio in summer, if you are short of space. They like fairly generous watering and feeding, but in winter they like to be kept nearly dry and at a minimum of 5°C (40°F). Watch out for the sap, as it's an irritant and tends to leak out if the plant is injured.

1 *Bougainvillea glabra.*
2 Brugmansia.
3 *Geranium maderense.*
4 *Plumbago capensis.*
5 *Stephanotis floribunda.*
6 *Nerium oleander.*

Abutilon (7) is a rather upright, bushy shrub with large, bell-shaped flowers in apricot, yellow or red that appear throughout summer, and, in some cases, all winter as well. The dark red 'Nabob' is especially good. The leaves are large and attractive, making this a striking plant for a large tub, given a cane for support. Its only fault is that it's a bit prone to greenfly and whitefly. Feed and water generously in summer, less in winter. It needs a minimum of 5°C (40°F). Repot, when it's needed, in early spring.

Jasmines (8) have a hefty scent that percolates the entire room, and they'll twine themselves round trellis for support. *Jasminum polyanthum* is commonly sold as a houseplant and has pink buds opening to white flowers in spring, but it'll reach 3m (10ft) and isn't much to look at when it's not in flower. You'd be much better off with *J. azoricum* from a specialist nursery; it's more compact, evergreen, and has fragrant white flowers all the year round. Avoid pruning it if possible. It needs 5°C (40°F) in winter.

7 *Abutilon* 'Nabob'.
8 *Jasminum polyanthum.*
9 Citrus (× *Citrofortunella microcarpa*).
10 *Passiflora edulis.*
11 *Acacia dealbata.*
12 *Tibouchina urvilleana.*

Citrus plants (9) are *the* must-have conservatory plants nowadays, but to be honest, they aren't the easiest to grow. Keep them in pots barely big enough to hold the roots, and repot them in spring only when they are pot-bound. Use John Innes No. 2 potting compost with 25 per cent potting bark or large perlite pieces added – citrus need a rich but very free-draining mix. When repotting, only go to a pot one size larger than the last. Feed with a special citrus feed, or use general-purpose liquid feed, not tomato feed, and water thoroughly when the compost starts to feel dry. Don't use the little and often technique for citrus. In winter, they'll need a temperature of 7–10°C (45–50°F), and you can cut down on watering quite severely. I know it all sounds a right fiddle, but citrus are worth all the effort once you get the hang of them – home-grown oranges and lemons score maximum brownie points when the neighbours drop in for a drink, and the blossom smells divine.

Passion flower (*Passiflora*) (10), in their tender forms, are becoming popular as conservatory climbers for covering a wall – although they're fast growing, they cling to trellis using tendrils, so there's no need to tie them up. The flowers are similar to the outdoor passion flower, but often bigger and in other colours, including red. If you are going to grow a passion flower, you might just as well grow one with edible fruits as well as attractive flowers, in which case *Passiflora edulis* is probably the best. Grow it in a large tub, feed and water it generously in summer, and prune it in early spring, as for bougainvillea, to stop it growing too big. The fruits are ready to eat when they are purple and wrinkly; the proper way to eat them is just like a boiled egg – slice the top off and dive in with a spoon. Give it 5–7°C (40–45°F) or more in winter.

Acacia dealbata (11) is the florist's mimosa; the one with ferny foliage and lots of tiny, fluffy yellow balls of flower in late winter. It makes an elegant conservatory tree that can be stood outside in summer. Treat it the same as abutilon, but start applying liquid tomato feed as soon as you see buds appearing. In a mild area, you might get away with it in an unheated conservatory, but it normally needs to be frost free.

Tibouchina urvilleana (12) looks quite exotic, though it's really quite tough; it's a naturally bushy conservatory shrub with large, oval evergreen leaves and big velvety-purple flowers all summer. Give it a large pot or grow it in a tub, feed regularly in summer and keep the compost moist all the time. It doesn't want to dry out completely, even in winter, when it needs a minimum temperature of 5°C (40°F).

Under-cover nursery

Once you have a greenhouse, instead of just dabbling at plant production, you can really go to town. A greenhouse traps the sun's heat and acts as a natural 'propagator', so summer cuttings root easily and seeds of hardy plants germinate readily inside it. But if you want to propagate plants early in the year, or you want to take more difficult cuttings, then you'll need an electricity supply and a few extra items of equipment.

Propagators

A heated propagator looks like a big, clear plastic box that sits on a solid tray containing embedded heating cables. By combining steady bottom heat, humidity and protection from draughts, it provides ideal conditions for root cuttings or raising seedlings. It needs to stand on staging inside the greenhouse, with a nearby power point to plug in to. Some models are big enough to hold four standard-sized seed trays while others hold only two. You can simply fill the interior with small pots if you want.

Before you use the propagator, spread a 2.5cm (1in) layer of damp sand over the base and switch it on so the inside warms up. If you use it in winter or early spring, even with background heating to keep the greenhouse frost free, you'll probably need to set the propagator thermostat to the maximum to maintain 15–18°C (60–65°F). This is suitable for most seed germination and rooting softwood cuttings. In an unheated greenhouse, it's best to wait till spring when the temperature is naturally warmer.

As you fill the propagator with pots or trays, push them up close together to make the best use of the space, and re-wet the

After all these years, I still get a thrill watching seeds germinate. Lupins come through in a matter of days.

sand regularly to keep it damp. As well as distributing the heat evenly, this creates the humidity that sustains a good growing environment. Although it sounds like a waste of heat, keep the ventilators in the lid of the propagator open on all but cold nights to keep the air inside moving, to help avoid fungal diseases.

When you take young plants out of the propagator, remember that they've been used to perfect conditions, so don't put them straight out into the garden. Grow them on in the greenhouse for a while first and then 'wean' them gradually to outdoor conditions.

Cold frames

A cold frame is handy if you grow a lot of frost-tender plants that need hardening off before you can plant them out in spring. You can't take frost-tender bedding plants out of a warm greenhouse and expect them to acclimatize to outdoor conditions overnight. Hardening off lets them get accustomed to moving air and fluctuating temperatures gradually.

Stand the plants out in the cold frame 4–5 weeks before you expect the last frost, open the lid every morning and shut it each night. If it's going to be cold overnight, cover the lid of the frame with hessian or several old newspapers for insulation. If you don't have a cold frame, the alternative is to move plants out of the greenhouse on fine days and move them back at night for 2–3 weeks before it's safe to plant them out. Choose a spell of settled, mild, still weather to plant out tender plants.

A cold frame is also a good place to propagate hardy annuals and perennials from seed, or strike semi-ripe cuttings taken later in summer. With its lid open, use it to grow on young plants, such as polyanthus, cyclamen or winter bedding, during summer; these are plants that need intensive care but at lower temperatures than they'd have under glass. Once you have a cold frame, you'll find it invaluable for all sorts of 'overflows' from the greenhouse.

Other handy propagating kit

If you only propagate plants occasionally, you can get by just using seed trays with rigid plastic lids – unheated propagators that keep seeds and cuttings humid and protect seedlings from draughts and pests. Alternatively, make your own propagating covers by cutting the bottom off plastic bottles and sitting them over the top of flowerpots – unscrew the cap for ventilation.

In the garden, you can root a lot of easy cuttings in summer in well-prepared ground in an odd corner of the garden underneath a plastic cloche – or plant out single cuttings and push a bottle-propagator into the ground over each one.

Cold frames are indispensable as a half-way house between the greenhouse and the great outdoors.

Propagation methods

The quickest way to propagate most plants is from cuttings. You can have a new plant flowering within a few months from a cutting, when to grow the same type of plant from seed might take a whole growing season. Some plants take several years to flower when they are grown from seed, but a cutting that is taken from a mature, flowering plant is already mature, so it starts flowering straight away – you've just cut out the juvenile phase. Many hybrid plants do not come true from seed, but cuttings are always identical to the parent – the original clone.

Seed is useful for growing plants that don't produce good cutting material, or that won't root from cuttings, and it's the best way to raise large numbers of bedding plants, which flower quickly from seed. People often get confused by all the different types of cuttings and when to take them, but it's a lot more logical than at first it seems. It's mostly down to how firm the current season's growth becomes as the season progresses – softwood cuttings come first, semi-ripe come next, with hardwood cuttings last.

You can always tell a real gardener's greenhouse by the amount of clutter it contains, and the amount of plants being grown from seeds and cuttings.

How to... **take softwood cuttings**

Softwood cuttings, also called tip or stem tip cuttings, are taken from the tips of soft young shoots in spring and summer, before the tissue has turned woody. This type of cutting is used to propagate bushy plants that root quickly and have reasonably long stems. They are rooted in trays or pots. Use this method of taking cuttings for argyranthemums, fuchsias, osteospermums, pelargoniums, penstemons and tender perennials and greenhouse pot plants.

Softwood cuttings of most plants will root at any time between late spring and late summer or early autumn. Midsummer is the very best time for more difficult plants; if you want to take all your softwood cuttings at once, instead of spreading the load over the season, that's the time to do it. Cuttings of frost-tender plants should be taken in late summer so that they can be kept in a heated greenhouse through the winter and so be saved for the next year.

> ### What you need
>
> - *sharp penknife or craft knife with disposable blades*
> - *8cm (3in) pots filled with seed compost*
> - *hormone rooting powder*
> - *large poly bag or propagating lids to cover cuttings*
> - *pencil or dibber*

1 Remove soft shoot tips from suitable plants with a sharp knife. The cutting should be 5–8cm (2–3in) long when prepared (see step 2), though fuchsias may only be 2.5cm (1in) long. Tricky cuttings (and there are not many of them) can have their cut stem bases dipped in hormone rooting powder but it is not usually necessary.

2 Remove the lower leaves and make a basal cut just below a leaf joint. Fill an 8cm (3in) pot with seed or cuttings compost and tap it to settle the contents. Dib the cuttings around the edge of the pot – three cuttings will normally be happy in a pot this size. Don't bury the cuttings too deeply – the lower leaves should be clear of the compost. Water the cuttings in.

3 Either fasten a polythene bag over the pot and cuttings with an elastic band, or use a rigid, plastic transparent top sold especially for propagating. Stand the pot in a heated propagator, or on a warm windowsill, not in the scorching sun. Check the pot regularly and remove any rotting cuttings. Pot up the young plants as soon as they start to grow away and when tapping them out reveals a healthy root system.

How to... **take semi-ripe cuttings**

Semi-ripe cuttings are similar to the softwood type, but they are taken later in the season – in late summer or early autumn, when this year's new growth has started to go woody at the base, where it grows out from an older stem.

You should use semi-ripe cuttings for evergreen herbs, conifers, box, heathers and many shrubs. They are usually 'struck' in prepared soil in a cold frame. If you have only a few, you could use pots, or prepare a patch of soil out in the garden to put the cuttings in, and cover them with cut-off lemonade bottles or cloches instead.

1 In late summer and early autumn, select shoots that are young and vigorous but quite firm to the touch. They should be pliable but not sappy. Cut them off with a pair of secateurs and keep them in a polythene bag while you are collecting more material. In the case of branching bushy plants such as box and yew, strip off this year's stems from older branches so that they peel away with a 'heel' of old bark attached to the base.

2 Trim the base of the cuttings below a leaf joint and remove leaves from the lower two-thirds of the stem, as well as thorns from prickly plants. Pinch out any sappy shoot tips. The prepared cuttings should be about 10cm (4in) long. With heel cuttings, simply trim the heel to remove any long whiskers. Insert the cuttings 8cm (3in) apart in trays of cuttings compost (multipurpose compost mixed with its own volume of sharp sand to improve drainage). Hormone rooting powder can be used on tricky subjects.

3 Water the cuttings in and stand the tray in a cold frame that is kept closed but can be opened a little to allow ventilation in fair weather. Most cuttings will root during winter and spring and can be potted up or planted out in May. Some may take rather longer and can be left until autumn.

How to... take hardwood cuttings

Hardwood cuttings are usually taken in mid-autumn, around the time the leaves naturally fall from deciduous plants, though you can still take them until early spring.

Hardwood cuttings should be used to propagate easy-to-root deciduous shrubs with long, straight stems, such as roses, *Cornus*, willows, fruit tree rootstocks, *Rubus* and hazel. They are slow to root and most kinds need to stay put until the following autumn before being moved. The big benefit is that you don't need any special facilities.

> **What you need**
>
> - *secateurs*
> - *spade*
> - *sharp sand or silver sand*
> - *spare patch of ground in the garden*

1 Cut long shoots from the plant so that they include the woody base of this year's growth, and trim the tops off to leave them about 20cm (8in) long. If you want cuttings to grow into trees, in the case of willows for instance, leave them their full length with the top untrimmed; you can take cuttings 60–90cm (2–3ft) long with willows.

2 Remove any leaves. Dip the base of the cuttings in rooting powder – choose the strongest kind available for use especially on hardwood cuttings, as they contain more of the active ingredient. Choose a patch of bare ground in an open, sunny spot. Make a slit trench with the spade, by pushing it vertically down to its full depth, then waggling it backwards and forwards to open up a 5cm (2in) wide V-shape, and sprinkle a 2.5cm (1in) layer of sand all along the bottom of it.

3 Push the base of each cutting down firmly into the slit trench, leaving only the top 5cm (2in) sticking out above the ground in the case of 20cm (8in) cuttings (more for longer ones). Continue pushing cuttings in 8cm (3in) apart until they are all in, then close the trench by firming the soil down from either side of it with your foot. Water well.

How to... **root leaf cuttings**

Leaf cuttings are used to propagate plants that don't have any stems, and they can be taken at any time during the late spring or summer. They are rooted in trays, and are usually ready for potting 6–8 weeks later.

Leaf cuttings are suitable for *Streptocarpus*, *Saintpaulia* (African violet), *Begonia rex*, and many succulent plants.

What you need

- *sharp knife*
- *seed tray*
- *cuttings compost*
- *transparent propagator lid*

1 *Streptocarpus* (the Cape primrose) has long, tongue-like leaves that can be chopped up to make several cuttings. Cut a healthy, rich green leaf from the parent plant. Avoid any that are pale yellow or showing signs of browning.

2 Taking care to remember which is the top and bottom of the leaf, slice it up into sections about 3cm (1½in) long. (Leaves of *Begonia rex* can actually be cut up into square sections larger than a postage stamp, but their polarity – top and bottom – is still important.)

3 Insert the cuttings into the seed compost so that they sit up rather like gravestones. The bottom 1cm (½in) of leaf section should be buried and the rest left protruding. The cut surface which was nearest the parent plant (i.e. the bottom) should be inserted and the top edge is the one still visible. Keep the cuttings in a warm propagator. They can be dug up and potted individually when a new young plant has been produced at the bottom of each of them.

Many succulents can be propagated from leaf cuttings.

Variations on the leaf cuttings theme

Entire leaves of *Begonia rex* can be cut from the parent plant and laid on the surface of cuttings compost in a seed tray. Secure them with opened-up paper clips bent open to make U-shaped pins. Take a sharp knife and push it through the main veins to make a slit about 1cm (½in) long. Place the tray in a warm propagator and make sure that the compost and the atmosphere do not dry out. In a couple of months' time, tiny new plants will arise from the cut tissue and when they are large enough they can be dug up and potted on individually.

With *Saintpaulias* (African violets), cut off a whole leaf complete with 4cm (1½in) of leaf stalk, and push the stalk into a pot of seed compost. Keep it warm and humid, but don't cover with cling film as it will rot. A cluster of plants will grow from the base of the stalk: pot each singly when they are big enough to handle.

Leaves of some succulents, such as the echeverias, root naturally when they drop off the plant. Choose young, whole, fully expanded leaves and barely press the end where they were attached to the plant into a sandy compost (made by mixing equal parts silver sand and seed compost). New roots and shoots will grow from that point.

Secret of success

Green fingers have nothing to do with it – the trick is to stop cuttings dying of dehydration or rotting before they root.

To prevent dehydration, check often to see if cuttings need watering and aim to keep their compost just moist all the time. Cover all but hairy, felty or succulent cuttings with a lid to keep them humid.

To prevent rotting, don't overwater, and ventilate regularly to keep air circulating. Pick off dead or mildewed leaves often, and remove flowers and buds – they divert energy from root production.

Softwood cuttings need protection from the elements, so invest in a corrugated plastic cloche to keep them safe.

Propagation tricks

When you don't have a lot of propagating kit, or you want to take a few cuttings of things that are expensive to buy but difficult to root, it's always satisfying to know that are there are tricks and short cuts that you can use.

Softwood shrub cuttings in sun frames

A wide range of shrub cuttings can be rooted easily by taking 15–20cm (6–8in) softwood cuttings in late June or July and putting them outside in the ground under a 'sun frame'. Choose a sunny spot and prepare the soil as for semi-ripe cuttings (see page 300).

You need a rigid plastic cloche with a square of rigid plastic to cover each end, so that it's totally enclosed. Paint the outside with greenhouse shading, so your cuttings don't scorch. Prepare softwood shrub cuttings as before (see page 299). Push them into the ground about 5cm (2in) apart. Water them in thoroughly and cover with the cloche. Seal the ends up, and pile soil round the edges, so that humidity builds up underneath – you want to be able to see condensation forming on the inside. Lift the cloche off once a week, to remove any mildewy leaves or cuttings that have gone rotten, and water the cuttings so the steam-bath effect continues. After about 6–8 weeks, start to increase the ventilation and after three months or so remove the cloche entirely. The cuttings will root slowly and most should be ready to pot in autumn; leave the rest till next spring.

Difficult cuttings

As a general rule, if a plant is more expensive than other species of a similar size at the garden centre, it's usually because it is difficult to propagate. Some 'problem plants', such as named cultivars of Japanese maples (*Acer palmatum*) have to be grafted, but a lot of difficult plants can be easily increased by layering (see page 159). But if you have a greenhouse, it's worth trying cuttings of other hard-to-root kinds like camellias, rhododendrons, passion flower, wisteria and clematis in a heated propagator. Don't expect a high success rate, so take plenty more cuttings than you want, but if even only a few root, you can feel very pleased with yourself and you'll know you've saved a few pounds.

Take a mixture of softwood and semi-ripe cuttings in late June and July to hedge your bets, and in the case of clematis, take internodal cuttings (see box below). Always use the strongest rooting powder – the stuff for hardwood cuttings if possible.

Put three cuttings in round the edge of a 8cm (3in) pot filled with seed compost. After watering them, stand the pots on the damp sand inside the propagator and turn the heat up. Shade the propagator from the sun. Aim to keep a steady 21°C (70°F) inside, and close the propagator's ventilators to create 100 per cent humidity. Water the sand to maintain a steamy atmosphere but don't overwater the cuttings, and watch out for mildew or signs of rotting.

Cuttings will root at varying speeds, and none are quick. Pot up the rooted cuttings individually – any that haven't rooted or rotted at the base can go back in for a second try.

Offsets

There are some plants that are no trouble to propagate at all, because they virtually do it themselves – they are the ones that produce offsets, as many cacti, succulents and bromeliads do, or those that build up big clumps, such as clivias.

With offsets, simply detach as many as you need when they are big enough to grow independently, at the start of the growing season in spring, and pot them up.

Spring is also the best time to divide clump-forming plants, but here you'll need to tip the parent out of its pot and work your fingers in between to separate part of the original plant, complete with its roots.

Treat a newly potted offset or division like a cutting that is only partly rooted. Give it extra care while it grows itself some more roots – keep it warm and draught-free, don't let it dry out and don't overwater it. That said, it's the easiest way you'll ever find to propagate plants.

Clematis cuttings

To make internodal cuttings, remove a length of this year's stem and cut off the soft material from the end leaving semi-ripe wood. Keeping the top uppermost, divide the rest of the stem into cuttings with two pairs of leaves. Cut cleanly just above the top pair, and 2.5–5cm (1–2in) below the bottom pair – it's important to keep them the right way up. Dip the base in hormone rooting powder and push into pots as usual.

Caring for young plants

The average garden-centre plant tends to be quite large so that it has a better chance of surviving the pitfalls it's likely to meet when planted in the garden, such as slugs, drought and competition from other plants. A rooted cutting or young plant wouldn't stand a chance – it's like sending a boy out to do a man's job. No, young plants need growing on in almost nursery conditions until they are roughly the same size as you'd buy them at the garden centre – only then are they ready to plant out.

Cuttings rooted in the garden

Hardwood cuttings that you've rooted outside in the garden are already quite well acclimatized, as they've been grown in the open from start to finish. Other types of cuttings that you've rooted outdoors in a cold frame, or other temporary cover, need to have the ventilation gradually increased over 6–8 weeks. That way, they slowly get used to wind and weather in easy stages before you take away their protection entirely.

The best way to grow them on is to 'line them out', as nurseries call it. In autumn or early spring, dig them up from their rooting place and plant them in well-prepared ground in the vegetable garden, or in a special nursery bed. Plant them 30–45cm (12–18in) apart, with 60cm (2ft) between the rows. Water them in and leave until they are big enough to transplant to their final positions, any time between autumn and spring – when they are dormant.

If you don't have a suitable spot, or you need your plants to be portable, dig them up and put them into pots to grow them on. You'll need to water and feed them, so it makes more work, but it suits some people better this way.

Cuttings rooted in pots or trays under cover

Plants that have rooted in pots can be potted up any time during spring, summer or early autumn. Delicate plants that aren't keen on root disturbance are best moved in spring or autumn.

Tip them carefully out of their propagating pots, and pot one cutting in the middle of a 12cm (5in) pot. If you have lots of cuttings of the same sort, plant three close together in the middle of the pot: you'll have a big bushy plant in less than half the usual time. Stand the plants in a shady part of the greenhouse or cold frame, or put them in a plunge bed. Keep them watered and give them liquid feed once a week. To encourage a good shape, 'stop' them once or twice by nipping out the growing tips.

Making a plunge bed

A plunge bed is like a topless cold frame, half-filled with sand. Its job is to act as a nursery bed for hardy plants in pots that need somewhere safe to keep growing until they are big enough to plant out in the garden. Although not essential, keen propagators find it very handy. If you buy a lot of plants, it comes in very useful for 'holding' them until you are ready to plant them out. It can also be turned into a low cold frame for rooting semi-ripe cuttings just by laying a sheet of plastic over the top as a lid.

Stand the base on loose, bare soil, half-fill it with sand, then rake it level and water well. Water the plants, then sink their pots to the rims in the damp sand so they can take up water as needed. Dampen the sand every few days: it's much quicker than watering lots of pots one at a time.

Epilogue

Well, that's it. Two television series and two books later, I hope you feel more in tune with plants and gardens than you did when we started. You'll keep making mistakes – we all do – and I'd not be telling the truth if I didn't admit to being irritated by my own errors of judgement. But at least now you might know what your intentions should be, and that's the most important thing.

I've been gardening for a living now for almost forty years, and if anything, I enjoy it now more than ever. Each spring rekindles a childish enthusiasm for sowing seeds, and the mindless task of mowing becomes a safe haven for daydreams.

To some, gardening may seem like a harmless sort of pursuit that is of little real importance in a world where mightier issues grab the headlines. I don't agree. When power-crazed world leaders have long since been forgotten, foxgloves will still emerge in the shade, and water lilies open their starry flowers in the sun.

I believe passionately that gardening is the most important thing in life. Growing plants is, for me, the ultimate reality, the real thing, and something that anyone can do on the smallest patch of earth. Think of your own small garden as a patch on the larger quilt that is the British countryside. If we all looked after our patches, what a quilt we would have.

Heigh-ho. Grow well and enjoy your garden.

Raising your own plants is really the best feeling there is.

Index

Page references in *italics* indicate illustrations.